AWAKENING ASHLEY

AWAKENING ASHLEY

Mozart Knocks Autism On its Ear

Sharon Ruben

iUniverse, Inc.

New York Lincoln Shanghai

Awakening Ashley
Mozart Knocks Autism On its Ear

iUniverse, Inc.

For information address:
iUniverse, Inc.
2021 Pine Lake Road, Suite 100
Lincoln, NE 68512
www.iuniverse.com

The views and opinions of various therapeutic interventions stated in this book are strictly that of the author and only represent beneficial outcomes of the child described in this book. Furthermore, the information presented is to inform and educate not diagnose or cure. The author strongly recommends consulting with qualified, licensed health professionals when choosing any therapeutic interventions.

The names of various therapists and specialists have been changed to protect their identity.

ISBN: 0-595-30780-9

Printed in the United States of America

Contents

▼

Acknowledgments

This book and Ashley's recovery would never have been possible if it weren't for the special people in my life and the doctors, therapists, teachers and other acquaintances I met along this journey. I've learned from you all, and it has enriched both my life and Ashley's. Thank you for taking the time with Ashley and molding her just so and for giving me strength, support, guidance, education, and most of all, love to see this recovery through.

To Dave. Our love has withstood one of the most difficult times of our lives together—this journey. Thank you for being my rock and supporting my relentless pursuit to get Ashley well.

To Kacey, Ashley, and Sydney. Mommy's done writing. Let's go out and play!

To my parents, sister and brother, and in-laws. Thank you for absolutely everything you've done for me during these last three trying years of my life. A family support system kept me going throughout all of this.

To the members of my therapy team. Dr. Conlon, Dr. Wieder, Dr. Layton, Kelly Dorfman, Lindsey, Diana, Brenda, Shelly, Tina, and the staff at the Spectrum Center. Thank you for instilling all your knowledge in me and guiding me along this journey. Your expertise was instrumental in making Ashley well.

To Kathy L. You are responsible for lighting the fire in me and connecting me with a world of information and the best network of specialists. Thank you for giving me that push forward.

To Mr. G. and Mrs. Rojas. Thank you for welcoming Ashley into your Montessori program. A sensorial approach combined with practical life exercises has been beneficial for Ashley's coordination and concentration. Now, she is reading, writing, learning, and excelling thanks to your dedication to teaching.

To Don Campbell. Thank you for your assistance with the book and bringing Mozart into my life—I'm a believer in the Mozart Effect.

To Dr. Michael Palmer. Even as a busy doctor, New York best-selling author and Dad of a son on the spectrum, you still found the time in your schedule and compassion in your heart to guide me with my book. Thank you for taking me under your wing and helping this Mom carry her message.

To Katie, Matt, Mable, Sandy, and Sara at NBC. Thank you for a wonderful segment on Ashley's recovery and bringing her story to the attention of your viewers.

To Valerie Dejean. You brought Ashley back to me, and for that, I'm forever grateful.

To Dr. Tomatis. I wish I had known you. Thank you for your brilliant research. Ashley wouldn't be where she is today without it.

To Ashley

You are the bravest little soul I know,
and are living proof, early intervention is key to recovery.

I love you.

Mom

To My Readers,

When I first decided to write this book, I wondered what I would include in it. I had so much to say. I wanted to tell the story about my daughter's journey since being diagnosed with Pervasive Developmental Disorder Not Otherwise Specified (PDD-NOS)—an autistic spectrum disorder. I also wanted my readers to be able to obtain usable information from our experiences.

As time passed, I saw great progress with my daughter through the many therapies we employed, both conventional and non-conventional. I became passionate about sharing with others how much she has been through—how much we have all been through—and how it has changed me forever.

We all play many roles in our lives. My role as a Mom to three girls, wife of a man I call, "Mr. Wonderful," daughter, sister and that of friend, has been forever altered because of this journey. The way I view life now has been forever altered. And yet I've grown in a way I never imagined, and I have become stronger and more knowledgeable about this disorder than I ever thought possible.

Everyone in my life has been touched by Ashley's diagnosis in one way or another. I enlisted everyone's help and relied on all offers to get me through each day. Whether it was playing with Ashley and teaching her new words and socialization; babysitting my other children so I could take Ashley to therapy; or even helping with the housework and cooking, I relied on all of the people in my life during this time of need. To me, it really does, "take a village"—even more so for a child with special needs.

In return, I educated them—possibly to ad nauseam—about this disorder; the characteristics, the signs and symptoms, the interventions and the truly complex nature of the autistic spectrum.

But more importantly, I found I was educating myself in the process. Every spare moment I had—after taking care of three children, a husband, a house, and attending daily therapies with Ashley—was spent immersed in a book about autism, or on the Internet collecting information. I read medical literature and visited Internet chat boards. I read about vitamin supplements and herbal remedies. I read autism success stories and the not-so-successful stories. I compared everything I learned to what I saw going on with Ashley so I could help her—help us—rise above this disorder.

The people in my life have been so supportive of my efforts, and when I was having bad days, they gave me their ear and listened and their shoulder on which to cry. It is not easy on the heart or the wallet to be a parent of a child with special needs. I never knew my life would take such a turn. But, we are taught to steer in the direction of a skid to put us back on course, and that is how my husband and I approached this.

Ashley's disorder meant our energies and resources had to be focused on getting her proper treatment. We were determined not to let this diagnosis crush our family, and we refused to live in denial. Ashley would not have benefited from any of that.

Once the initial shock and denial wore off from receiving such a blow, I immersed myself in finding the right team of specialists to work with Ashley. The more I talked to the professionals and other parents, the more specialists I found to join our team. And that's literally what we had—a therapy team for Ashley.

Although I consider Ashley's journey now over, my dedication to the cause remains. I will continue to reach out and help those touched by autism. There is no other choice to be made. That is my mission now.

This ride has been bittersweet. What I once thought was an insurmountable, often heart-wrenching journey filled with daily struggles and fear of the unknown, has turned into the recapturing of the moments I always envisioned having with Ashley, and a heartwarming renewal of the love I carry for her.

I wish all of you a journey filled with strength, love and support from your friends and families, and especially a new perspective on the human spirit. We can do amazing things when put to the test. But more importantly, our children with special needs are the true heroes. For all of the medical testing they go through, for all of the nine-to-five doctors' appointments and therapies they endure, for all of the medications and vitamin concoctions we hide in their sippy cups, for all of the squeezing to calm them down, for all of the swinging to rev them up, they are the absolute true heroes in this battle. This is my story.

CHAPTER 1

▼

ARRIVING AT TODAY

I nervously paced the floor of the lobby alternating between looking down at my watch and out the window to the street.

"Where is he?" I wondered. "I thought he was supposed to be here at seven o'clock."

It was 7:08 a.m. I was getting worried.

"Ms. Ruben, your car is here," the doorman finally said.

I looked at Dave and gave him the nod. It was time.

Dave folded the sports page he had been perusing and tucked it under his arm. He seemed quite calm. I was filled with an exorbitant amount of anxiety.

We pushed our way through the revolving door of the Essex Hotel and slid into the black Lincoln Town car reserved for me.

"Good morning. Thirty Rockefeller Center, please," I said to the driver. Our eyes met in the rearview mirror.

He knew exactly where we were going. He was in possession of a voucher for my fare.

We made our way down Central Park South past the horse-drawn carriages.

"I'd love to take a carriage ride later," I said to Dave.

We turned right onto Fifth Avenue. This was my favorite city—New York—full of shops and eye-popping buildings and television and movie stars, whom I always sought out (and on some occasions) even met.

It was such an electrifying town to me. I had been here many times before. As a teenager, I marched in the St. Patrick's Day parade with my high school band. There were trips made to watch the U.S. Open tennis tournament, trips made to take in Broadway shows, trips to be part of the audience of various television shows, and the times I went to the top of the World Trade Center to get the breath-taking view of the city below. I was a typical tourist on those occasions. But today, I felt special being here. It was a special day.

Before I knew it, the driver parked. Dave and I got out of the car and headed toward the door to the NBC studio building.

"Hey, are you…?" a man said, holding out a piece of paper and a pen.

"Uh…no," Dave said, brushing off the advance by the man.

"Hey, he just thought you were Tom Cruise!" I said, laughing at the ridiculous thought of someone asking my husband for his autograph.

Well, Dave does look like Tom Cruise—there is a resemblance, and I can see where the man may have mistaken Dave for Tom. But it was just so ironic. I was the one going to NBC for the interview, and Dave was the one being asked for his autograph.

We entered the building. I walked past the window overlooking the plaza and saw the infamous crowd that gathers daily. I, too, had been part of that boisterous ensemble on various visits to the city. Today, the crowd was no different. They were loud and begging for air time with Al Roker while he was doing his 7:30 a.m. weather segment.

Dave and I were escorted into the elevator and up to the Green Room. As we stepped into the Green Room, it was smaller than I had envisioned, and it wasn't green at all. We sat down, and I was immediately given instructions and paperwork to fill out by a couple of NBC assistants. We were told to help ourselves to the refreshments—which had already been somewhat picked over by the seven o'clock guests. I was too nervous to eat anyway.

"Sharon, you'll be going on at 8:13," an NBC assistant said, giving me other instructions as well.

I sat there with Dave and was quite in disbelief of where I was at the moment—the Green Room of the *Today Show* with Katie Couric and Matt Lauer. Wow! I usually dream big, but this time, it was *really* happening!

"Sharon, it's time for wardrobe and makeup," the assistant said to me.

I walked down the hall and walked into a closet full of clothes. The man there looked at me and gave me the nod of approval. I had dressed perfectly already—no need for him today. I walked across the hall to get my hair and makeup done. I sat down in the chair and told the woman to make me look beautiful.

With tinted foundation smoothed just right on my face and newly-acquired cheekbones through the magic of makeup artistry, I headed back to the Green Room and sat nervously with Dave. I watched the television screen mounted in the corner of the ceiling.

"Coming up, how special music and sound therapy has become a turning point for an autistic child. But first, this is *Today* on NBC," Katie said, heading into a commercial.

"There she is!" I exclaimed to Dave, watching the clip for my upcoming segment.

It was our daughter, Ashley, during a therapy session wearing headphones and drawing on the board. Just as fast as the clip appeared, it was gone. A commercial played. The butterflies flitted through my body. I was shaking.

"Okay, Sharon and Valerie, let's go," the assistant said to us.

Valerie Dejean was accompanying me for the interview. She is an occupational therapist and owner and director of the Spectrum Center in Bethesda, Maryland, where Ashley had been treated.

I kissed Dave. He would stay and view the segment in the Green Room. Valerie and I were escorted down the steps and into the studio to the interview couch. The television studio was cold, just like everyone says it is. Katie Couric was waiting for us.

"Hi, I'm Katie. It's nice to meet you. Your story is amazing," she said, shaking my hand.

I sat on the couch and a stage-hand attached a microphone to my sweater.

"Don't be nervous," Katie said to me.

I could hear another segment going on in the front of the studio. Katie whispered instructions to us so her voice would not be heard through the microphone.

A commercial ended prompting the cameramen to turn their cameras to Katie. My stomach took a leap.

We were on the air!

Katie looked up from her notes and read from the teleprompter.

"More than a million and a half Americans are diagnosed with some form of autism—a complex and often baffling developmental disability that affects the way a person communicates and interacts socially. While there are a variety of therapies available—to date—there is no cure. But today, the story of one little girl and her journey—with the help of Mozart!"

I turned to view the monitor. With the first sight of Ashley's baby picture, tears fell from my eyes. Katie pulled out some tissues from a box on the table next to her. I dried my eyes and tucked the tissues under my leg. I turned back to watch Ashley's segment on her unbelievable journey—the product of two days' taping at my house, Ashley's Montessori school, and her therapy sessions a month earlier. But I had not seen the full, edited, taped version—until now.

KATIE (AT THE RUBEN'S HOME SITTING IN THE DEN): To her parents Sharon and Dave, Ashley was perfect—the second daughter they always wanted.

SHARON: She looked beautiful! She looked perfect! I was elated! I wanted another child so Kacey could have a playmate. They were 14 months apart. I thought Kacey would be a great role model for Ashley.

KATIE: But Ashley had a different idea. At 16 months, she preferred to be left alone.

SHARON: She would tune us out when we'd call her name—kind of be in her own world. I couldn't imagine that there'd be something wrong with my child!

KATIE: But there *was* something wrong with Ashley. After a hearing and speech evaluation, it was determined that, while her hearing was fine, her speaking ability—at 19 months—was the equivalent of a six-month-old.

SHARON: My heart just sunk!

KATIE: Dr. Chuck Conlon, a neurodevelopmental pediatrician at Children's Hospital in Bethesda, Maryland, examined Ashley.

DR. CONLON: We really looked at the hallmark of her social interaction abilities and her communicative abilities—it was autism spectrum disorder.

SHARON: Autism? Ashley's not autistic!

KATIE: While devastated, Sharon was also determined to find help for her little girl. Around her second birthday, Ashley started speech and occupational therapy. But despite a 20-hour-a-week program for almost a year, she made little progress. So, Sharon decided to try a special listening program developed by French doctor, Alfred Tomatis, who theorized that autistic children have under-developed inner ears that can be re-trained through intensive sound therapy. Leslie Neale, a recreational therapist at the Spectrum Center in Bethesda, Maryland, explains.

LESLIE: The Tomatis Method is really looking to help your ear to listen better and to perceive sound better and in doing that, to help start language emerge.

KATIE: At the Spectrum Center, Ashley was exposed to music of Mozart—after it had been filtered to bring out the high frequencies.

LESLIE: Mozart carries higher frequencies in the music, and the instrumentation carries along very consistently with the human voice. (*A high-pitched noise plays in the background.*)

KATIE: Ashley also listened to her mother's voice after it had been modulated.

LESLIE: With the mother's voice tape, we simulate for the children what it sounded like to them when they were in the womb.

KATIE: It's in the womb that hearing develops. The fetus picks up only high-frequency levels of the mother's voice and other sounds. The Tomatis therapy is designed to replicate those sounds heard in-utero in order to re-awaken the ear's natural ability to listen and ultimately stimulate the brain's desire to communicate.

LESLIE: For some kids, it's really opening another new door to them in an entirely new world.

KATIE: For Ashley, the result was nothing short of miraculous!

SHARON: The second day, I really remember. We got into the car, and we were driving home. All of a sudden, she said, "I want cookie!" She'd never said anything spontaneously like that before. Dave and I just looked at each other like, 'What did she just say?'

KATIE: After more than a year of Tomatis listening therapy combined with interactive games, Ashley is now part of the crowd.

ASHLEY: Gimme a high five! (*Ashley holds her hand up to receive a high-five from Leslie after a round of therapeutic humming*).

LESLIE: You're doing…super! (*Leslie slaps Ashley's hand with a high-five.*)

SHARON: She learned to talk, she learned to pretend play, she learned to hug, and she learned to love us. Tomatis was just that…switch!

KATIE: But autism experts caution against false hope. They stress that the Tomatis Method is not a cure; it's not science; and it's not meant for every autistic child.

DR. CONLON: I don't think I could make this a treatment recommendation from the standpoint of definitely do this, until there's more evidence to suggest there's good clinical science to say this works.

KATIE: But for Sharon and her husband Dave, this is all the proof they need.

ASHLEY: I love you, Daddy![1]

Coming out of the taped video segment, the cameras turned toward Katie, as she introduced Valerie and me for our live interview. The butterflies in my stomach took flight again.

KATIE: Sharon Ruben is Ashley's mother—very emotional this morning, understandably. Valerie Dejean is an occupational therapist and director of the Spectrum Center in Bethesda, Maryland. Good morning to you, both. It's nice to have you.

SHARON AND VALERIE (in unison): Hi.

---

1. ©National Broadcasting Company, Inc. 2003, All Rights Reserved

KATIE: Valerie, I know the Tomatis Method has been around since the 1960s, but it seems as if we're hearing more about it these days, and people are more interested. Why is that?

VALERIE: Well, I think there seems to be an increase in the amount of autism, and parents are really researching what they can do, and they are not just taking the answer that there is nothing available for them.

KATIE: I know we heard the music go from before filtering to after filtering. Tell me how this high-pitched noise actually stimulates the inner ear or helps autistic children—in layman's terms, please.

VALERIE: Well, how the ear learns to listen to language starts in the womb. As early as seven months of age, the fetus learns to recognize all of the sounds or phonemes—the building blocks of language. If they don't recognize those sounds, it's very hard when they're born to attach meaning to language and learn to develop language, because of that—they don't hear it, they don't understand it.

KATIE: So is this a one-time deal, or does this kind of therapy have to continue as a child ages?

VALERIE: It depends on the child and the severity. Some children—like Ashley—do wonderfully. I feel if we can get to a point with a little bit of maintenance, they will do very, very well. But some children are more severe and need more on-going work.

KATIE: How is Ashley? I hear she's in a Montessori school.

SHARON: Yes, she's been released from all of her therapies. She no longer has speech or occupational therapy. She's been released from the special educator from the county. She's in Montessori now, and she has just fallen into place like any other four-year-old.

KATIE: This must be the answer to your prayers. You must be so grateful and relieved as Ashley's mom.

SHARON: She loves us now. She calls me Mommy. She calls Dave Daddy. It just opened up a whole new world for her—and for us—we're a family now.

KATIE: Now, she's had other therapies, though, we want to point out. She was also on a special diet for some time. Why are you convinced, Sharon, that it was the Tomatis Method that really was responsible for her vast improvement?

SHARON: There's not a doubt in my mind that Tomatis really gave her that boost she needed. We had stopped her speech and occupational therapy during those loops of Tomatis. Every day of Tomatis, we were seeing brand new things emerge from her. She was eating new foods. She was spontaneously talking. She was hugging us and loving us. She was just...being re-born...almost. It was an amazing process!

KATIE: Valerie, a lot of experts on autism say that, while the Tomatis theory is sound, its therapy has not been scientifically proven to work for autistic children, because of the lack of controlled clinical studies. What is your response to that; and I'm just curious, if this therapy has been around for so long, why haven't there been controlled clinical studies?

VALERIE: I agree. We do need the controlled clinical trials. That's a very important piece of work that needs to be done. And I have many anecdotal stories—like Ashley's—but they're anecdotal. I think doing research takes a lot of skill. I'm a clinician. I've been building my practice. But we're trying to form collaborations with universities, with researchers and graduate students to get that work underway, because it is important.

KATIE: But we can't give false hope to all parents of autistic children. What percentages of children respond to this therapy?

VALERIE: Well, I'd say a good percentage respond. I think about 80%—but they're not all Ashleys. And it depends on their degree of severity. For some parents, having a child who now sleeps through the night, or who starts to toilet train or who wants to be with them for the first time is major improvement. But it's not at the same level as we saw with Ashley.

KATIE: We're almost out of time, but I know you're writing a book about your journey. What's your one piece of advice to parents?

SHARON: Heed the warning signs. Sometimes, parents just brush off some delays that they see in their children. Go to the doctor, go to the pediatrician, and just check it out. Don't give up, and don't be in denial. There's hope out there. I hope I can share that with everyone.

KATIE: Well, I think you have this morning. Sharon and Valerie, thanks so much. And we'll be right back.[2]

I got up from the couch. I hugged Katie and thanked her. Valerie and I headed off the set to the backstage door. Matt Lauer flew past us.

"You guys did great!" he said, sprinting to his next segment seeming late to the set.

I went back to the Green Room and met Dave. I hugged him. The butterflies had subsided. I was thrilled the segment had gone so well—that I hadn't cracked under pressure. I cried a few tears, but that was human of me.

I wasn't just talking to America that day about Ashley's recovery with a promising sound stimulation therapy. This was the first time I had actually come out and disclosed Ashley's disorder to even our friends. They didn't know about Ashley's diagnosis at all—until that segment.

For more than two years, Dave and I kept it a secret. Our friends knew Ashley was in speech therapy and on a special diet, but that was the extent of their knowledge.

After the segment, I called the house to check on our daughters. Apparently, the phone had not stopped ringing. All of our friends were calling to leave messages.

2. ©National Broadcasting Company, Inc. 2003, All Rights Reserved

"Sharon, you're my hero," one friend said in a message left with my mother.

"We are so happy for you and Dave—that Ashley is better. You should be very proud of yourself," another friend said.

It was almost cleansing having told our story to millions of viewers. I felt a weight had been lifted. The fact NBC was interested in Ashley's story was even that much more remarkable. But if Ashley's recovery from an autistic spectrum disorder at the age of four wasn't a human-interest topic, then I don't know what was. I hoped I touched a lot of people across the nation that day.

And then I found out I had. That week, the Spectrum Center received hundreds of phone calls and e-mails from parents who had viewed the *Today Show* segment. I had given hope to a lot of parents by telling Ashley's story—hope that often seems elusive when one is on a journey such as this. I enlightened them to a technology that, perhaps, they were previously unfamiliar with, and gave them another treatment option to consider for their children on the autistic spectrum. And, I changed a small business—Valerie's—forever.

Valerie was soon swamped. But she was very excited at the opportunity to treat so many new children—children described to her as being "just like Ashley." Inquiring parents were astounded that Ashley had ever presented on the autistic spectrum after seeing the television segment and her remarkable metamorphosis.

But before Ashley was typical, she was atypical—quite different from her sister who is 14 months older—quite different from peers her own age.

CHAPTER 2

▼

SUBTLE NUANCES

"Bye, Ashley! Bubie and Grandpa are going now," my mother said, as she and my father assembled their bags at the front door. It was the summer of 2000. They had come for a brief visit.

Ashley, 16-months-old at the time, stood fixated on the Barney video she was watching. Her back toward us, she did not gesture or turn around to acknowledge my mother's good-bye.

"We can't compete with Barney, either. Don't take it personally—she loves that purple dinosaur," I said, innocently.

"Ashley, come and give me a kiss good-bye!" my mother said, trying a second time.

But her attempt fell short again. Ashley remained mesmerized by the color and movement of the characters on the screen without so much of a flinch to acknowledge her grandmother. My mother gave up.

"Sharon, I think you should get her ears checked to see if her hearing is okay," my mother then suggested.

I shrugged off a reply to the motherly advice thinking to myself, "Her ears are fine. She's just a toddler enjoying a toddler show."

Little did I know, this motherly suggestion would set the wheels of our journey in motion—a journey the likes of which no one in the family could have ever imagined we were about to take!

The old adage, "Mothers are always right," kept a vigil in my mind for days after my parents had packed up and gone home. As I went about my daily routine with the girls, I was continuously haunted by my mother's suggestion of getting Ashley's ears tested. It was such a preposterous idea to me—an outlandish thought that there might be something wrong with Ashley. But I just couldn't bring myself to believe that. What agitated me more was that my mother had never steered me wrong when I was growing up—she always seemed to have the right answers. Maybe this was the one time my mother was mistaken. With all of the advice she'd given me, surely she could be wrong—just once!

But all it took was watching Ashley day to day; her lackluster demeanor, her disregard for everything non-Barney, and her isolation from all of us, to make me grow ever so uneasy with my mother's instincts. She was on to something—and I hadn't picked up on it—like she had.

But as new Moms, we want to be the first to notice things about our children, not have someone, even a caring family member, stumble upon it before we do. What kind of Mother would I be if I didn't notice these things in my children first? Did I not answer my mother because it was unsolicited advice? New Moms hate unsolicited advice. Did I not answer her because maybe she was right, and I just couldn't face the truth about something possibly being wrong with my child? Did I not want to come to terms with such a possibility?

I think, back then, I thought all of these things. I even thought, not my child—she's beautiful! How could she have any problems? Okay, Ashley didn't seem quite right, but she didn't seem quite wrong, either. But if my mother's suspicions of a problem were borne out of being around Ashley for a few hours during that short visit, why wasn't I more attuned to it? I am with Ashley all day, everyday! Where were *my* maternal instincts?

So, I heeded my mother's advice. I felt obligated to do so as well as to quell the persistent pounding in my head that wouldn't let me shake the notion of a possible problem with Ashley.

I began to test Ashley's hearing myself, not wanting to get a specialist involved at this premature stage. I followed Ashley around the house like her shadow, clapping my hands so vigorously they turned black and blue. I dropped toys on the hardwood floor, purposefully kicked some of the play things already strewn about, and yelled her name, as if trying to find her in a crowd. I made all kinds of noises just to see if she could hear them hoping she would turn to me.

She didn't—for the most part. She ignored me, preferring to meander about the room looking for the next best toy to occupy her mouth—she mouthed everything. There were fleeting moments, however, when she would turn around and look back at me. I took these momentary glances to mean she heard the clamoring and clattering of spoon-against-pot-in-my-hand—that she wasn't deaf at all. But they were looks as if she wanted to blurt out, (if she had that ability), "Lady, you are weird! *Stop* that noise! *Stop* your insanity! And *stop* following me!"

If she could hear me and turn around, even once, from the sound of an object I sent crashing to the floor, I figured she did not have a hearing problem—my mother's original concern I now thought I could put to rest. Somewhat comforted by *that* revelation, it was still vague to me why Ashley continuously tuned us out when the simulated noise was no longer there. She just didn't seem to be all together in mind and spirit with the rest of us in the family—she seemed more like that of a lost, little soul.

The Early Years

We often assume when our child is handed to us at birth with a full set of fingers and toes and no physical deformities, that they are "healthy." Our worries from the last nine months are extinguished. We breathe a sigh of relief. We have no reason to believe otherwise. We put a lot of stock in physical appearances.

But it's really not that way at all. A beautiful, healthy-looking baby on the outside can start to have developmental problems on the inside. And more frightening, these problems can go unnoticed to the most attentive and doting mother. Even a trained pediatrician may shrug off a possible developmental delay, suggesting it is just a natural variation in development from one child to another. I've come to learn and witness *this* first hand.

Ashley is our beautiful, blue-eyed daughter, her hair naturally highlighted with splashes of blonde. She is the middle child of three girls. How she got the light hair and blue eyes is still an unsolved mystery. The rest of the family has dark hair and dark eyes. But genetics are hard to figure out.

I started noticing some peculiarities with Ashley while she was growing up, which didn't set off too many alarms, each one taken individually. I figured as Ashley matured, these things would just work themselves out naturally. But piecing them all together, as time elapsed, started to weave a story in Ashley's development that we would soon come to discover.

The Bottle Battle

The immediate thing I noticed was Ashley wouldn't take a bottle when she was a baby. I tried every nipple on the market, but she refused them all. I didn't know if she was refusing the liquid in the bottle or the nipple. All attempts I made to introduce a bottle to her were met with flailing hands and gagging. I found it unusual, because I had never had any trouble with her older sister, Kacey, taking a bottle. I thought all babies took bottles! Now, all of a sudden, mine didn't! I was more than confused. Where is the section in my baby book about not taking a bottle, ever? I looked for it. It's not there. Someone out there assumes there are no problems with this—now, I know better. Back then I thought it was just Ashley's nature to want to be nursed as opposed to taking an impersonal bottle. I thought it warm and sweet of her to always want me. But it was not always convenient when she wouldn't take a bottle. It was hard for me to leave Ashley with anyone.

Slip Sliding Away

As a baby, I noticed Ashley just didn't have a lot of meat on her bones. She wasn't a "pleasingly plump" baby. Her legs and arms were thin. I could see the veins underneath her skin quite vividly. And she was a floppy baby—very floppy. She would nearly slide out of my arms each time I held her. When I propped her up on the couch to take her picture, she would slither down the cushions. I'd prop her back up, she'd slide back down. She was like a jellyfish.

At birth, her weight was normal, around the 75th percentile on the growth chart. But by six months of age, she was below the 50th percentile. From then on, her weight and height crept at a snail's pace, and put her in the 10th percentile by the time she was one-year-old. I was concerned with her petite, frail-looking body, quite undersized in comparison to other children her age. But Ashley's pediatrician seemed to shrewdly pacify my anxiety. He was only concerned if she was to fall below the chart, which she hadn't—yet. She was just teetering on the border. I am small-framed. Maybe, she had my genes! Again, "the tricky genetics," I thought! That was the only reason I could think of to explain her dwindling size.

I remember going in for Ashley's one-year checkup. The nurse thought Ashley was there for her six-month checkup, until she looked down at Ashley's chart. Her size must have been so obviously small for even a trained nurse to make such a comment.

Two Left Feet

Ashley sat and crawled within the normal developmental timeframes—albeit at the latter end—but still normal by our pediatrician's standards. Ashley learned to walk within the normal developmental limits as well, but again at the latter part of the milestone range. She always seemed gingerly in her movements, her legs too weak to support her. She was quite clumsy. Again, I thought the clumsiness must have been my genetics hard at work. I carry around a trait my loving husband refers to as being a "klutz"—a term of endearment he lovingly labeled me with the day I met him in college. Fortunately for me, he was able to see past that uncontainable flaw and made me his wife, nonetheless.

As Ashley toddled about trying to figure out how her legs worked, she never quite grasped the understanding that putting her hands forward would break her fall. Consequently, her forehead always found the hard floor or the cement of our driveway. I would watch her forehead swell into a mass of black and blue from the impact and always in the same place as the previous fall. As I carefully and motherly positioned an ice pack on her boo boo, her hands vehemently swatted me away, dueling with my efforts at immediate first-aid. I cried along with her and tucked her head under my chin. I could feel her pain, and was so angry at myself for not being there sooner to catch her before the fall.

Loose Lips

With her legs weak and unsure of their role on her body, I soon noticed her mouth and lips were not very adept at drinking. When Ashley made the transition to a sippy cup at a year old, the spill-proof tops proved quite challenging for her. She couldn't master the sucking technique. I had to put a top on the cup that practically spilled the drink into her mouth. She also had trouble using a straw. Not knowing what else to do with the straw, she would chew it. In restaurants, I would watch other children her age, or even younger, being given a sip from a straw or an open cup by their mothers. "Why can't my daughter drink like that yet? What's wrong with her?" I would ask myself.

A Cut Above The Rest

As Ashley was cutting her teeth, she didn't get the two bottom teeth first, as I read is customary. She got one top tooth and one bottom tooth at the same time. I thought this too, a bit odd and out of line with normal child development. I tried to find a cause for this in my many baby books, but I couldn't find anything. Only a mother would park such information in her brain. I didn't place too much emphasis on it at the time. The others came in fine. I have since learned from Ashley's pediatrician, it is the sucking pressure distributed on the gums that is responsible for babies cutting their first teeth. Supposedly, the bottom gum gets more pressure during nursing or sucking on a bottle promoting the bottom teeth to break through first. Since Ashley had sucking difficulties, it was odd pressure nursing on me that apparently made a top and bottom tooth cut first.

This displaced oral pressure was just another link in the chain. She had weak suction nursing, she couldn't suck on a sippy cup well, she couldn't suck on a straw, she couldn't drink from an open cup, she cut her first teeth out of order from the norm, and she constantly sucked her thumb. Something more was going on in her mouth than the little meaning I attached to these early on in her development.

The Ears Have It

By 15 months, Ashley had suffered as many as five ear infections. I thought that excessive. The pediatrician, however, didn't think it was worrisome. Then again, it wasn't he who was up with her on those horrible, sleepless nights. We were. We paced for hours trying to get her to go back to sleep, trying to stop the blood-curdling screams, trying to make the hurt go away. The doctor defended his nonchalance toward her ear infections using the reasoning that the size and position of a young child's Eustachian tubes do not allow for effective draining of fluids that collect in the ear. Therefore, the ear is vulnerable to infection. And he was quick to point out that babies who spend an inordinate amount of time on their backs can be even more prone to ear infections—and was she spending too much time in this position?

Outside of those ear infections and bottles and bottles of antibiotics she gagged on when we squirted the liquid down her throat with a baby syringe, Ashley seemed otherwise healthy. (We did become aware of an allergy to amoxicillin during one of her bouts with an ear infection. She broke out in a rash all over her body.)

Good Girl!

Ashley was always such a "good" baby, and I considered myself a rather cool-headed Mom. Ashley never really fussed. She was easy going. I always thought if one had a quiet baby, it was something of which to be proud. Somehow that parent learned the art of calm that others had not yet studied—a calm parent, a calm baby. When Ashley was a toddler, strangers would remark at what a 'good girl' she was—how well behaved she was in public places.

"Is she always that good?" a mother curiously asked me, grabbing the candy her little terror had just stripped from the shelves at the checkout aisle.

"Yes, she is a very good baby. I'm very lucky!" I said, taking it as a compliment to my mothering.

Ashley was just the opposite of that rambunctious child. She was low key, never made a noise, never meddled with things, and never, ever, upset a grocery display—a rather pleasant shopping companion. I took her everywhere!

Opposites Don't Attract

I don't know why I didn't pick up on Ashley's quiet demeanor sooner. I always thought this was a rather refreshing break from that of Kacey, who was entrenched in the "terrible twos" stage at the time, and could be quite a handful. But, despite the terrible twos, Kacey was really quite easy to mother, I have to admit. If I placed something in front of her, she ate it. If I told her to go to the potty, she went. (She was potty training at 18 months.) If I sent her to time-out, she willingly complied. She knew when she had done something wrong, and that I was angry—she could read my facial expressions.

Kacey was very much into books. She loved curling up with Dave and me to have her favorite books read to her, no less than five times in a sitting. She loved to play "school" and could be very creative with her play. Playing just came naturally to Kacey. She would pull us into her little world and pretend to be the teacher. She made us sit in "circle time" and recite the days of the week, while she pointed in the air with a stick, tapping an imaginary calendar. She even put us in time-out occasionally, exercising her teacher privileges. What a crafty two-year-old!

Since the two girls were only 14 months apart, I thought they would become great buddies. Kacey was a great role model and teacher for Ashley. I thought Ashley would follow cues from Kacey and want to do all of the things her big sister did. Or, if not follow her big sister then, maybe Ashley would take the lead (like Kacey had done when she was younger) and show me what she was all about.

But I never got the lead from Ashley, and she rarely followed protocol, either. The toys we had didn't seem to interest her, except for the purposes of chewing them. Unlike Kacey, she didn't understand what to do with a doll. Ashley didn't know how to feed it, brush its hair, put it to bed, or even give it a kiss. She didn't know how to have a tea party or play hospital. She couldn't throw or kick a ball, or even jump down the last step of stairs.

Ashley never cuddled up with us to have a story read like Kacey did. In the coziness of our laps we bonded with Kacey as she turned each page of the book. This intimacy with Ashley could never be realized. Ashley found solace in turning the pages of an opened book by herself from across the room, away from us. She had no idea there was a wonderful story within those pages—one, we so desperately wanted to share with her.

Ashley had no interest in playing with Kacey. She chose to be alone. She found insignificant things to occupy her time. She always scoured the floor examining the crumbs I missed on my pass through with the broom. The crumbs intrigued her. She also migrated toward shoestrings and played with them, for whatever little joy they gave her in return. Why did these mundane objects interest her so much? What kind of satisfaction was she getting out of them, more so than being with us?

Video Zombie

Kacey enjoyed watching Barney videos, and Ashley quickly became a fan—finally something they could do together. Barney was their absolute favorite. We named our living room the "Barney Room," a place where the girls would sit and watch their videos. Once a video started, it swept Ashley up, and there was no tapping into her attention. She was like a zombie in front of the television. Ashley could watch an entire video with her sister and not get up or be distracted by other things. I can't say I know many toddlers with such staying power! I don't think she understood the videos, she just watched them in an absorbed state, all the while sucking her thumb and tuning out the rest of the world.

I noticed sometimes it didn't even matter if the volume was turned down. It was the picture that captivated her—not the sound—not the music. Yet, sometimes, Ashley would cry inconsolably when a certain puppet in one of the videos appeared on the screen. I didn't know if it was the look of the character that scared her, or the sound of its voice. But it immediately traumatized her, and she would break down and cry. Even as I stood in another room, I knew from Ashley's sudden eruption into tears which part of the video they were watching. It was like clockwork. Something was setting Ashley off.

Ashley never danced along with the characters on the screen or laughed at something funny on the videos like Kacey did. Ashley couldn't sing, but she started to hum the tunes. I noticed when a character came on that she seemed to enjoy, Ashley got really excited and jumped up and down. She flapped both hands, as if she were a bird about to take off from its perch and got up on her tippy toes. She did this a few seconds and then stopped. When something seemed exciting to her again, she started flapping her hands and got back up on her toes. I thought this was either normal reaction to something exciting, or maybe, she was finally imitating movements the characters were doing. I didn't know it would become clinically significant—I was to find that out later.

Sometimes Ashley watched the television from a most peculiar side angle. I couldn't imagine how she saw anything from that perspective. I always repositioned her in front of the television. Yet, she preferred to revisit that angle time and time again as she watched from her peripheral vision. She also stood extremely close to the television screen, for what reason, I'm not sure. Again, I always moved her back to a more suitable distance.

Sometimes, if Kacey wasn't in the room with her, I would find Ashley sitting in front of the television watching the "snow" on the screen after the video was over and had rewound itself. If someone wasn't there to tell her the video was over, she just sat there. Ashley never came to find me so that I could turn the television off, and she never gestured for a new video. She never gave me these signals—she didn't know how.

The Crib Potato

Each time I went into Ashley's bedroom to get her from her crib—though wide awake—she was always on her back. She never sat or stood up to greet me. She remained on her back with her toes woven through the railing, sucking her thumb looking skyward. She never played with the toys attached to her crib. She never looked at the books I placed at one end of the crib. Rarely did she make noise to let me know she was even awake. Ashley seemed content not needing anyone or anything—except for that left thumb. It was as if she were thinking, "If they get to me, great. If not, I'll just wait." I couldn't imagine after a long night's sleep or a refreshing nap, she could still be tired enough to remain on her back—but that's where I always found her. She spent so much time on her back in the crib, she was probably thinking, "They should really do more with this ceiling!"

If It's Not Crunchy, I'm Not Eating It!

One day I was feeding Ashley strained baby food. She seemed to tolerate it just fine. It was like any other day during her solid food stage. Then, the next day, it stopped! She completely shunned it. She made it abundantly clear she was through with strained foods. I was totally unprepared for it. I was gearing up for a slow transition off of strained foods and into table food. But Ashley had a very different timetable for me—hers was now!

I thought she was giving me a message that she was now ready for grown up foods. I was just a little bit mistaken. From that point on, she became very picky and wouldn't eat anything we placed in front of her. She wouldn't eat fruit, eggs, cheese, meats, or bread. She absolutely wouldn't take mushy, gooey, runny, or sloppy foods. She had been on baby food for months—it doesn't get much gooier, sloppier, and runnier than that! But now, if she happened to get a dab on her finger, she cried like it was fire burning her to the bone.

The girl would not eat! I found a crunchy vegetable snack made of spinach, tomato, and potato that went over big with her. I thought this was a good way to get vegetables into her diet, even if it was in the form of a snack food. It seemed nothing else worked. This snack food turned out to be one of a few limited things she ate for months and months. And when she finished eating them, she got more. I know my parents thought we were spoiling her appetite, but it was literally one of the only things we could get in her. She ate Cheerios and crackers and some snack foods that were primarily crunchy. "What was it about this craving for crunchiness that made her refuse all other textures of food?" I wondered.

If she wasn't going to eat, I thought she had better drink. I started giving Ashley whole milk when she turned one-year-old, just as I had done with Kacey. I always thought the introduction of milk was a special time—like a right of passage into toddlerhood—my big girl could now get milk. I was probably overgenerous with the milk, knowing she needed calcium, because she was not currently getting it through foods in her diet. She gulped it down in cupfuls. So, Ashley lived off of a diet of veggie snacks, Cheerios, crackers, milk, and juice for a very long time. And I slipped a multivitamin in her sippy cup to narrow the gap for the lost nutrients in her diet.

It wasn't the healthiest of diets, I know. I was an emotional wreck over the fact that something wasn't right with the way she refused food.

Meal times were excruciatingly difficult for Ashley and me.

"Ashley, you need to eat, sweetie!" I would say, welling up with tears trying to get her to taste something—anything!

But Ashley just sat in her high chair and gave me blank stares. She seemed bored out of her mind. She was not the least bit interested in what was on her plate—not touching even a morsel. All she did was suck her thumb. I was worried sick over her lackadaisical behavior. She was weak and thin and had no energy or desire to do much of anything.

Everything I read about toddlers and their picky eating habits made me think Ashley was just in a stage that she would soon outgrow. But as her pickiness continued for months, I became worried. She went many meals without eating anything—even veggie snacks were tiring after a while. She was already quite small for her age, and her head circumference was not growing very much. (I know this, because I was overly obsessed with measuring her head on a daily basis, hoping for the slightest change in growth.) And when I noted no change in her head size, I grew more uneasy with what I saw happening to my little girl.

Affection Rejection

Ashley never took the initiative to show us any affection. Sometimes, when we hugged her or picked her up, she screamed and squirmed her way out of our arms wanting to be put down. She had a gymnast's back bend—near that of a perfect ten—which she used to escape our hugs. It was difficult to understand what she wanted. We offered her things we thought she needed, but all she did was balk and run the other way. She couldn't communicate with us.

When friends or family visited, she screamed. Just having someone say, "Hi, Ashley, how are you?" sent Ashley into a tail spin. I reassured them she was either having a bad day, (a cover-up, because I knew it was always like this), or that, because she didn't see them on a regular basis, was unfamiliar with them, and to not take it personally (a feasible answer I conjured up).

But how could they not take it personally? Both sets of Ashley's grandparents seemed very disappointed knowing that the affection they came to give her on those visits would never be received or reciprocated—and none of us could figure out why she acted that way.

"That's okay, she'll come to me when she's ready," my father always said, to bring an end to the horrible scene. But she never came to him on that visit—or any of the ones to follow.

So, my parents and in-laws moved on from one grandchild who shunned them—Ashley—and migrated toward Kacey during their visits. Kacey could speak and relate to them and, frankly, was exceptionally bright for her two and a half years. Ashley ended up playing by herself and did not join in the fun. In the interest of wanting to maintain the peace, Dave and I just let her isolate herself, since we didn't want to make more of a scene than what had already been made.

Ashley seemed out of touch with us and everyone with whom she came in contact. She preferred wandering in her own little world with her own agenda, keeping us and others at a distance. She seemed to be in a thick fog that would never lift. Horrible as it may sound, Ashley was more like a pet than a child. Then again, pets at least crawl up on your lap and love you. They don't squeal and take off running when you pay them attention or show them affection. They seek you out. Ashley was in our house, but she really could have been under the bed slumbering like a cat for all she participated in our family!

We failed in our attempts to communicate with her. We couldn't get to know who this little girl was and what she was all about. She wouldn't let us into her tightly-guarded space.

Even trying to take her picture was a fiasco. I always got the back of her head. She never faced forward to look at me. If by chance, I got lucky enough to "time the shot" when she did turn toward the camera, she looked like a deer caught in the headlights. She was frightened and stiff lipped. She never smiled. I don't even think she knew how to smile. I never saw it.

That's Puzzling!

Ashley could work a puzzle like no other toddler I had ever seen. She had found her forté. She shocked us all when she did three-to six-year-old children's puzzles, sorting numbers, colors and shapes, before she was two-years-old. I thought she was quite bright to do this! She quickly learned her ABCs, 123s, colors, shapes, animals, and even musical instruments by doing the puzzles over and over again. (But, I don't think she knew that number two came after number one, or that letter B came before C in the alphabet.) Ashley was visually able to read the shapes of puzzle pieces and match those shapes with their corresponding counterpart on the empty puzzle board. I thought it was wonderful that she was learning from these puzzles—she had finally started to take an interest in a purposeful, educational toy. It took her out of the comfortable chair she liked to dissolve herself into, and kept her hands busy so she didn't think about sucking her thumb. When she completed the puzzles, she turned the boards upside down, spilled the pieces on the floor in disarray, and then started the puzzles over again—and again—and again.

But I never knew that the amount of time she spent playing with the puzzles would ever become clinically significant. They were educational—or so, I thought!

My Computer Geek in the Making

Ashley also quickly became very skillful at using the computer. We introduced Ashley to the preschool software that Kacey had begun to use. At first, it seemed hard for Ashley to manipulate the mouse, because she had such dainty fingers. However, it only seemed to take her a few days to figure it all out. Soon she was clicking the cursor and painting pictures on the screen like a pro, and becoming quite adept at it, for being only two-years-old. She really enjoyed the software's animation and music. I was all for the time she spent on it. She was learning.

But I felt caught between a rock and a hard place. The puzzles and computer seemed enjoyable to her, yet they provided nothing in terms of interaction with us. However, these tools brought out a potential in Ashley we had never before seen. We noticed she was really quite a brilliant, little girl inside! She was very visual and seemed to have acquired skills way above her age level.

What was missing? She couldn't talk to us!

The Sound Of Silence

Ashley wasn't developing her speech and communication skills as well as I remember Kacey doing. Ashley said 'Dada' once around seven months, but little else—she just grunted a whole lot. I kept a keen ear out for 'Mama,' but it never arrived. I kept waiting in eagerness for 'cup' and 'ball' and 'doggie.' Those were words never spoken.

And yet, I thought it wasn't Ashley's time to talk. We all have our developmental timelines. Maybe Ashley's pace was just slower than that of Kacey, who met every developmental milestone early. I didn't want to compare her to Kacey. They were two, totally, different little girls. Ashley didn't deserve to be compared with Kacey just because she was younger. But older siblings are really the only comparison for development that we, as parents, have. So, it was only natural to notice the differences in achievements between them. But I compared them as loosely as possible. I didn't become overly concerned, at that point in time, when Ashley didn't quite meet the standards that Kacey had set by being the first born. I just gave it more time.

I remember my mother-in-law calling on weekends when Ashley was little. "How's the baby? What's she doing? Is she talking yet?" she would ask, trying to catch up on her granddaughter's development.

"No, she's not talking yet—just making grunting noises," Dave would reply. The next week she would call and ask the same thing. The reply was the same. "No, she's not talking a whole lot yet."

My mother-in-law never mentioned her concerns about Ashley's lack of talking when she would call back then. Perhaps she didn't want to meddle with our parenting or say anything that might alarm us, yet she instinctively had that gut feeling something was not right with Ashley. Having recently moved to live closer to us, I learned of her worries about her granddaughter's development.

"Sharon, every time I called, Ashley was still not talking or babbling. I thought that wasn't normal. I remember going with you on one of your doctor's appointments with Ashley. It was Christmas time, and we had come to visit. I believe it was her nine-month checkup. I was just waiting for the doctor to see what I saw in Ashley—this lifeless little girl who didn't make a sound—didn't make a gesture. But he didn't! He didn't mention anything! I was concerned every time I changed her diaper—she never kicked her legs or reached for things like Kacey had done at that age. Kacey would pull my glasses off my head. She would reach up and grab the little bottles above her changing table as I changed her. She was into everything and would wriggle out of my grasp every time she had her diaper changed. Ashley didn't move a muscle—she just lay there and didn't mind—didn't fuss—didn't show a whole lot of happiness. It worried me!" she confided.

She sensed from a thousand miles away that Ashley was having problems—problems Kacey never had.

Then again, my mother-in-law compared everything about Ashley's development with that of Kacey's. Kacey's extraordinary ability in meeting every developmental milestone extremely early, coupled with the way she instantaneously picked up on learning, seemed to afford her a gleam in my mother-in-law's eye as being "a very smart little girl." With Kacey so blatantly bright, it appeared almost like black marks against Ashley when she compared the two—Ashley was just not following suit.

But to my mother-in-law's credit and her instincts four states away, Ashley wasn't babbling. Her speech wasn't progressing. And she wasn't attaining her developmental milestones—irregardless of the bar that Kacey had set so high. Something was prohibiting Ashley from developing, communicating and getting to know any of us.

I had no idea what that something was—until it hit me *(smack)* in the face…like an unexpected, frozen snowball…leaving me just as cold and numb.

In short, Ashley wasn't becoming verbal.

"How did I miss that one?"

CHAPTER 3

▼

THE BLAME GAME

Having passed my unsophisticated and makeshift hearing test, my opinion was Ashley could hear—albeit, she seemed to have selective hearing. But, I thought that's how most toddlers acted. However, the issue of not always being able to capture her attention on my terms became more commonplace than not. As hard as I tried, Ashley rarely sought me out or tuned me in. I caved in to my mother's instincts. I made an appointment to see Ashley's pediatrician.

Ashley's primary doctor was not in the office the day of our appointment. I saw one of the other doctors in the pediatric practice.

"My husband and I have become concerned with Ashley's hearing. She ignores us when we call her name. She really won't interact with us on any level. I've tried making all sorts of noises, and she does turn around on occasion. But she doesn't speak yet; she has this grunt about her like she's trying to talk. She's up a lot at night just crying, and we can't console her."

"And she's how old?" the doctor asked, unfamiliar with Ashley, looking back through her chart.

"She's 17 months. I don't see her tugging at her ears, so I don't think her ears are bothering her. But something is," I told the doctor.

"Let me take a look in her ears and see what's going on in there," she said, putting her otoscope together.

She checked both ears.

"They look good to me—free of fluid, wax, and infection," she said, without hesitation.

"Actually, they are some of the nicer looking ears I've seen today," she smiled, recapping her long day of seeing screaming toddlers with ear infections.

I was oddly surprised! Rarely did we ever come out of that office without a prescription for antibiotics to treat an ear infection. The doctor's findings weren't only surprising to me, they were worrisome. As twisted as it may sound, I was hoping for at least an ear infection or wax build-up. That would at least explain why Ashley was having attention difficulties and language problems, and why she often cried like she was in pain.

Back when Ashley was ten-months-old, I took her to have her ears checked for a possible infection. The nurse practitioner couldn't see into Ashley's ears due to a build-up of wax. With a small instrument, she tried removing the wax without success. She had a nurse bring in, of all things, a Water Pik!

"Is that safe?" I asked myself, trusting their peculiar medical practices.

While I did my best to pin Ashley down on the examination table, the nurse positioned the Pik in her ear and turned on the pulsating stream of water. After a few seconds and a lot of wrestling holds on my part to keep Ashley still, a chunk of wax dribbled out of her ear. I gasped! I watched the wax float in a puddle of water that had collected on the table near Ashley's ear.

I thought that maybe having an excess of wax in her ears back then, at such a crucial point in her development, could have been cause for her hearing and speech difficulties now.

"Did the pressure from the Water Pik damage a nerve in Ashley's ear? Was this the nurse's fault? Was I being too trusting by letting them shove that Pik in her ear back then? Was this the usual protocol for removing wax from an infant's ear?" I wondered, trying to reason it all out.

I just wanted some answers. But I wasn't finding any that day. Her ears were beautiful inside—quite a rarity.

The pediatrician agreed that Ashley's speech was a bit delayed for her age and advised us to get a BAER test. She explained this hearing test, known as the Brainstem Auditory Evoked Response (BAER), detects electrical activity in the ear and auditory pathways in the brain in much the same way an antenna detects radio and television signals, or an EKG detects electrical activity of the heart. The doctor wrote a prescription for the test and sent me on my way.

I never followed through with the suggested BAER test. Ashley just seemed too small in my mind to be hooked up to wires. It sounded too frightening at the time. I didn't think there was that much cause for concern—enough to subject my little girl to a test like that! I figured I would give it just a little bit more time.

A month later, we returned to the pediatrician's office for Ashley's scheduled 18-month well-exam. This time, we were able to see Ashley's regular pediatrician. I told him about our visit a month earlier to have Ashley's ears checked and that she hadn't yet begun to talk or even babble. I informed him of our suspicions of a hearing problem. He thumbed back to the pages of our previous visit and read the progress notes from the doctor who had seen Ashley.

"She doesn't have *any* words?" he asked.

"None," I said, worry filling my voice.

"She should be saying many words by now," he informed me. "How do you know what she wants?"

"I don't most of the time," I said, shrugging my shoulders. "We just give her what we think she needs. We put more food on her tray when it looks like she's getting low—if she eats at all. We fill up her cup when it is empty. We put a stash of toys in front of her. It's quite a guessing game," I told him.

"It sounds like you are always there meeting her needs before she gets a chance to ask for something."

"But she can't ask! She has no words! She doesn't communicate with us! I don't think it is a case of me beating her to the words. As much as I try to imitate language for her, she doesn't grasp it and use it back to me the way Kacey did when she was learning. Frankly, she avoids interacting with us."

How did he think Ashley was going to ask for anything if she didn't have the vocabulary to do so?

I acknowledged his point about meeting all of Ashley's needs before she could ask me. I absolutely *was* doing that. But I was doing it because clearly there was something going on with her communicating with us—she couldn't. I felt I had to make up for it by providing her with everything—it was being done out of necessity—not from a spoiling standpoint. I wasn't a first-time Mom! I did know *something* about parenting. I didn't feel like I was spoiling Ashley. I gave her things without her cuing me first, because those attempts had failed. She had to eat! She had to drink! She had to play! So, I gave her those things. When I had done the same things for Kacey when she was younger, she used her language just fine. For some reason, I felt I had to talk for Ashley and give her things I thought she needed, since she couldn't put the words together and communicate them herself.

But I played devil's advocate with the doctor. Granted, he had a plausible reason for Ashley not talking, and I could see where he was going with this. I almost felt the need to duck, sensing he was winding up a pitch to sling the blame my way. Maybe he was right. Why should she talk? There was no motivation for her to speak. We did everything for her. She was getting everything from her big sister and us.

But that was a short-lived thought on my part. I didn't think that was the case at all. With all of the concern recently about Ashley's hearing and her lack of attention, I was really becoming swayed that there might be something more going on here—something medical.

After looking in her ears—which showed no sign of infection—I think I convinced the doctor enough so that he, too, looked genuinely concerned. He opened his prescription book and wrote a prescription for Ashley to have a speech and hearing evaluation, and referred her to an ENT (ear, nose, and throat) specialist for further assessment.

"Well, let's see what these evaluations tell us," he said, handing me the prescription.

"You have a tough road ahead of you. This is going to take a lot of work on your part," he said with a most serious face.

He closed Ashley's medical chart and clutched it under his arm along with his small medical bag.

"Keep me informed. Please have me copied on all of the reports. Call me if you need anything."

He opened the door and left the room.

While I waited for the nurse to come in and administer Ashley's scheduled immunizations, I wondered to myself what Ashley's having a speech delay meant in terms of my having a tough road ahead.

"Wouldn't Ashley's speech just come in on its own? Wasn't it just a little tardy? Wouldn't she be able to catch up to her peers?" I asked myself, staring blankly at the prescription he had written.

I folded the paper and put it in my bag. I sensed things were getting a bit more serious than Ashley just being a late bloomer, or me being too doting of a mother. I think he, too, sensed this by enlisting the professional opinions of those at Children's Hospital. But I would wait with baited breath, as he would, for the results of the work-up and for our questions to be answered by the specialists.

A few weeks later, Dave and I walked anxiously with Ashley into Children's Hospital for her speech and hearing evaluation. It was October of 2000. I had never been to Children's Hospital, but I had heard great things about it. We sat in the waiting room with other parents and their children. We put Ashley down on the carpet, and she played with some toys. I observed all of the other children around Ashley's age romping around making normal noises—some were even speaking small sentences. I looked at Ashley. She wasn't making a sound. She was concentrating on a toy she had found. I was a bundle of nerves waiting and wondering what we were going to discover through this testing. I watched the goings on around me, from the shuffling of papers at the admissions desk to the many doctors calling out their next patient's name and escorting them off down the hall. It was quite crowded—or maybe it was always like that.

"Ashley Ruben?" I popped up and grabbed our bags.

"Hi, I'm the audiologist. I'll be seeing Ashley today."

"Come on Ash, it's time to go," Dave said, scooping her up and walking behind me.

Ashley did not appreciate being pried away from her toys. She began to cry. Her cry got louder and louder as we followed the audiologist down the winding corridor.

We entered the soundproof room. It was dimly lit.

"Why don't you go ahead and sit down with Ashley," the audiologist directed me.

I took Ashley from Dave's arms and sat in a chair opposite a glass window. Ashley was still crying. The audiologist removed a pair of headphones from the wall, extended them, and placed them over Ashley's golden locks. I held Ashley's arms so she didn't interfere with them. The headphones immediately slid down her baby-soft cheeks still dripping with tears. I repositioned them back up over her ears and tried to tighten them. They were already adjusted to the smallest size. I placed my chin on top of the headphones to hold them in place. They seemed gigantic on her small ears. She continuously tried to remove them.

Ashley was not at all cooperative. I can't say I blamed her. This was apparently not on her list of fun things to do that day. Dave and I wrestled with her to stay put. The audiologist walked into the control room behind the glass window opposite my chair. Reflections from the soft light hit the glass window so I could faintly see her at the control panel.

Then all of a sudden, a little bear appeared out of a small box high up in the corner of the wall. Ashley perked up and looked at the stuffed animal. She settled down. I could hear faint beeps and tones in her earphones as I hugged her tight to keep her from squirming out of the chair.

Each time Ashley heard a sound, she was rewarded with seeing the bear. One bear came out on the right side of the room. Another bear appeared on the left side of the room. This happened for a few minutes. All of this apparently gave the audiologist data on Ashley's hearing ability.

After a few minutes, the audiologist left her control panel and walked back into our room. Ashley and I turned around in the chair, and the audiologist unraveled some tubing that had been resting on top of another machine. She inserted an earpiece in Ashley's left ear and pressed a button. She explained to us this test indicated if there was any fluid in her ear at that moment. A certain curve on the graph gave her this indication.

"She looks good in this ear," the audiologist remarked.

She removed the tube from the left ear and tried to position it in Ashley's right ear. Ashley's right ear seemed a little smaller, as the tube did not fit as comfortably. The audiologist placed a smaller earpiece in the right ear, but was met with resistance from Ashley, who reached up and yanked the tubing free. Trying my best to insert it back into her ear, screams of protest ensued.

Ashley had made it abundantly clear her participation was now over! We decided to call it quits with the testing. It was fine by the audiologist. She apparently obtained enough data to make her conclusions.

The final results revealed Ashley's hearing was within normal range for the development of speech and language. Reassuring, to say the least, but not full of information to understand why Ashley wasn't talking, or why she ignored us when we talked to her.

"I will write up my report and send it to your doctor," she said, opening the door for us to leave.

We made our way back to the waiting room to pass the time before our next appointment with the speech and language pathologist. We watched Ashley play and roam aimlessly about the room. She was much happier in this setting, no longer crying, having forgotten what she had just gone through.

"Ashley Ruben?" a woman holding a manila folder called.

We followed her to her office, and she closed the door behind us. We introduced Ashley and ourselves.

"You can sit in a chair or on the floor; it doesn't matter," she said to us.

"Do you need us to play with her?" I asked.

"I'm just going to observe her for a little bit. You can sit down for now," she said, gathering her test papers.

Dave and I sat down on the floor with Ashley as the speech therapist gave us a brief rundown of what she planned to do to assess Ashley.

"Hi, Ashley," she said, trying to create a bond with her.

The therapist unlocked her cabinet doors with a key she wore on her arm as a bracelet. She pulled out some toys to occupy Ashley while she took a history from us.

Right away she could see Ashley wasn't interested in the toys and didn't really know how to play with them. Ashley wandered around for a little while making a grunt sound that had become familiar to Dave and me.

"Ashley!" the therapist called.

Ashley ignored her.

"Ashley!" she called in a firmer voice.

Again, Ashley did not respond to her name.

"Look Ashley, a duck. Do you know what a duck says?" But Ashley didn't care for it.

"Ashley, I have some blocks. Do you want to build something?"

Ashley sat down. The therapist tried to get her to build a tower with wooden blocks, but Ashley was unable to stack one on top of the other. She preferred putting them in her mouth. I was quick to point out to the therapist that Ashley could stack the jumbo plastic interlocking blocks at home. But apparently that didn't show the therapist whatever it was she was looking for with stacking the wooden ones. Those blocks were "cheating" in her opinion—so much for my attempts at trying to secure Ashley some points!

Ashley wandered about the room toddling quite wobbly and taking in what little scenery there was. She was not particularly interested in any of the toys on the floor.

"Is this how she plays at home?" the therapist asked, referring to Ashley's limited play, mouthing of the toys, and grunting sounds.

"Yes," we said in unison.

"This is pretty much it. She puts most everything in her mouth, and she sucks her thumb a great deal," I added.

The therapist gave a small ball to Ashley who immediately put it up to her mouth.

"Can you give the ball to Mommy?" the therapist asked.

I knew she couldn't, because she didn't know the word Mommy—much less identifying the name with me. I had come to accept that.

Then, I held out my hand and asked her for the ball. Surprisingly, it somehow landed in my hand. I was shocked!

"She's never given me a ball before just now," I said, enthusiastically.

I wanted to give Ashley back any points she had lost by not doing it upon the therapist's request.

"Good job, Ash!" Dave said, quite in disbelief himself.

"I'm looking for her to do this on a consistent basis as a measure of her receptive language skills."

"Oh," I said, feeling a bit deflated by her comment.

The therapist was not as impressed as we were about what had just transpired. I thought it was huge! But it was another failed attempt on my part to slide some points Ashley's way.

Maybe it was a fluke that the ball ended up in my hand. But thinking more about it, Ashley seemed to understand the request more when she got a visual prompt—me holding out my hand to receive the ball. Having the therapist ask her to put it in my hand just didn't register like it did with a visual.

I started to sing some songs with hand gestures and Ashley seemed to respond to that immediately. She was even trying to imitate with her hands. Songs seemed to be how I could captivate her attention.

After about 45 minutes of testing and note taking, the speech therapist gathered her thoughts and summarized what she had observed. As Ashley wandered around scanning the room, we listened closely to what the therapist had concluded during her observations.

She told us Ashley's play skills were limited to exploratory play with limited functional play skills. Ashley's eye contact and interactions were limited with her and with us. Her pragmatic skills (the use of communication for social purposes) were also limited. Ashley couldn't vocalize to express comment or label things. She did, however, express protest by pushing away from a non-desired object on occasion. She mouthed toys and did not use them for their intended purpose. She also sucked her thumb continuously. Okay, we knew these!

The consonants Ashley had were limited to /n/, /h/, /d/, and sometimes /g/. With respect to expressive language (what Ashley could communicate), Ashley was unable to point, and she could not demonstrate the ability to imitate speech sounds, non-speech sounds (animal or environment), or words. She was unable to say her own name, or anyone else's.

With respect to receptive language (what she understood), Ashley loved music or singing (i.e., finger songs such as "Where is Thumbkin?") and responded to a sound source. She responded to "no" most of the time and would maintain attention only when we played finger songs with her.

She was not able to identify two body parts when asked. Although, I again spoke up for her telling the therapist she was able to do these at home. Ashley did not respond to gestures such as "come up" or "want up." She did not respond when her name was called. She did not wave "bye-bye." She did not demonstrate the ability to follow simple commands.

The therapist scored Ashley's overall speech and language ability at a six-month-old level. In short, Ashley was a 19-month-old child with language and communication skills similar to that of an infant!

"She's like an infant?" I said to myself, not understanding any of this.

Somehow, Ashley had not developed her language skills beyond that of when she was six-months-old.

I inhaled a deep breath and let it out slowly with my lips pursed together—a cleansing breath I had learned in Lamaze class. I tried to slow my heart rate down; I felt it beating faster with each word the therapist spoke. Tears pooled in my eyes, but I fought them back by tilting my head toward the lights in the ceiling. I didn't want to break down right there, in front of a stranger, so I forced myself to be strong and keep a cool head and try to understand everything the therapist was telling us.

Still, my heart sank. This was such a dismal report. I knew Ashley wasn't responding to us, but to compare her to an infant was just numbing. I was very confused.

Ashley never really had any trauma to her that I knew of, except tripping resulting in a few bumps on her forehead. Was *that* enough to delay her speech? I had a normal pregnancy, but had an emergency C-section, because I couldn't push her out. The doctor was becoming worried about her vital signs, so we decided it best to have the surgery. Did something happen during my pushing or delivery? Was this my fault?

How could this be possible? How could I have not seen this earlier? How do we fix this? *Is* it fixable? Or would Ashley just be considered of low mental capacity all her life?

A million things swirled in my head at that moment. I hoped Dave was still paying attention to the therapist, because I had mentally left the conversation. I could hear the therapist speak, but I wasn't listening.

I imagined pictures in my mind of Ashley growing up and being a cheerleader like I had been. I saw her hitting aces on the tennis court making her tennis pro Daddy proud of her. I saw her winning swimming awards like I had won. I saw her immersed in drawing and art like I had a passion for. I saw her at the piano— she loved music. I saw her in a wedding dress—perhaps it was the one I wore. I saw her holding a baby—my grandchild? I saw them all in a few instantaneous seconds—and saw them fade away just as quickly.

What was happening? Why was this slide show of Ashley's life racing through my mind? What was the speech therapist telling us that made me think Ashley was not going to grow up and achieve things like this and have a fulfilling life? I zoned back in and re-focused on the conversation.

"Is this a type of…mental retardation?" I asked the therapist with a lump in my throat.

I don't think the therapist wanted to touch that one—but I could read her poker face.

"I'd like to refer you to our neurodevelopmental pediatrician, Dr. Conlon. I think it would also be a good idea to see our psychologist."

"My God!" I thought.

The titles of these doctors were not painting a pretty picture in my mind.

"What's going on with Ashley? Just tell us!" I so desperately wanted to scream out at her!

"She needs a psychologist? And a neuro something or other? Huh?" I said to myself.

I had no idea what a neurodevelopmental pediatrician was, but my background in biology did not like the sound of "neuro" at all.

Both doctors were located down the hall from her office, and both had waiting lists three-months long.

"How can you make a 19-month-old child wait for such an evaluation?" I thought, angrily.

I didn't realize there were so many children who saw neurodevelopmental pediatricians and psychologists that the doctors booked patients three plus months in advance. They were obviously very busy with very large patient loads. It almost made me think Ashley's problems were typical of a lot of children seen at this hospital.

The therapist recommended Ashley start intensive speech therapy sessions—two to three times a week—immediately. She, too, had a full load of patients, but Ashley was placed on her waiting list. I knew my health insurance company would only cover an initial evaluation, so treatment by this therapist was not within my insurance network. I would have to go elsewhere to find covered services.

But the therapist made some suggestions which we were to start implementing at home until we found services for Ashley:

- We were to work with Ashley by engaging her in finger play ("Itsy-Bitsy Spider," "Where is Thumbkin?" and "Wheels on the Bus"), since she responded so well to music.

- We were to initially manipulate her hands and body to participate in the song, and then slowly fade our prompts.

- We were to design an environment with as many communicative opportunities as possible in our home. This was to be done by keeping toys and desired objects out of reach, so Ashley had to initiate the request of these objects through gesture, vocalization, or better yet, through words.

- When Ashley was finished playing with a toy, she was to use the phrase "all done," either verbally or signing, to help her develop a sense of termination instead of just walking away and moving on to the next best toy.

- When we gave Ashley food, we were to give her only a few pieces at a time to encourage her to develop requesting through pointing or saying "more."

- We were to develop her joint attention by following her lead and commenting on what she attends to. We were also to point out items of interest in order to encourage her to follow our lead.

- We were to model language above her current level (which was obviously quite low). If she just used approximations, we were to praise her at each attempt she made, regardless of the quality of the imitation. It was important for Ashley to understand why we were praising her by saying, "good talking" or "I like the way you said 'more' or 'nice words.'"

- We were to work on her social skills by encouraging her to use "no" by shaking our heads back and forth to express protest.

- We were to teach her sign language for words such as "help," "please," and "more," so she could have her wants and needs met.

Wow! This was a lot to digest. We were not speech pathologists by any stretch. It all seemed quite overwhelming. Ashley couldn't say a word. How was I going to get her to request something off a top shelf or say "all done" when she was finished playing? How was I ever going to teach her sign language? That seemed way too hard to do!

Talking is a natural, progressive process with most children. It seemed like I was going to have to rig Ashley's environment to tease the talking out of her—something I thought a little sneaky and somewhat unnatural.

It really was going to take creativity and a lot of time and effort on our part to ignite her verbally. It then dawned on me what Ashley's pediatrician must have meant. I guess this was the "hard work" message he was trying to impress upon me.

Would the average parent take these steps to get their toddler to talk? Holding Elmo hostage on the top shelf until the decibels of Ashley's screaming broke the sound barrier or my wedding crystal, (whichever came first), was not something I was looking forward to or even thought practical.

We arrived home from the hospital, and it was time to begin the battle. I spent about three hours on the phone to the health insurance company trying to find the recommended neurodevelopmental pediatrician and psychologist within my health care network. Knowing how expensive this journey would get if I didn't stay in-network was weighing heavy on my mind.

A few hours earlier, I was told my daughter was developmentally delayed and required many hours-a-week of therapy. That was enough to bring me to tears. But to add to the misery, the health care world was chipping away at my already-fragile state, telling me these specialists were not in my network!

"What do you mean there's no one in my network?" I said, nearly ready to explode over the phone. "I can't keep my daughter waiting for these services. She's not even two-years-old!"

"Please hold Ma'am," the cold and seemingly uncaring voice on the other end of the phone said.

I grew more livid each time I was put on hold.

"Please be patient, your call is important to us. We will be with you shortly," the annoying recording on the phone repeated.

I wanted to cry again and hang up. So, I did both.

Meanwhile, I could hear Dave and Ashley upstairs. He was singing "Five little ducks" to her, and she was imitating the quack sound by saying, "cack, cack, cack." I had never heard her do that before! It was wonderful! She couldn't imitate animal sounds for the therapist a few hours before, but now she could? But now, it was in the context of a song, not the question, "Ashley, what sound does a duck make?"

It was becoming clear to me that Ashley was more responsive when she heard singing and music. Obviously, she had just proven it. She knew exactly what sound a duck made.

"Does she get those points back?" I wondered.

I just wanted her to talk—we all did. But she was exhausted, and so were we. It had been a very long day; one of the longest and most heart wrenching days of my life.

The next day, I was still getting nowhere with the insurance company. I called the speech therapist we had seen and left a message on her voice mail. I told her I was willing to go out of network if she could accommodate Ashley in her schedule. Actually, I never heard back from her—ever!

I spent many hours a day "on hold" with the insurance company. When the "holding" music turned into a disconnection, I threw up my hands in disgust. Was someone on the other end intentionally hanging up on me when their extension rang? It was pitiful no one wanted to take my call. That's no way to run a business—much less a business dedicated to helping others with their health! I was getting nowhere!

Nearly at the end of my rope, I turned to Dave's employer. Working with the health care administrator from Dave's workplace, I switched health plans. Within my new network, I could now find the specialists I needed for speech as well as the recommended developmental pediatrician and psychologist. I felt much better knowing the monetary burden had eased up somewhat. But it still seemed like we were headed into a storm with what I imagined lie ahead in terms of making Ashley better.

I called a rehabilitation office to inquire if the speech therapist was accepting new patients. I was transferred to a woman named Shelly who was the speech and language pathologist. I told her a little bit about Ashley's speech delay. She had an opening in her schedule, and I set up a time to meet with her. Finally, someone who cared!

The day of our evaluation, Dave and I dropped Kacey off at his parents' home. We headed up the highway. Shelly's office was about twenty miles away.

I was armed with all of Ashley's medical records, a scrapbook of milestones, and a bag of her toys and puzzles.

Shelly greeted us, and we went into her office. Dave and I sat on the floor while Ashley and Shelly sat at a kiddy table. Shelly explained she was going to assess Ashley's auditory comprehension and expressive communication skills using a standardized test for children Ashley's age. We already knew where Ashley's language and communication skills fell, since we had just come from Children's Hospital a few weeks earlier, but we knew Shelly had to start with her own baseline. We sat, observed, and answered questions as they arose.

I was quite surprised that Ashley took an instant liking to Shelly. Ashley was not usually comfortable around anyone and had only recently become comfortable with us. Shelly had a sweet, caring voice. She made Ashley feel relaxed and at ease. She also had a great stash of toys that Ashley zeroed in on as she stepped into

Shelly's office. Ashley didn't fuss or scream in the way she normally did when recognizable family members would visit.

I expected Ashley to start to cry and run straight for the door. But to do that, she would have had to trip over us first. She didn't, and there was an immediate connection between Shelly and Ashley. I could now relax and let out the sigh of relief from the anxiety that had built up inside of me during the twenty mile trip to her office.

I watched Shelly intently as she administered her test. First she put a piece of cellophane against Ashley's ear and crinkled it to see if Ashley reacted. She did, faintly. Shelly wrote something down.

"Ashley, do you want to play with my bear?" she asked, enthusiastically.

Shelly took a teddy bear and walked it across the table and let it drop off the edge.

"Uh-oh! Where's the bear?" Shelly asked, trying to engage Ashley.

Ashley didn't follow Shelly's gaze to the bear on the floor. Ashley's attention wandered to the pile of toys underneath the table. She went rifling through them.

Shelly let Ashley play freely with some of the toys while she elicited responses from us.

"Does Ashley laugh?" she asked us.

"She's just starting to laugh while watching her Barney videos," I answered.

Shelly marked this down on her testing sheet.

"Does she respond to "no"?

"It has to be a very loud and firm 'no'," I replied.

She handed Ashley some keys on a ring.

"Ashley, can you give Miss Shelly the keys?"

Ashley held onto them, and then put them in her mouth. Shelly took out a spoon, a cup, and a sock.

"Ashley, can you hand me the spoon?"

I knew Ashley couldn't do this. I had not introduced Ashley to a spoon, because there was no need for one, given the limited finger foods she ate. I was certain she didn't know which one was a spoon. Ashley turned the other way and didn't respond to the question.

"Ashley can you please hand me the sock?"

Ashley didn't. I knew Ashley understood a sock went on her foot, but she couldn't follow the one-step direction.

"Does Ashley have any words?"

"No," I replied.

"She used to have Dada, but I haven't heard that since she was about seven-months-old," I added.

Shelly wrote something more on her sheet. She went through a few more tests and then gave us her thoughts.

Shelly's evaluation more or less revealed what the first speech therapist at Children's Hospital had concluded. Ashley scored in the second percentile for auditory comprehension—an age equivalence of zero to eight months. She scored in the first percentile for expressive communication—an age equivalence of zero to five months. Her total language score put her at zero to seven months—severely delayed.

Shelly diagnosed Ashley with "speech delay." I knew Shelly's services would be covered by our health insurance so I scheduled Ashley's therapy sessions.

"I will write up her short and long-term goals and will have those for you at her first visit," Shelly said.

Ashley ran out of Shelly's office, and we headed her in the direction of the waiting room.

"It was a pleasure meeting you," Shelly said to us. "Bye, Miss Ashley. I'll see you soon. We can play some more with my toys, okay?"

Dave picked up Ashley, and we thanked Shelly.

From Shelly's conclusions, and that of the previous speech therapist, there was no denying Ashley definitely had a speech delay. We were accepting of this. I was still confused as to why she was delayed. But that had to be put aside at the moment. The most important thing was to get Ashley the best help available for her problem. We left feeling confident that from Shelly's rapport with Ashley, therapy was going to work out well.

We started to see Shelly regularly beginning the following week. Ashley remembered being there as was evident in her finding Shelly's office all on her own. She seemed excited to see Shelly again.

"Well, hello Miss Ashley. Are you ready to play?" Shelly asked.

I followed Ashley into Shelly's office and closed the door. Shelly handed me a piece of paper that mapped out short and long-term goals for Ashley. I took a seat on the floor and read through them as Shelly started her session with Ashley.

- Demonstrate five different sounds during play in five therapy sessions;
- Use variation in loudness, pitch and rhythm patterns during three sessions; and
- Imitate sounds /b/, /p/, /m/ with 80% accuracy.

These were quite elementary. But that's where Ashley needed to start. Ashley saw Shelly twice a week. During those sessions, Shelly used a lot of Barney and Tele-tubbie books to engage Ashley in play, since these were her favorite characters. She tried feverishly to get Ashley to imitate farm animals with the See-N-Say. She tried to get Ashley to point to body parts while singing the song, "Head, Shoulders, Knees, and Toes."

Progress was slow. Many, many sessions passed with Ashley sustaining attention for only about a quarter of the time. She tired easily and got bored quickly. She wasn't at the point of repeating words that Shelly asked her, but some new consonant sounds were starting to surface.

Through the use of finger play songs such as "Where is Thumbkin?" Shelly worked on Ashley's imitation skills. Ashley learned to make her fingers "run away" behind her back as the song cued her to do so. This made us smile!

Shelly seemed to penetrate Ashley's world without Ashley thinking it too intrusive. Shelly was so patient with Ashley. She always saw great potential in her, even during the really non-productive sessions. And there were many. But each session produced something new, if only a sound or an imitation of a word. And each session seemed to add to the previous one. Ashley was starting to make strides. They were very small strides, but strides packed with big efforts from a little girl.

While playing with plastic zoo animals—taking them out of a basket and putting them back when play was done—Ashley said what we believed to be approximations of her first words, "in" and "out." She later found the words "up" and "down."

We were all quite amused that Ashley's first words were not the usual "ball" or "cup" heard in most children. My child's first words were prepositions! It was quite laughable to us and proved what we always knew to be true about Ashley—she was one-of-a kind!

But they were words or approximation of words nonetheless. I would take them without question. And Shelly considered them real as well. They helped Ashley meet her goals.

Dave and I often talked to Shelly about what she saw as the reason behind Ashley's speech delay. Shelly surmised that an inner ear problem was at the root of Ashley's delay. With as many ear infections as Ashley had had when she was younger, this led Shelly to believe it was connected somehow—that there was some type of blockage preventing Ashley from connecting with language. The histories of some of the other children Shelly saw were similar to that of Ashley's, which enriched her belief that Ashley's ears, somehow, played a very important role in her speech problem.

We kept that in the back of our minds. We knew Ashley wasn't deaf, and we knew the audiologist's findings stated her ears were in proper working condition for the acquisition of speech. For some reason, it was just taking Ashley a little longer than usual to learn to talk.

But with the new sounds she was making, some imitative finger play, and her first prepositions, Ashley met her beginning goals in two months. It took her a little longer than the five sessions Shelly had stated in her initial plan of care, but we had no timetable on Ashley. She just took it one session at a time—and so did we. Ashley saw Shelly twice a week.

At twenty months of age, I took Ashley to an ear, nose and throat specialist hoping the doctor could shed some light on what we all were thinking was an inner ear problem. Again, I was armed with the progress notes from Ashley's medical records indicating all of her ear infections and all of the antibiotics she had taken.

I was hoping to make a case to the doctor that the number of ear infections Ashley had had could have played a role in her speech delay, and ask whether she should she have tubes inserted. I had previously spoken with one of our friends who told me that after her son had tubes inserted in his ears, his speech improved, and he was no longer having problems with acquiring language. Because of this positive outcome, I wondered if Ashley could also benefit from the insertion of tubes. At this point, I was grasping at anything.

"Could Ashley's hearing have been impaired from these ear infections which occurred at such a crucial time when babies start to develop language? Could her fetish of thumb sucking have anything to do with her not talking? How can she talk if her thumb is constantly in her mouth?" I barraged him with questions.

"Even children who suck their thumb do acquire speech," he explained.

He examined Ashley and found her ears, nose, and throat to be clear and saw no physical reason—on that day—why there would be inhibited speech production.

So what was Ashley's reason for not acquiring speech? He didn't know!

With the previous hearing test being normal, he concluded that the peripheral auditory system was functioning well, but she was clearly missing milestones for speech. He mentioned if Ashley had had difficulty with serious ear infections in the past—and they were present for long periods of time—those ear infections could be a contributing factor to speech delay. However, he did not recommend tubes since her ears were free of fluid and infection at that visit.

I found out nothing from him! I collected my files and took Ashley away in my arms. I left not knowing anything more than when I had stepped into the examination room. How polite of him, though, to compliment me on my organization of her records and my knowledge of her history of illnesses! For that, I got an A+!

I was livid! Why didn't any of these specialists know anything specific to Ashley's problems? Why did I go to them? I was no more informed now than when I started this whole thing. Their alleged expertise was apparently not that of my child's present problem. Was Ashley's speech delay something so inexplicable that no one had good reasoning for it? Why was I baffling every specialist I went to with my concerns? I couldn't imagine that they really knew something, but just weren't telling me. That would be pretty unethical, I thought.

Since no answers landed in my lap after seeing an audiologist, two speech therapists, an ENT and a pediatrician on numerous occasions, it was time for me to rely on the only person I could trust to find the answers—*me!*

It was at that point in time where my role as a parent took its sharpest turn—that of being Ashley's advocate. I was the only one left to figure this whole thing out. My determination was my fuel. Nothing was going to stop my heavily invested interest in this for Ashley's sake and her future—a future I still didn't know was certain. So I hit the ground running—and hit it hard!

CHAPTER 4

▼

KNOWLEDGE IS DANGEROUS

After long and exhausting days of commuting back and forth from therapy sessions and preschools, maintaining the house, bathing the girls, reading to them and finally tucking them into bed, it would seem like the perfect opportunity to unwind and relax with Dave—but my gears kept turning.

I felt compelled and obligated to find out what was happening to my little girl. When the girls went to bed, I was holed up in my office for hours. I was consumed with learning all I could about Ashley's speech delay—why it had come to be and how I could facilitate it coming in normally.

On some nights after falling asleep, I would pop up in bed wide awake, my mind racing with unanswered questions and concerns for Ashley's future. It didn't matter much to me that it was the middle of the night. Knowing another long day filled with therapy sessions or doctors' appointments was just hours away, did not hinder my insane efforts—at equally insane times of the night—to become as well-informed as possible. To me, it was uninterrupted time when I could take as long as I wanted without the girls vying for their turn on the computer.

I would creep downstairs trying not to make too much noise. But the creaky door to the office always gave me away.

"Dave really needs to fix that," I would whisper, closing the door so the light wouldn't wake anyone.

I started looking for answers on the Internet. I burned the midnight oil—a mixture of perseverance and dedication to finding answers to the many questions I held inside.

One evening I put in "speech delay" in a search engine and was caught off guard by the results. The word "autism" appeared in their descriptions.

"Did the computer not understand my request? I wanted to know about speech delays, not *autism!*" I pondered, looking confused.

I vaguely heard of the term autism from Dustin Hoffman's portrayal of an autistic savant in the film *Rain Man*—but my knowledge was very limited.

I thought back when I was younger, playing with my brother. He used to tease me, as brothers do, about my artistic ability. He used to call me "autistic," not "artistic." I wondered at that moment, if my brother really knew the meaning behind the word he would jokingly use when we were growing up? I wondered if *I* even knew the correct meaning. I always equated autistic with retarded, because that's kind of in the context of how he meant it. As children, we would joke that way.

I clicked on some titles from the results. What I read told me if someone had a speech delay, there may also be an underlying issue of autism.

I could feel my heart race.

"Ashley isn't autistic," I mumbled to myself.

"She isn't Rain Man, or even Rain Girl!"

I wasn't quite sure what constituted being autistic, so I went to some autism sites just to see what they had to say. There was information on autism. There was information on what autism wasn't. There was information on something called PDD-NOS (Pervasive Developmental Disorder, Not Otherwise Specified). There was information on something called sensory integration. There was information on therapies and treatments.

"Oh, good, it's treatable," I thought.

The information stated that autism was more prevalent in boys than in girls. The symptoms ranged from mild to severe. It was a life-long developmental disability resulting from a neurological disorder that affected brain functioning.

"Life-long? Brain disorder?" I said, becoming nervous.

I sat up straighter in my chair and re-read the description. The information also stated that autism wasn't mental retardation, because some autistic people may be very intelligent—that evidence existed to suggest that Albert Einstein might have been autistic.

It stated autism wasn't savant syndrome, although some autistics are savants (i.e., instant calculators), but most aren't. It stated some autistics are "gifted" with a high level of intelligence. Some are of normal intelligence, and some may be retarded. It also stated that some autistics have some disadvantages, but some live very happy and rewarding lives.

"This definition is all over the place!" I said, becoming more puzzled each time I re-read it.

My research took me to more specific information on the characteristics of autism. I read it all, but really had no idea what it all meant. Yet frightfully, what I read seemed remarkably similar to what I saw in Ashley. Clearly, she had impairments in social interaction and pretend play. She didn't form peer relationships. She had poor, if any, eye contact. She couldn't gesture.

"Restricted, repetitive behavior, what exactly does that mean?" I wondered.

I thought of how Ashley repeatedly opened and closed the front door. But she did this so infrequently I didn't know if it warranted being lumped into this repetitive category.

She often fixated on the most insignificant objects such as string or dirt and sometimes laughed for no reason at all.

"Repetitive motor mannerisms," I read on.

Ashley would flap her hands when she got really excited, but she didn't go around the house all day long doing it. It only happened when she watched videos. She would, though, get on the floor and do some amazing twisting moves with her limber body. She would often spin around not seeming to get dizzy, as well. But I didn't think she did these to excess.

She was definitely showing characteristics of what this website was defining as autism. Though strange as her behaviors were to me, they weren't all inclusive, suggesting she really had autism. I couldn't bring myself to determine that. Ashley had some traits, but not others. And what traits she had were still pale in comparison to the wording of these criteria. So was she? Or wasn't she?

I didn't know! But I had to be fair to the criteria and acknowledge their merit as a medical tool. I couldn't deny I saw these things in Ashley. It was just to what degree she was fitting into these categories that I found perplexing.

What I had apparently just stumbled upon was enough to instill panic in me—maybe unnecessarily—but possibly, right-on-the-money. I could feel my legs shaking underneath the keyboard.

"I should never have even begun this search. I really have no business trying to fit Ashley into this category without a medical degree," I thought to myself.

But, I also thought being a Mom should entitle me to at least try and learn what I could about what was going on with my little girl; to take a stab at diagnosing her—even without a license to practice.

But if I were to play that game, I told myself, I had better be prepared for the consequences that came with it, namely scaring myself to death—or worse—coming up right!

I was starting to get dizzy from all of the incomprehensible literature. Why was I was putting myself through this misery? I thought it best to just shut down the computer and return to bed.

But I couldn't submit just yet. I found myself riveted by this information. And, I was already in too deeply to quit. I would *never, ever* be able to rid my mind of what I had just read and what I had just learned.

But I was a glutton for punishment. As the night grew later, I pursued other titles in the search—my thirst for answers still not quenched.

I visited another site and found myself in conflict with what I was reading. This site went so far as to state that people who were autistic wouldn't want to be cured, as that would be like erasing them and replacing them with different people.

I was just taking a stab at diagnosing her, but if it turned out this was what was happening with Ashley, *I did want her cured! I wanted her back!* Why else would I be so entrenched in this on-line research? Why was I investing so much time and getting so little sleep, if not to find answers to her problems? Why wouldn't I want to do everything in my power to change how she was—to make it better for her? Why shouldn't I find a way to afford her every possible treatment and every opportunity for a normal life? Why should I give credibility to this notion that by trying to help Ashley, I would be erasing her being?

Ashley couldn't relate to us and do the normal things toddlers do. She couldn't communicate her wants and needs. She couldn't climb stairs or go down a slide. She couldn't run without falling down. She didn't play with other children. She didn't eat anything resembling a normal diet. She had uncontrollable tantrums. And she didn't have the attention span to sit in circle time with her peers and listen to the days of the week—all those things that make children learn and grow.

I wasn't about to sit idle and be faced with the possibility that what I was seeing in Ashley (presently), was all I was going to get from her for years to come. I wasn't trying to *replace* Ashley. I was trying to *find* Ashley!

Ashley seemed to be lost somewhere within herself—without an identity of her own. I'm not sure she even knew who she was. She never looked in the mirror. She didn't know her name. She had no sense of her body. She was "frightened" by daily activities, such as brushing her teeth or giving us a good morning hug—running away as I approached her. But I knew she was in there somewhere. I just had to find a way to get to her.

At times she would go haywire on us. Nights were especially difficult. She would wake up crying and become inconsolable. It took a toll on us. Sometimes we would pace the floor for hours holding and rocking her to calm her down—our arms turning numb after hours of this routine. Dave and I would take turns with her. Just when it seemed like the right time to put her down, (thinking she had fallen fast asleep), the slightest change in our body position would send her back into a flailing tantrum. Out of what we thought was a deep sleep, she would awaken, and it would begin again.

"What did I do? What's wrong? I just want to sit down, Ashley! Just...let me...sit down!" I would say, feeling exhausted and frustrated.

We just wanted to rest our aching backs and our weary arms! We barely made a motion! But that was enough to start the routine all over again—back to the pacing, back to the wincing from the muscle spasms that soon overtook Dave's back. For months we got very little sleep, and we were becoming resentful.

My search took me to a website about developmental delays—the delayed achievement of one or more milestones affecting a child's speech and language, fine and gross motor skills, and/or personal and social skills.

Skimming the list of developmental milestones gave me another unsettling feeling in my stomach.

"She can't do most of these things," I whispered, squinting at the screen.

I would periodically take my baby books off the shelf and read and re-read the monthly milestones a normally-developing child was expected to attain. But the books were often ambiguous, stating all children develop at different rates. The books steered away from mentioning at what point an unmet milestone turns into a developmental delay—that was left up to the reader's interpretation. For some reason, the information on this website appeared more reliable than my books. It presented the information from the perspective of a delay; not meeting various developmental milestones by the stated timeframes.

It was becoming apparent that there was not just a problem with her speech and language, but Ashley was showing delays in quite a few different areas. At ages considered appropriate to master these tasks, Ashley hadn't. It wasn't primarily she couldn't say "mama" or "dada" or "cup" or "ball," she couldn't imitate us or use gestures to let her wants and needs be known, such as pointing. Rarely, could she respond to simple one-step directions. She couldn't throw a ball. She couldn't drink from a cup without a top. She didn't use a spoon or fork. She couldn't even pull off her socks.

I sat back in my chair and reflected on Ashley's development during the past two years. There wasn't even an ounce of curiosity in Ashley to want to do these things. We did them for her.

I revisited in my mind the argument with her pediatrician about me being too doting—his reason for her not acquiring speech. I don't think this ever had merit. According to these websites, Ashley had real medical cause for not communicating, exploring her independence as a toddler or getting to know others—even me—the one who carried her for nine months, the one who loved her before I could see her, and the one who agonized over her delivery for hours trying to bring her into this world, so I could form an everlasting bond with her.

I printed all the information I gathered. There was enough information here to keep me reading for the next three months. I just couldn't believe for a minute that Ashley had some form of autism like these website were hinting at. But it seemed I had stumbled upon a word that identified Ashley to a frightening "T."

"Does the average person delve this deeply for answers about their child's development," I wondered.

I was alarmed, shocked and scared. Either, I was naïve in believing a medical condition could not possibly be tagged to my beautiful daughter, or something was definitely brewing inside of Ashley that seemed to have a tinge of developmental delay to it—*or possibly worse, autism*—a larger problem than anyone had ever led me to believe!

I kept this information to myself. I was, after all, just in the beginning stages of educating myself. There was no need to sound alarms with Dave until I understood this better and could talk to him rationally and intelligently.

I tiptoed back upstairs and carefully negotiated myself over the locked gate at the top of the steps. I got back into bed in hope of picking up sleep where I left off—four startling hours earlier!

CHAPTER 5

▼

SHATTERED

After a long three-month's wait for an appointment, the day finally came to see the neurodevelopmental pediatrician at Children's Hospital. We dropped Kacey off with Dave's parents and drove to our appointment about an hour away.

I wasn't exactly sure what a neurodevelopmental pediatrician was or what he would tell us. I packed Ashley's puzzles as I had done many times before when we visited specialists. I wanted the doctor to notice Ashley had come a little bit further with her play skills from what the first speech therapist at Children's Hospital had written in her report. I carried a copy of the report to give to the doctor.

By now, Ashley was (to our amazement) completing an entire alphabet puzzle, and she could put shapes onto a shape sorter pegboard without blinking twice—a three-to six-year-old skill. Ashley was twenty-one months. She spoke a few prepositions, but needed prompting. She couldn't spontaneously talk. Her diet was still limited to crunchy foods, but she was beginning to eat some cut up hot dog. We were climbing the food pyramid!

Dave and I sat in the waiting room of Children's Hospital with other parents of children who were playing with toys. I wondered why these children were here and who they were seeing. Right away, I found myself comparing these children to Ashley, as I am sure the other parents were sizing up their children with mine.

How old is your child?" I asked the father of one child, who looked about Ashley's age.

"Sixteen months, and yours?"

"They're very close in age," I said, not sharing with him that Ashley was almost six months older but not nearly as verbal, tall, or filled out as his child.

I often contemplated lying about Ashley's age. If I were to back her age down about a year, she would seem normal in all respects—verbally, emotionally, and physically—and then we could pick up with her development from there. She wouldn't seem so different then, and she wouldn't be considered needing any type of therapy.

"What would be the harm in forgetting her age and making one up for her?" I thought to myself.

I can't believe I spent time even considering this—but I did. I thought it might be an answer to ease what we were going through.

We were called from the waiting room. Dave grabbed Ashley, and I gathered our bags. We went down the hall to have her weighed, measured and vital signs taken.

Ashley simply wanted no part of that. She screamed and cried when the nurse touched her. She refused to have the blood pressure cuff put on her arm. We couldn't get her height, and we couldn't successfully get her head circumference measured. The nurse got what vital signs she could.

We returned to the waiting room, sat down, and watched Ashley play until Dr. Conlon walked in and greeted us. We shook his hand, introduced ourselves, and followed him to his office.

"This is Ashley," I said to him.

"Hi, Ashley!" he said, but she ignored him and busily inspected his office. We all sat down and watched Ashley.

"So, tell me why you're here?" he asked.

"Our pediatrician referred us to Children's Hospital to get a speech and hearing evaluation. Ashley's not talking yet. The hearing test was normal, but the speech therapist told us Ashley's speech and language was at a six-to-nine-month-old level. The therapist seems to have greater concerns about Ashley than just her speech. So we were referred to you. Ashley often tunes us out. She doesn't play well. She doesn't seem to want to be with us or anyone. She's just off in her own world," I told Dr. Conlon.

He asked us a lot of questions about her infancy and toddlerhood. We told him the things we saw in Ashley—the lack of language, the poor eating habits, the uncontrollable tantrums. He seemed to know exactly what we were talking about, as we reeled off her peculiar behaviors one by one.

"Does Ashley flap her hands or walk on her toes?" he asked, demonstrating for us.

"Yes," Dave said, nodding his head.

Having done extensive research prior to seeing Dr Conlon, I learned some things about the characteristics of autism that Dave didn't know. I hadn't yet shared with him any of the information I had stayed up nights reading and collecting. I most certainly didn't mention the word autism, because I wasn't sure myself how Ashley fit into that picture.

But I knew Dr. Conlon's question was not asked in a positive light, having previously learned that hand flapping, toe walking and continuously spinning around were repetitive mannerisms characteristic of autism. Not knowing these were traits of the disorder, Dave answered the question in a manner suggesting, "Yes, she can do that."

"Boy, I wish he hadn't said that," I thought to myself.

That surely would open up a can of worms. But the worms were already out. It was now up to Dr. Conlon to do what he would with that information.

In my mind, these were not good things to be flaunting in front of a neurodevelomental pediatrician. Most certainly this would result in a black mark against Ashley. Yes, she did these things, but I thought it wasn't to the point of suggesting a repetitive behavior in her, so I kept mum.

But Dave was quicker with the affirmative response than I was with the denial of it. I was almost trying not to be forthcoming in her behavioral issues. I wanted to protect Ashley from what I feared the most—the "A" word—like my reading had hinted.

But Dr. Conlon specialized in developmental disorders. He knew we were there due to concerns that Ashley wasn't meeting all of her developmental milestones. Nothing I was going to say or withhold was going to sway his medical opinion. But I felt he was sizing her up for one of those little categories I had stayed up nights researching.

Then, he threw the words, Pervasive Developmental Disorder (PDD) at us. I vaguely remembered that from my reading, but didn't spend too much time on it. But if it came from my reading, I surely knew it wasn't good news. I seemed to only read the bad stuff!

He briefly discussed this term with us. In addition, he talked to us about something called the "autistic spectrum." Boy, was my research ever right on the money! Out came the much-feared word—"*autistic.*"

The fears that resided in my mind during those late-night Internet searches were being validated before my eyes! But how did he label Ashley so quickly— even before getting to know her or seeing what she had to offer? I hadn't even opened the bag of puzzles I toted with me! He hadn't yet seen our puzzle genius at work!

After the discussion, I unpacked Ashley's toys, and she played while he observed her and asked us more questions. He glanced down at her playing on the floor every now and then and made notes on his paper.

I immediately pointed out all of Ashley's strengths. I wanted Ashley to get points right out of the chute. I flaunted the fact that she had become very adept at puzzles and knew her ABCs, shapes and colors. He gave me a sense of being impressed as well—being able to see for himself her proclivity for puzzles.

He then unlatched the fasteners to his big, black examination case and took out his own puzzles and testing materials. He put a puzzle on the table in front of Ashley and mixed up the pieces. I imagined he wanted to see how she would fare with unfamiliar puzzles, as he may have thought she had memorized hers by now.

"Ashley, can you do the puzzle?" he asked.

Ashley completed the puzzle sprightly and with confidence. Dave and I looked at each other and smiled. We knew she was in her element.

Dr. Conlon turned the puzzle upside down.

"Ashley, can you do it this way?" he asked, taking the pieces out again.

Ashley picked up the pieces and put them in their respective positions without hesitation. Dr. Conlon was awed by her ability.

"She's very visual," he remarked.

He then placed a card with colored circles on the table and took out round chips, the same colors as the circles on the card. He handed Ashley the colored chips. He didn't need to ask Ashley to complete the puzzle. She instinctively knew what to do. She instantly placed the same colored chip on the corresponding color on the card.

"Great job, Ashley," Dr. Conlon remarked.

Dr. Conlon took a piece of paper and on it, drew a vertical line with his pencil.

"Ashley, can you make a line like mine?" he said, making a downward stroke.

Ashley grasped her pencil with her fist and drew something similar to his mark, but with more of a curve. He thought this was good enough. Then he reached for a small glass jar filled with beans.

"Ashley, can you pour the beans out?"

Ashley shook the glass jar, but no beans came out. He showed her how to pour them out, and they spilled onto the carpet.

"Ashley, put the beans back into the jar," he said to her.

Ashley didn't understand. He helped her do it. Upon his request to pour them out again, Ashley just shook the jar feverishly until the beans came spewing out.

"Okay, that's one way to get the beans out," he said, and wrote something on his testing sheet.

I guess Dr. Conlon was looking to see if Ashley could follow directions. She couldn't. She just played with the jar and didn't have any idea what was being asked of her.

Next, Dr. Conlon took out some simple black and white drawings.

"Ashley, where's the dog?"

Ashley couldn't point to it.

He asked her to point to another picture, but she took no interest in it.

"Does Ashley do any pretend play? Does she hold a phone up to her ear and pretend to talk to Mommy or Daddy? Does she pour a (pretend) cup of tea and drink it?" he asked us.

"No, she's really not that interested in those types of toys. I don't think she knows what to do with a phone," I replied.

"Kacey, our older daughter does a lot of pretend play, but Ashley doesn't seem to be into that. She's never poured a pretend cup of tea and sipped it. She doesn't feed a doll a bottle or put it to bed like Kacey does. Ashley likes to carry around a handful of things. She sometimes carries five or six dolls loaded down on her and walks around with them sucking her thumb. She doesn't actually play with the dolls, she just carries them—as if they are security to her," I said.

Finished with his questioning, Dr. Conlon began a physical exam on Ashley. He measured her head circumference that the nurse was unable to obtain. (It was rather small.) He performed a Wood's lamp test looking for cutaneous lesions using a black light over her body. These lesions, if she had them, would show up under the light as pigmentations and may be indicative of other disorders. He did not find any. That was a relief!

He examined her from top to bottom noting nothing disfiguring about her. But he did describe something about her joints which he called hypotonia or "decreased muscle tone." He explained to us her joints were very flexible, and that at rest, her muscles didn't give back a whole lot of resistance when manipulated.

He described low muscle tone as not something too alarming, but that it isn't seen by itself, but rather in conjunction with other symptoms of a problem. He told us Ashley sits on the floor in what is called a "W" position where her knees are positioned in front and her legs are spread out to each side.

I noticed Ashley would sit this way, but didn't think a whole lot about it. I was more focused on Ashley's bigger issues like being non-verbal and non-social. I was a gymnast in my younger days and had the same flexibility and sat the same way. My parents often wondered how I could sit in that position and not be in excruciating pain. But I thought it was a natural position to get into. *My* parent's weren't concerned about the way I would sit. They never knew it meant anything such as what this doctor was suggesting in Ashley. Maybe I was just breeding a gymnast in Ashley to explain her limberness.

He finished her physical exam then let her play with the puzzles while he talked to us. Cognitively, he was impressed with her abilities. Her thinking skills fell in the 24 to 30-month range. Being only twenty-one-months-old, we thought this was great! He remarked at her ability for completing puzzles reiterating her visual acuity.

But he was quick to point out her language and social skills were far below that for her age level. She inconsistently followed one-step commands and wasn't able to point or gesture. The four or so words (all prepositions) she did have were not as impressive to him as they were to us. He remarked they were all learned through speech therapy in a rote manner and were not used in a functional sense. In other words, he thought she may have memorized them, did not comprehend their meaning, or use them in their proper context.

He told us Ashley lacked pretend play skills. I knew she didn't play as well with toys as Kacey did, but I hadn't realized the magnitude of her not being able to pretend. Evidently, it is very important in a developmental sense.

When a child plays "house" or "dolls" or "you be the Mommy, I'll be the baby," she isn't just playing a game. She is "role playing" and using her imagination to conjure up a fantasy world and taking play to a new level.

The child temporarily removes herself from her own world and puts herself in a different role or scenario using props or dress-up clothes and becomes "somebody else." She makes a gigantic jump into the world of make-believe and then returns when she is done playing. This is easy for most children and is essential for growth and development. Ashley's lack of role playing spoke volumes to Dr. Conlon.

He mentioned it was hard to capture her attention during the testing (calling her name or giving her a problem to solve, like picking something up off the floor when it fell.) At times, he remarked, she seemed aloof and had little eye contact with him or with us—as if she weren't connecting at all. She would occasionally walk on her toes and flap her hands during the tests and seemed obsessed with the contents of his opened examination box.

His overall impression was Ashley had an autistic spectrum disorder. It was characterized by joint attention difficulties and delayed, atypical language development involving social communication deficits with some restricted, repetitive behaviors.

I looked down at Ashley playing. She was so non-suspecting. She didn't know there was anything wrong with her. She didn't know we were talking about her. She just went about investigating his black box all the while tuning us out.

Dr. Conlon pretty much confirmed it. Our sweet little girl was definitely held hostage by a disorder I had suspected from my research. I still didn't understand how a disorder like this had come to take up residence within her.

I was just so baffled. Kacey was healthy and thriving. Ashley was not that way at all. What had happened to cause all of this? Why was Ashley prone to this disorder and not Kacey?

Dr. Conlon went into great detail about the autistic spectrum. He described it as a continuum, with one end being that of very mild issues, while the other end was the more severe form of the disorder. Within each condition on the spectrum, there were even more variations of severity. The disorder was not clear cut from what I gathered.

He gave Dave and me reassurance that he saw Ashley at the very mild end of the spectrum with what he called Pervasive Developmental Disorder-Not Otherwise Specified (PDD-NOS). PDD-NOS is a label given to children who meet some of the criteria of autism, but not all of them. That now shed light on why I didn't think Ashley had all the characteristics of autism I read about, and why I was confused by the ones she did have. Some of her behaviors—which I didn't think were happening with enough frequency to be able to conclude she was autistic—were apparently still enough to warrant being considered on the autistic spectrum.

In other words, her behaviors were clearly not readily seen in normally developing children, but they weren't to such a degree to classify her with severe autism. She warranted a less-stringent label, but still had a serious disorder on the spectrum—PDD-NOS.

The overall compliment Dr. Conlon made was that Ashley "truly has strengths in the visual-motor-perceptual area."

"Thank goodness for small favors," I thought to myself.

If her cognitive skills weren't so high, it would have been more concerning to him and a bleaker picture for Ashley.

It was difficult to learn from Dr. Conlon what I suspected. No one wants to be told there is something medically wrong with their child. I'd rather it be a problem with me than for my innocent daughter to be afflicted with a medical issue. But that's not how it was unfolding. Ashley was definitely different than normal children her age. The testing proved it; being with her everyday proved it; and witnessing the differences from that of her sister and peers proved it. It was now time to accept this diagnosis. But would I be able to?

I wanted to understand this very complicated language the doctor was using with us. It was very confusing, even with as much as I had learned staying up nights reading about the characteristics of autism. Since I had not shared with Dave (to this point) what I had found during my research about autism, he must have been dazed and confused listening to all of this. He was hearing this raw, for the first time. I, at least, had an inkling. But I wanted to keep my research and suspicions to myself for fear of prematurely setting off too many alarms. I didn't want to discuss it with him until I understood it fully and knew for sure this situation had a place in our lives—at least to the point I needed to share it with him.

Yet there in Dr. Conlon's office, it seemed like I was oddly enough being given the nod by the doctor to divulge to Dave all of the information I had been researching on autism during the wee hours of the morning—that there was now the real presence of the disorder in our lives such that I needed to be forthright with him.

I had so many questions. I could have spent days asking them to Dr. Conlon. As it was, he spent more than his allotted time with us and rushed in and out of his office collecting material and writing referrals for additional medical testing.

He recommended additional medical and laboratory evaluations to include thyroid testing, lead levels, high-resolution karyotyping to conclude if she had all of her chromosomes, a DNA probe to rule out Fragile X Syndrome (an X chromosome defect that causes mental retardation and a wide range of associated signs and symptoms), and a panel of other metabolic testing.

He referred us to the Autism Society of America (ASA) and recommended an occupational therapy evaluation. He noted Ashley had strong visual motor skills and might benefit from a sensory motor program to help with her overall attention span.

He suggested two books, *Thinking in Pictures* and *Emergence*, both by Temple Grandin, a gifted animal scientist who is autistic. Dr. Conlon thought these books would help me learn about life with autism through the author's experience—a powerful and inspiring story to give me hope for Ashley's future.

He also recommended Ashley see the psychologist at Children's Hospital for further psychological testing. He thought she should undergo a sleep-deprived

EEG (electroencephalogram) to rule out any seizure activity of the brain—since it was hard to capture her attention, and because her speech wasn't developing.

Lastly, he provided Dave and me information on the early intervention services that the county I lived in offered children with special needs. I was to contact the county office to set up an evaluation.

It was difficult for me to accept Ashley was now considered "a child with special needs." To me, that was always a child with overt problems. No one on the street would have thought Ashley was a "special needs child" by looking at her. But the doctor had given us his opinion. He was the expert. And this…we *had* to accept!

As we left the building, we were in disbelief and full of questions. Dave carried Ashley through the windy parking lot. The day had turned colder and darker while we were inside. We walked to the car in silence.

We settled Ashley in her car seat. She appeared quite tired and worn out. Dave and I looked at each other.

"What just happened in there?" I asked.

We had gone in the hospital two hours earlier with a puzzle genius and came out with a daughter labeled autistic! Something had gone terribly wrong. What we thought to be a problem with Ashley's hearing somehow turned into a disability with perhaps a bleak outlook. And we were now parents of a child with special needs! We were stunned from the blow.

We turned to look at Ashley and found she had fallen asleep. What a trooper she was. We had just subjected her to a very long testing process. She did what she could in terms of her ability for the doctor. We couldn't be disappointed with that. The rest of the questions would be answered from the results of the additional testing Dr. Conlon recommended.

"How did he determine she belonged on the autistic spectrum just by observing her for a few hours?" I asked Dave as he started driving.

"She doesn't even know him, and yet, he wanted to see her look at him more and come up to him more than she did. She was in a strange place with a strange doctor. Why would not opening up in that environment be held against her?" I rambled on.

"I know, Sharon. But you know, she didn't look at us much either," Dave said in all honesty.

And I guess that was the point the doctor was making. And her lack of being able to point was apparently a tell-tale sign of a problem. Not pointing meant not engaging us in something she found interesting—not bringing us into her world so we could enjoy something with her.

"But he thought she was exceptionally bright! She can do puzzles better than the kindergartner down the street!" I said, trying to make some sense of all of this.

"She's very smart, yes! She just does things her own way and at her own pace," Dave tried to reassure me.

"You know, Sharon, I'm not much of a social butterfly myself. Maybe she takes after me. I'm pretty reserved. I don't care for big parties and socializing. She's very laid back, and so am I. Didn't he say if she keeps developing with high visual skills, he only saw great things for her to the tune of possibly an 'engineer's mind'?" he said, trying to give me some hope.

"Do I want her to be an engineer?" I asked, sarcastically.

"That's not the point. He meant she could grow up to be very smart and perhaps embrace a career such as that—engineers are very creative and brainy. It was a compliment, Sharon!"

"But how can he forecast what she may become in the future? He thinks she'll go far with her visual talents, but he just placed her on the autistic spectrum due to a variety of social and behavioral deficits. That's like taking one step forward and two steps back. It makes no sense to me," I said, becoming a little discouraged.

I was stressed. We were stopped in traffic. I shut myself down and stared out the window not looking at Dave. It was a very long ride home in silence.

What we were taking away from all of this was that Ashley had some autistic traits that put her on the autistic spectrum. But the doctor apparently had every expectation of Ashley going far in life, despite what we all saw that day.

I guess Dr. Conlon's experience seeing children on the autistic spectrum allowed him to forecast these expectations for Ashley. He was encouraged by her cognitive ability and wanted us to be clear as well about her visual gifts. But his position on labeling her left me too stunned and confused to see a brighter picture just yet!

We were putting all of our trust in this doctor and our daughter's life in his hands—a man who we didn't really know. As his words changed the course of our lives as we knew it earlier in the day, we hoped we were trusting in good faith. For he had just altered Ashley's life and ours—forever!

We arrived at Dave's parent's house to pick up Kacey. His parents knew the day had been a drain on us and had removed the burden by preparing dinner. We shared with them Ashley's diagnosis.

"Does this have anything to do with why she tunes us out?" his mother asked.

Dave's mother took exceptional resentment to Ashley's inability to tune into her.

"Well, she's getting a little bit better with us at home. But she didn't really want any part of the doctor today. He noticed that right away. But he saw how gifted she was with puzzles. He was impressed with her cognitive skills," I told her.

"She's very visual," Dave said to his mother.

"Oh yes, I know. She seems very smart," his mother responded. "You know, my cousin has a son who has three autistic children."

This was the first I heard about this, and Dave didn't know these cousins at all.

"I believe they are three, five, and seven. The oldest two are really severe. The younger one is moderately affected. They have issues with their behaviors and diets I remember my cousin telling me," his mother continued.

We explained how the doctor thought Ashley would go far due to her giftedness. He saw great potential in her.

"Oh, I hope so. My cousin tells me the children are not progressing very well," she said in a rather dismal tone.

"They have therapists coming into their house all day, every day to work with these children. It's extremely hard on the parents. It's all-consuming," she said, filling my mind with all sorts of dreadful pictures.

I didn't know if my mother-in-law was preparing me for the days ahead using these children as a frame of reference for the work and patience it would entail on our parts, or if she was worried that this disorder could place a tremendous burden on our marriage. Or maybe she was trying to communicate both of these to us!

Well, I guess only time would tell. I'm sure no two children are the same in these situations, and I didn't know if, at some point in time, Ashley would display any of the behaviors that these children showed. We knew nothing about what would be or what could be—only about what was.

"Now, is this doctor who saw Ashley reputable? Do you think you should get another opinion?" Dave's mother asked.

"I think he knows what he's talking about. But we may seek out the opinions of other doctors. We do have a lot of additional testing to put Ashley through to rule out other medical issues which could look similar to autism," Dave said to his mother.

We finished dinner. The girls were looking quite tired. We were exhausted as well. The day was wearing on us. We packed our bags and said our good-byes. We brought the girls home and tucked them into bed. It had been a very draining day, physically and emotionally. We were still shocked and in disbelief.

That evening, I told Dave about the information on autism I had researched, and how I instinctively suspected autism in Ashley, but was frightened to say anything to him.

I told him I thought he misinterpreted Dr. Conlon's question about Ashley flapping her hands or walking on her toes—that it wasn't a *good* thing she did this—that my reading suggested it was a characteristic seen in autism.

"Well, I didn't know where he was going with that—sorry!" Dave said.

"Do you think Ashley will get over this? Is this something you get over? Will she be all right? Will she learn to talk?" I asked him.

"What do you mean? Of course she's going to talk," he said with a hint of annoyance in his voice.

"I mean, I read that some children with autism never learn to talk—that this is a life-long disability. What does this mean in terms of getting along in school? What if she needs a special school? I always thought our girls would be together in school one day, holding hands and running on the playground," I said, starting to cry.

"My dreams—my dreams are gone!" I said, and turned away from Dave.

"Sharon, Dr. Conlon seemed very impressed with her! Don't be so negative!" he said, in Ashley's defense.

"Dave, she can't do *a lot* of things!" I said, turning back to look at him.

"Am I the only one who sees this? She can't even pull off her socks! An infant can do that! She's helpless in a lot of ways! And she's way below her peers, not just in speech. She doesn't understand us *all* the time. She doesn't even want to be hugged! She's just not here with us. I agree with Dr. Conlon. Ashley's aloof, she's not social, and her diet is horrific! She has a lot of these autistic characteristics I read about. That's why he labeled her. And I researched developmental delays too, and she's delayed in most everything!"

"Give the girl a break. She's not even two!" Dave said, acting like I was coming down too hard on Ashley.

"I'm scared! I think you are too! You just show it differently!" I said, my sleep deprivation and crankiness showing in my tone of voice.

"Sharon, I want you to stop reading and stop researching! You are way too obsessed! There's too much information out there on the Web. Most of that information doesn't pertain to Ashley—all of it seems like bad news! Go find some positive news, will you? You're filling your mind—and mine—with all of these gloom and doom stories. *Enough!*"

His annoyance turned to anger, and he stormed out of the room and went upstairs to bed.

The day had obviously caught up with us, and we found ourselves fighting with each other at a time when we needed each other most.

I went to bed, too. All the questions from the day went to sleep with me. And just as fast as I closed my eyes and fell asleep, they all haunted me and woke me up.

My mind was racing. I went back downstairs and turned on the computer. I found myself re-visiting the websites that had taunted me weeks earlier. But now, I felt justified in being on the websites. My daughter was now *officially* labeled!

The next day, I called my mother to inform her about Ashley's diagnosis. No sooner did she say hello back to me, there was dead silence on my part.

"Sharon? Sharon? What's wrong?" my mother yelled at me.

I couldn't answer her. I broke into a hard cry.

"Sharon, are you okay? What's going on? Is someone hurt?"

I sniffled my way through my sentences.

"It's…it's Ashley. She's…autistic!" I said, sobbing into the phone.

"Okay, Sharon, tell me what the doctor said. Just take a deep breath for me and calm down."

I couldn't speak.

"Sharon, I need you to talk to me," my mother said, trying to bring me back into the conversation.

I took a deep breath and tried to calm down.

"He…he tested her and…she's…she's really smart…but…but he thinks she belongs on the autistic spectrum—she has no social communication."

I didn't have the strength or the wits about me to go on. I dried my eyes with what little dry part of my sleeve I had left.

Do you want us to come up?" she asked, sensing a need to have my parents with me.

"Yyyy…yes," I said, sniffling.

"Okay, we'll be up shortly. Let us pack a few things."

"No. Tomorrow. Come tomorrow. Don't rush," I said, trying to calm myself down.

"Are you sure? Why don't we just come up now?"

"I'll be okay," I tried to reassure her.

"Where's Dave? Is he home?" she asked.

"Yes. He's here. He's with the girls."

"All right, call me back later. But we'll be there tomorrow morning," my mother said.

She told me she loved me, and I hung up the phone.

I took a minute to pull myself together. I picked up the receiver and called my brother to give him the news. My brother is four years older than I, but we are very close. He took the news amazingly well. He reassured me things would be okay.

"Sharon, we'll get her the help she needs. What can I do?" he graciously asked.

"Nothing," I whimpered.

"She's just so young! I'm scared." I said, crying again.

"I don't know if this helps any, but a friend of mine has a relative who was diagnosed with autism not too long ago. I'll call and get a phone number and an e-mail address for you. Maybe you can contact the Mother. Maybe she can give you some information," he said, trying to be helpful.

I wanted to call and talk with her, but not anytime soon. I wasn't exactly ready to share my personal heartbreak with anyone outside of my immediate family just yet. I couldn't even digest it myself.

"Let me know if you need anything. And I mean anything!

I love you!" he said, as he always did before ending our conversations.

My brother was always there for me if I needed *anything*. And I always relied on him for advice of every kind. He was so intelligent on many fronts. He lived a few states away, but I knew he would be here at a moment's notice if I just said the word.

Our relationship had come a long way from the days when he teased me using the words artistic and autistic interchangeably. Granted, it had been nearly twenty six years since his menacing days. He vaguely remembers those days of teasing me. I obviously remember them well.

He has since grown up to be a most generous guy. Despite the harassing—which came with the territory of being my brother—he always looked out for me when I was younger. And he still does today.

When I got off the phone with my brother, I called my sister. She is six years older than I, and as we have grown older, we have become best friends. She took the news with amazing strength and composure. I can't say the same about me. I broke down and cried again.

My sister lived about an hour and a half away in the same state. She too, was ready to drop what she was doing with her two children and come and comfort me. And she was always there to put things into perspective for me.

Rather ironically, she mentioned that she too, had a friend down the street that my nephew played with who was also autistic. He was seven-years-old, but had been diagnosed at eighteen months. My sister suggested that, when I was ready, I should speak with her friend—that perhaps she could lead me to the right specialists or give me insight into the disorder and how her friend has dealt with it for nearly five years.

My sister also mentioned that my brother-in-law's cousin had a son who was autistic who actually lived in my area. She gave me her name and number to get her perspective on this and to have her share her story with me.

Suddenly, I was finding out that Ashley was not the only one diagnosed with autism! In a mere day and a half between my mother-in-law, my brother and my sister, I had just learned about six other children with autism—that it wasn't just my Ashley who was diagnosed with this disorder!

But to me, it felt like it. I didn't know anyone in my inner circle of close friends who had an autistic child or a child with any developmental delays—and I felt all alone.

My friends all had healthy children. I couldn't turn to them yet. What would they say to me? How would they comfort me? How would they relate? I couldn't bear the thought of telling my friends about Ashley on a "Girl's Night" out and then have them return to their happy, talkative, loving child—while I went back to mine who shunned me and who couldn't say my name yet. They didn't have issues like these that had just been placed on my shoulders. They wouldn't be able to offer me anything I needed. I was instantly jealous of their easy, blissful lives and their cheerful, healthy children. So, Dave and I kept Ashley's diagnosis from our friends—a lie we would have to repeat over and over when they would casually ask how our girls were doing.

And yet, seeing how busy all of the specialists were that we had seen, there was obviously prevalence with this disorder to which I was previously oblivious. Were people just not talking about autism—as I had chosen to do? Did they think it wasn't for public consumption, like I, too, thought? Why is it that I had never before met anyone who had a child on the spectrum? I guess unless one is part of the autistic community, it remains unknown to the rest of the public just how many people out there are touched by this disorder. Prior to my travels down this road, I never needed to know who out there had autism. It's not like strangers just instantly shared that information with me.

But suddenly I was finding out that it was omnipresent. And with Ashley now as my source of reference, I know what to look for in its characteristics. I have radar to it. And now knowing what I know, I suspect a lot of parents out there probably have children who fall on the autistic spectrum somewhere. And they don't even know it!

The next morning, I brought Ashley to the local laboratory facility to have her blood drawn for the recommended tests: thyroid, high resolution karyotpe, DNA probe for Fragile X, and quantitative plasma amino acids and urine organic acids.

The man at the admissions desk slid the glass window open and took the prescription for the blood work and my insurance card. After looking at the prescription for a second, he handed it back.

"Ma'am, we don't accept this referral form here."

"What do you mean? I was told to come to my local lab and get my daughter's blood drawn. Why don't you accept this form?" I asked in a harsh manner.

"This is on a Children's Hospital requisition form. We don't accept this. You need to go to Children's and have these drawn," he said in a most insensitive tone.

"But this is what the doctor gave me," I replied innocently.

"But it needs to be on a requisition form like this one," he said, holding up a sample.

"But I don't have one of those! This is what he gave me! I don't understand why I can't have the labs drawn here! I can't go to Children's now—I was told I could come here!"

"Do you want to call your doctor and have him fax over the appropriate requisition form?" he asked.

He handed me the phone through the window opening. I sat Ashley on the counter of the admissions window. I called Dr. Conlon's office which was located in another state. Perhaps he could just fax a new requisition form and end this ridiculous discussion with this insensitive man in a lab coat.

I got a recording and hung up.

"Excuse me," I said, getting the man's attention.

I handed him back the phone.

"My doctor's not in. There's no answer," I said of my efforts to facilitate a solution to the problem.

I implored him to accept the requisition—that I didn't know there had been a mistake made with the form—that my daughter needed these labs drawn today!

The entire waiting room was now privy to my predicament. He called the office manager into the room to look at the prescription. After more pleading and begging on my part, she accepted the form with some hesitation.

I sat down with Ashley and waited for her name to be called. I could hear a few of the technicians in the office scrutinizing the form.

"Mrs. Ruben?" they called me back up to the window.

"Okay, what is it now?" I wondered.

"Mrs. Ruben? What are these tests for?"

I played dumb not wanting to explain to them (and the audience that was now focused on me) that these were tests the doctor recommended, having just diagnosed my daughter with autism—a word I'm sure no one in that room knew—a word I was still trying to add to my vocabulary.

"I don't know! These are just the tests that he ordered for my daughter! I thought that was your job!" I exclaimed in an angry, exhausting tone.

The line behind me had since backed up, and I could hear the heavy, impatient sighs being released.

"Ma'am, just have a seat and let these other people through. We'll call you when we find out how to draw these labs," the assistant suggested.

I sat back down. Ashley shimmied out of my arms and ran around the room. I chased her from place to place. She seemed to like crawling into the big empty space inside of the television stand that was playing an infomercial on a heart medication. To get inside of it, she had strewn medical pamphlets all over the floor. I picked them up with every weary eye in the waiting room staring at me— so much for the "good girl" compliment I always received by total strangers!

I waited and watched the clock. I watched as those who had been waiting in line behind me were called to have their blood drawn. They did so and left. I was still waiting and wondering. I could hear the laboratory technicians talking about how they had *no idea* what these tests were. Outside of the thyroid test, they had never heard of the other ones. They were apparently looking in their laboratory code books to ascertain what color tubes they needed to use. Not one of them could find these tests in their books. Not one of them knew!

I got up and continued to argue with them. I had been in this office a very long time and had seen a waiting room full of people come and go. There was now a room of fresh, new faces sitting and waiting. I had been there *that* long! One of the technicians got on the phone and called up the main lab that was cities away. They finally got some instructions on how to proceed with the tests. After nearly an hour of waiting, ranting, and raving, and total strangers gawking at us, Ashley and I were finally taken into the lab to have her blood drawn.

By now, I was the cranky one, not Ashley. I know these probably weren't common, everyday, diagnostic tests! I know I had thrown the technicians a curve so early in the morning! But these people didn't know my life had just been *shattered* with the news I received a day earlier. Nor would they care if I shared it with them. It was obvious that the burden of Ashley's disorder that I now carried around showed on my face. My anger was aimed full throttle at anyone who rattled me!

I put a urine bag on Ashley in hopes that drawing blood would trigger a sample they also needed for some organic acid tests. I sat down in the blood-drawing chair and had my arms and legs twisted around Ashley so she wouldn't escape. She knew something was up. The phlebotomist opened up the sterile syringes and alcohol pads. She prepped Ashley's arm. Ashley wailed!

She pressed on Ashley's veins to find a good juicy one. Having thought she found one, she slivered the needle into Ashley's arm. Ashley jerked with pain. I squeezed her to keep her from moving and put my cheek on her head.

"It's okay, sweetie. Mommy's here! It's almost over—I promise," I said, trying to reassure her.

The phlebotomist poked and prodded around underneath Ashley's skin. I know she must have been in so much pain! I hadn't seen any blood travel into the tube yet. I tried hard to keep Ashley in place. The nurse had come up dry. She missed Ashley's vein! She removed the needle and bandaged Ashley's arm.

"Can we try the other arm?" I asked her.

I felt like I was torturing my daughter. And I couldn't take her blood-curdling screams any longer. But these blood tests were crucial if we were to find out if Ashley had any other medical conditions. I was adamant about collecting it!

As misery loves company, Ashley's veins in the other arm were not cooperative either. The phlebotomist had struck a vein, but only got a trickling of blood from it—clearly there was not enough blood to fill the necessary tubes. I couldn't restrain Ashley any longer. She was nearly choking on her own tears that dripped into her mouth. *Game over!*

My poor baby! She had to endure more than any twenty-one-month-old should have to. She had given us all she could once again. It was all I could ask of her, as she had run out of arms and veins to stick.

After the other arm was bandaged, I picked her up and hugged her tight. That was too difficult to live through again—but feared I would have to. I was completely dissatisfied with the phlebotomist's incompetence and with the little amount of blood she had gotten. I knew we would be back in the not-too-distant future to try it again. I dreaded the thought. How could I put Ashley through *that* again?

I left the lab with Ashley still clinging to me and whimpering. I was given a few urine bags to collect a specimen at home. The one I had put on her at the beginning of the blood draw had not been successful. The urine seeped out of the bag and became absorbed by her diaper.

This had *not* been a good couple of days! My daughter had recently been diagnosed with an autistic disorder. I was fighting with Dave. I was fighting with people I didn't even know at the laboratory. I was subjecting my little girl to the pain of piercing needles. And I couldn't get a drop of urine in the place it needed to go. I was turning *mean* and *mad*!

My parents had since arrived at our house, and I greeted them with false bravery. They were there to help me, but I felt the need to keep busy and take my mind off of the diagnosis for a while. But each time I looked at the Band-Aids on Ashley's arms, I was reminded of it! Each time I tried to get another urine bag on her for failure of the previous one, I was reminded of it! Each time she turned the other way when my mother and father tried to hug her, I was reminded of it!

How did it ever come to this? Where did I go wrong? Where had it gone off course? Was I being blamed for something I did somewhere, at some time in my life? Was my life just too perfect and easy that I needed this challenge in it?

That night I lay in bed talking with Dave about it all. I broke down in tears again. As strong as I thought I was, I found I wasn't at all. I became pessimistic about everything and questioned Ashley's future and where it would take her. That's when I got the second lecture!

Dave was the strong one. He reminded me there was a beautiful little girl sleeping like an angel in the room next door.

He wouldn't let me forget that she was finally starting to do some really wonderful things. He wouldn't let me forget all the potential she held. He wouldn't let me forget the love we had for her and that with every ounce of energy he had, he would not let her fall victim to this disorder.

He reminded me again, that I was becoming too engrossed in my research and was scaring myself—and him. He reminded me that by my poor attitude and pessimism, I was bringing him down!

As his voice cracked, he was near tears himself with what may have been his breaking point—caused by me!

I suddenly realized, he was right!

I *was* a downer!

I was not seeing all the good in Ashley. I was only trying to guess how her future would play out—if *my* dreams for her would be realized. I was grieving as if I had lost Ashley. But he was there to remind me I hadn't—that we would, together, do whatever it took to make Ashley well.

I needed this reprimand from him. I sometimes got so wrapped up in the negative that the positive eluded me. But I was scared—scared of the unknown. She was our baby! But Dave brought it all back into focus for me. Now I know why I call him "Mr. Wonderful!"

Dave found it easier to fall asleep than I did. Our discussion played again and again in my head and kept me from falling asleep.

He was right!

He was so right!

Ashley needed us more than ever, and I needed to be braver and stronger than ever. I needed to pull it together if I was to guide Ashley through this.

But at that point, I couldn't. I was a complete wreck. I cried into my pillow as quietly as I could, trying not to wake Dave.

As much as Ashley needed me, I needed *my* mother. I got out of bed and walked down the hall toward the guest room. My mind was in conflict, as I stood in the doorway and watched my mother and my father sleep.

"Should I turn around and go back to bed? I'm a grown girl, what am I doing?" I thought to myself.

"Should I wake her or should I just wait until morning?"

I wrestled with my thoughts for a few minutes.

But I needed her to hold me. I walked to her side of the bed

"Mom!" I whispered, shaking her shoulder to wake her.

"Mom!"

She opened her eyes.

"I need to talk. I can't sleep," I said, starting to cry again.

She got out of bed, my father still sleeping soundly through my sniffling and crying. We walked downstairs and sat on the couch. I cried and cried as if I were a child again—like I had fallen off of my bike and scraped my chin. It hurt. It hurt a lot.

"Sharon, you need to be strong for Ashley. Kacey and Dave need you too," she said, holding me against her.

"You are now a Mom to two very adorable little girls. You need to put all of your energies into fighting this and looking forward and taking care of them. Don't think about the diagnosis. It might not have been what you wanted to hear, but maybe it's best that we finally know what the problem is so that we can start getting her better."

"I don't get it? How did this happen? Why me? What did I do wrong?" I asked, looking for answers I knew she didn't have.

"You didn't do anything wrong, honey. Don't tear yourself up inside wondering how or why? Let's just concentrate on getting her the treatment that she needs. We'll stay as long as you need us. Your father and I are here for you."

"Why is Kacey okay and not Ashley? What happened to Ashley?" I asked, brushing away my tears.

"I don't know, sweetie. This is all very confusing. But there are three people upstairs who need you very much. Don't let this eat away at you. That's not the answer. You need to calm down, Sharon. We all love that little girl. Moms will do anything for their children. You need to be strong and stop blaming yourself. That's not going to help Ashley. We'll make some calls tomorrow and find her the right people to see. But what you need right now, though, is some sleep. Get some rest."

"I can't sleep," I said, resting my head on her shoulder.

"Can I make you some tea?" she asked, trying to calm me down.

"Yes, thanks," I said, taking another tissue from the box she had placed on the table.

She walked into the kitchen to make some tea, and I stared at the pictures of Ashley on the mantle above the fireplace. I wondered if Ashley had shown signs when the pictures had been taken—around five-months-old. She looked fine in the pictures. At least I had thought so back then.

The slide show in my mind came back just as it had done at the speech therapist's office. But this time, it was rewinding. I went back in time and tried to remember every instance of a problem area in Ashley's life. Had I missed something along the way that I should have been more alarmed about? Was this due to a vaccination she had received? I had read about vaccinations, most notably the Measles/Mumps/Rubella (MMR) vaccine, being possibly blamed for cases of autism—that some parents noticed changes in their child around 15 or 16 months. That's when all of this with Ashley really came to my attention. But I didn't know this for certain. Or did she bump her head too many times when she fell? There were those peculiar things about her back then with her development. Were they the first indications of a problem that I didn't think warranted medical attention just yet? Was this again my fault somehow during labor and delivery? Did something happen that day to cause this?

I sat and thought about all of the possibilities with my knees bent and tucked under my chin.

My mother returned to the den with a piping hot cup of tea. The steam felt good on my cheeks. As I sipped, my tears fell into my cup—refilling itself with each sip I took.

"You need to get some rest, Sharon," she begged me.

I put the teacup on the table. I stretched out on the couch and closed my eyes. It was nearly morning, and I had been up all night. The lack of sleep and the new situation I found myself in were wearing on me physically and emotionally. My mother covered me with a blanket and watched me sleep.

I awoke a few hours later—the morning had arrived ever so quickly. My mother had awakened, too, at the other end of the couch. Dave had come downstairs. He was unaware that I had left our bed in the middle of the night. I stared at the teacup and the box of tissues on the table—a reminder of the night and the tears that I had cried with my mother.

I picked up the teacup with tears still in it. I walked out of the den into the kitchen. With renewed hope and strength for the challenge that lie ahead of me, and a night full of my mother's wisdom and support, I stood over the sink and poured out the remaining tea—my pessimism and denial poured out with it.

CHAPTER 6

▼

THE FOG BEGAN TO LIFT

Ashley was partitioned off from those around her by a thick layer of haze. It seemed somewhat of a protective barrier sandwiched between her world and that of a world she viewed far more confusing and threatening on the other side of it. As if the fog were a security blanket to her, she wrapped herself up in it, and she was nearly combustible if anyone was to try to slip underneath it to play peek-a-boo with her.

To provide her with more peer interaction, I enrolled Ashley in a day care program three days a week. Dr. Conlon thought that interaction with normal children would be good for her.

When I brought her to day care the first day, I kissed her good-bye and watched her from the window in the hall. Ashley didn't seem to care I had left her. The other Moms were busy consoling their crying children. One parent even remarked that Ashley didn't seem to have separation anxiety like her child had. What that Mom didn't know was that Ashley didn't even know that I was her mother. And that Mom certainly wouldn't have guessed that Ashley was autistic.

I don't think Ashley really knew where she was. The concept of day care was incomprehensible to her. She had never been with other children, except Kacey, so she didn't know what to do with them. She just retreated into her world. This new setting meant nothing to her.

I watched Ashley as she played by herself. I watched for repetitive behaviors. She turned all the knobs on a play stove and opened and closed the doors on the play microwave oven over and over again. She flapped her hands a few times. She didn't interact with the other children and often went over to a pile of plush pillows in the corner where she sat and sucked her thumb. It always seemed like she had little steam left in her even in the morning—and she always seemed content doing nothing.

Sometimes, I stuck my head inside the door and instructed the teachers to pull her back into the group setting. I wondered why I had to tell them this. Why, if they saw a child alone in the corner, wouldn't they pull her back into the group? I watched as children went to their cubby hooks and pulled down their coats for fun and put them on. Ashley couldn't do these things at this point. She didn't even know she had a hook or that her jacket belonged there!

During meals at day care, Ashley never touched the food they served—usually tuna casserole or stew. I can't say I blame her. Those were not high on my list of edibles, either. She sat in a high chair and nibbled on a cookie or cracker the teachers gave her, so she wouldn't go hungry.

Some of the children her age had outgrown a highchair. They sat at a kiddy table and devoured their tuna casserole with a spoon and sipped from their open cups. Ashley couldn't do these things like the other toddlers. I felt like this may not be the place for her just yet. She was developmentally behind these children her own age. I didn't think she knew what to do there like the other children did. She didn't even participate in story time or arts and crafts. She just wandered around the classroom without a plan, without focus and without words.

The other children seemed to be having a good time running around and screaming as toddlers do. But Ashley never joined in those activities. She couldn't initiate socializing, and as I observed, the teachers never brought her back into the action or hooked her up with a friend.

"The squeaky wheel gets the oil," I thought to myself.

To the teachers, she wasn't squeaky, so they never had to tend to her or discipline her. Ashley was mostly left to wander at her own discretion. As long as she was safe in the room, the teachers thought she was doing fine.

Ashley's daily reports always stated that she had a "good" day. But I knew otherwise. She didn't participate. She didn't talk. She didn't eat.

"How was that a good day?" I wondered. "Because, she didn't make them lift a finger to tend to her?"

The teachers didn't know anything about Ashley's diagnosis. And I didn't tell them. I didn't want them to possibly be prejudiced against her, and I didn't want management to tell me that they didn't have the time or staff to give her the special attention that she needed. It would just take so much explaining to enlighten them about what her difficulties were—her disorder. And if I told them, would they really understand the complexity of it all? I was still trying to understand it myself. So, I didn't touch that one with them. I thought that I would just try the day care setting, try to get her interacting with others, and if it didn't work, I'd take her out and move on.

I only had Ashley in day care part-time which amounted to half a day, three times a week. It gave me enough time to get some work done. I was working as a medical writer from my home office at the time. On some days I went by early just to observe her in the daycare room until it was time to pick her up. I wasn't completely satisfied with what I was witnessing.

Clearly, Ashley was like a fish out of water in that toddler classroom. She needed a classroom somewhere between the infant stage and the toddler stage—obviously there was none. I didn't think she was getting anything out of the time she spent there. She couldn't talk to the teachers and when they tried to instruct her, she ignored them. It was a flop. After four weeks of trying to make it work, I decided this day care situation wasn't working to my satisfaction and withdrew her. She was back at home with me while I pondered how to proceed.

At Ashley's next speech therapy session, Dave and I shared with Shelly, Dr. Conlon's diagnosis. Shelly's face completely froze at the word autism. She had not for a minute thought that Ashley fell on the autistic spectrum. She saw many autistic children in her practice. Ashley didn't quite fit that description to her. Shelly was completely taken aback.

"I thought all along that there was something blocking Ashley. I thought it was her ears—her ear infections. But…autism?" Shelly remarked, shaking her head in disbelief.

Shelly thought that if she could only jump-start Ashley somehow, she would progress nicely with the acquisition of language. Ashley had started to become a little more active in the therapy sessions. She was trying so hard with her words and sounds. But she was still quite aloof and non-responsive at times.

Shelly introduced me to Nancy, the occupational therapist at the rehabilitative center. Now having a diagnosis on the autistic spectrum, I flooded Nancy with questions about her background, and asked if she saw autistic children. She did have many autistic children coming to her for therapy, so I felt her experience with the disorder would allow her to address the necessary issues with Ashley. Nancy had an opening in her schedule, and we made an appointment for Ashley to see her for an evaluation following our next appointment with Shelly.

Nancy had testing material similar to that of Dr. Conlon. Ashley didn't fair too well on Nancy's tests. From stringing beads to building a tower of blocks,

Ashley was minimally interested or did not have the skill to perform a particular task. Nancy noted, as did the other specialists, that Ashley's attention span was poor with little comprehension of verbal instructions. Her fine motor skills (using her hands and fingers) and her gross motor skills (using her arms and legs) were delayed way below her 21 months of age, and she had difficulty with bilateral activities, using two hands together. Her ability to balance was also below age level.

When Nancy concluded her evaluation, she talked to Dave and me a little bit about what she thought were Ashley's deficiencies. She mentioned the terms "decreased auditory comprehension" and "sensory integration." I was not too familiar with either phrase, but had come across them during my online research and had passed them by.

What Nancy was telling us was that, in her opinion, Ashley showed signs of sensory integration dysfunction. Ashley was unable to fully process the information coming in through her senses. And these senses were not just the five that we typically think of: seeing, hearing, tasting, smelling, and touching.

There were lesser-known senses that we aren't in control over, known as the vestibular system (unconscious information from the inner ear about movement and position in space), the proprioception system (unconscious information from muscles, ligaments and joints) and the kinesthetic system (the combination of information from eyes, muscles, joints, and the vestibular system to form conscious awareness of one's body in space).

As a result of the organization of these senses, a child begins to develop and mature from lying on its back, to pushing up, to crawling, to walking, to running, to balancing and planning sequenced actions (motor planning). When the brain processes this information correctly, the body responds appropriately. It knows how to modulate, or regulate itself and thus, regulates our behavior to it as well. It doesn't overload us with stimuli we don't need (such as background noise that we usually ignore when doing something), and it doesn't "under" load leaving us without the needed sensory input. It balances the information it sends and processes it according to our needs. It does this pretty much unbeknownst to us.

Conversely, when the neurological system is not working optimally or is inefficient at processing the sensory information it receives, one can be very defensive to sensory stimuli and not be able to modulate one's behavior accordingly or be unable to plan those sequenced actions appropriately (like bringing a spoon to our mouth).

Ashley's central nervous system, with the brain being the primary organ, was apparently not analyzing, organizing, and connecting the messages it was being sent through all of her senses. Her responses to these improperly channeled stimuli resulted in disorganized behavior. She did not know how to react to something she thought was threatening, so she did so in the only way her body knew how—in a fight or flight manner. This explained why she flew off the handle at inappropriate times.

Her body also had difficulty with planning out everyday movements. These movements were not just related to walking, (as she was quite wobbly), but oral motor skills (being offended by most food textures and having difficulty using the muscles of her mouth to sip or blow bubbles), as well as gross and fine motor skills (having difficulty doing age appropriate tasks such as pulling off her socks or putting her arms through a shirt sleeve, stringing beads or manipulating Play Dough).

Since Ashley was having difficulty with her motor planning, she was not able to build higher skills, because she had not yet mastered the basic ones at her age appropriate level.

Ashley's low muscle tone that Dr. Conlon observed added to her difficulty in achieving these skills. She did not have the muscle strength or the lasting muscle contractions needed for even the simplest task.

I now understood that what I thought was flexibility in her joints—to the tune of maybe a gymnast's body—was turning out to be a contributing factor in her inability to acquire these motor skills. I wasn't aware that low muscle tone played such a major role in Ashley's life, but it was an underlying issue for her, coupled with her sensory integration dysfunction and her speech delay—all of which kept her from being that normal child on the playground; able to climb the ladder of the slide and slide down it; drink from a cup without a top, or communicate with others. These were things I watched all of her classmates do age appropriately and without difficulty.

Dave and I set up therapy sessions with Nancy, and Ashley saw her twice a week following our speech sessions with Shelly. To improve her bilateral and fine motor skills, Ashley worked on building a tower of cubes, threading beads, and snipping paper with scissors. To improve her gross motor skills, she worked on throwing and kicking a ball and jumping down from a small stool. To increase her socialization and attention skills, she worked on giving one of us a toy or throwing us a ball upon request, as well as trying to wave good-bye at the end of a session. To increase oral stimulation and decrease the sensitivities in Ashley's mouth, Nancy recommended several techniques such as massaging the inside of her cheeks with a vibrating toothbrush and stroking a baby gum brush over her tongue and inside her cheeks.

To increase overall sensory input and to modulate her, Ashley received a routine of daily skin brushing and joint compressions. This is called the Wilbarger Protocol. It is designed to increase one's awareness to sensory stimulation. The protocol is all about pressure touch and joint compression to the limbs of the body. The technique requires a special brush, which when used with a firm stroking motion in a specific pattern of direction, stimulates the tactile receptors of the skin. The joint compressions are given to key joints in both the upper and lower extremities to make the brain think the bone is about to be displaced. Proprioceptors, receptors sensitive to the position and movement of the body, fire to stabilize and protect the joint. Since muscles are controlled by proprioceptors, an influx of proprioceptive firing brings about a very calming effect on the body.

Some of the possible outcomes we were expecting to see from using the brushing protocol were: acceptance to touch (all over the body); increased participation in self-help skills (dressing); increased exploration of toys and textures; increased eye contact and visual attentiveness during tasks; and increased general alertness and a calm state.

Nancy demonstrated how to brush Ashley and give her joint compressions. She told us to follow this protocol every two hours for two to three weeks and then decrease the routine to three to five times a day. This protocol of tactile and proprioception sensation, along with the vestibular movement of bouncing or jumping, was to give Ashley a sensory diet that she was apparently lacking and one her body was craving. A sensory diet gives the brain information it needs to organize itself through these various stimulating activities. The brain's capacity to learn is based on adequate sensory integration.

Dave and I began brushing Ashley upon arriving home from our occupational therapy (OT) session. She withdrew and recoiled initially, not caring for it at all. She hardly let us touch her. But to be effective, we had to keep going and avoid repeated areas already touched by the brush or it would have a negative, disorganizing effect. We brushed her every two hours as recommended. This kept her in an optimal state of sensory modulation. We brushed—and we brushed—and we brushed.

And then it happened!

Ashley started to connect with me. While lying on her back, she now looked me in the eyes—something she rarely ever did!

"One, two, three..." I counted her joint compressions up to ten.

I moved to another joint and started again.

"One," I said, looking at her.

"Yun," she said back to me.

"She talked! And she looked at me! Wow, it really does work!" I said, being in total shock.

Ashley became more alert and started to relate to me more as I continued to brush her.

"Teh," she'd say when I got to ten.

Into a week of brushing, she had said one of her first real words, "bah" (ball), and it wasn't a preposition!

Dave and I noticed during the next few weeks that her eye contact, alertness, even her behavior were all improving due to this pressure touch and joint compression protocol.

On Christmas Eve of 2000, we decorated the house, and the girls helped trim the tree. Kacey left cookies and milk for Santa and his reindeer. We tucked the girls into bed. As they slept, Dave and I retrieved the packages we hid all over the house and put them under the tree. The tree shimmered! We hugged and kissed each other. We were going to get through this, we agreed…together!

As we made our way upstairs for the evening, we suddenly remembered we had forgotten something. We turned around and went to the rocking horse where Kacey had placed the cookies and milk. I took a big gulp of milk and Dave gobbled up the cookies strewing crumbs all over the carpet so the girls would see what messy eaters Santa and his crew were.

The next morning we carried the girls downstairs. Kacey was first to notice the presents—Santa had been there.

"Mommy, the cookies are gone," she said, excitedly.

"He must have been hungry. He had a lot of work to do. It looks like he loved the cookies we baked!" I added, seeing Kacey's face light up.

Ashley didn't really understand the concept of the presents under the tree or who Santa was yet. She wandered about sucking her thumb. But I think she knew something was different.

The gifts seemed endless, and we helped the girls rip the paper from every box. Kacey had fun and exciting toys. Ashley's presents were more along the line of her OT therapy—they were still fun, but I had a therapy theme in mind for her. She got a lot of toys that required her to exert some energy and work her muscles. They looked interesting enough to her, and she was not suspicious that there was an underlying method to Santa's toy selection. After all she was only 22-months-old!

Dave sat with Ashley and showed her how to hammer balls in the holes of one of her games. She would daintily tap the ball, it going nowhere.

"Hit!" we said, loudly.

Ashley seemed to understand the command. We gave her an enthusiastic "yeah" each time she hit the ball. But at times, she preferred to take two balls and clang them together seeming tired of the correct way to play with her new toy.

Kacey came over to show her how it was done in true big sister form. But Kacey seemed a little too intrusive in Ashley's space, and Ashley started to scream. But it didn't take Ashley long to master the use of the hammer. Putting her exceptional visual skills to work, she was quick to match up each colored ball to its respective colored hole. She gave the balls a *whack,* and down they fell winding their way through the maze and out onto the floor.

We marveled at this. By the time Christmas morning was over, Ashley had hammered the balls into the holes like a champ. It was great work on her arms and hands as well as on her motor planning. We noticed she went back and forth between using the left and right hands. A dominant hand had not yet emerged.

"Look, Ashley, Elmo!" I said, holding up an Elmo shirt and Elmo slippers so that Dave could get it on videotape.

She loved Elmo and would take her Elmo doll everywhere.

"Ashley, can you say Elmo? Who's this? Is it Elmo?"

"Em," she finally said, as I tried to put her slippers on. She balked at me for doing so.

As much as Ashley seemed to like the toys, she still just wandered about the room and paid little attention to her name. It was pretty much all about doing her own thing when she wanted to do it. We were making good strides with her, but we still had so far to go.

Ashley seemed to enjoy what OT was all about—playtime. She bounced on a large therapy ball. She bounced on a mini-trampoline. She swung and spun in a swing. These were all activities to increase her proprioception and vestibular (inner ear) stimulation.

She was working hard on her fine motor skills and her bilateral coordination. She still had difficulty separating and piecing together plastic pop beads. She worked on manipulating the buttons on a pop-up toy that required a turn of a knob or a button to be pushed up or down. Her little fingers couldn't get the buttons to work so well. She worked on cutting with scissors and threading beads down a long string. For a little toddler, she was really trying hard.

I watched Ashley intently during her OT sessions. I had acquired all the equipment, games, and toys Nancy had in her sessions, but I also studied her therapy techniques. Dave and I devoted many hours, many times a day to giving Ashley proprioceptive and vestibular input that had been missing all this time. Our basement was turned into an occupational therapy room. We brushed her.

We swung her. We bounced her—just like Nancy did. We put her hands in a bucket of dry rice and beans to decrease her tactile sensitivities. We put Play Dough in her palm and had her squeeze it as tightly as she could. We tried to help her build up those tiny muscles.

We started out a little slowly it seemed, as Ashley took a little longer than I think even the therapists expected to achieve some of her goals; but by four months into speech and OT, we were beginning to see some real signs of progress from Ashley. Her hands were becoming less defensive to textures, and she wasn't throwing as many tantrums out of frustration as much as she used to. Her motor planning had started to emerge as well.

She started to throw a ball to us "over hand" when cued, and she understood and followed simple commands. Her jumping ability had improved slightly, and she started to display problem solving abilities by stacking and nesting cups.

Ashley started to approximate more words like "bub bo" for "bubble blow" while playing with bubbles. She couldn't blow the bubble—she still couldn't pucker her lips correctly—but she was bursting the bubbles with her finger pointed (after many hours of work teaching her to point).

"Puh," she said, popping a bubble. She was starting to have fun.

I taught her to sign a few words such as "more," "all done" and "cracker." I was amazed at how fast she caught on to the concept. She could use it functionally.

With her expressive language starting to emerge, her receptive language was going even faster. She definitely seemed to understand us more than she could talk to us. Her eye contact got better each day. We were just thrilled with what we were witnessing.

"Could the brushing be doing all of this?" I wondered. The occupational therapist thought so. And, she was right on the money! What she told us to be on the lookout for, with respect to results from the brushing protocol, was coming at us fast and furiously—as if a cork had just popped. Ashley was slowly emerging out of her fog.

The year came to an end, and 2001 rung in. We were greeted with exciting news that I was expecting our third child. We planned on having more children and didn't want Ashley's diagnosis to be the cause for halting those plans.

Nonetheless, I had fears that I may be going through all of this again with the third baby. There were no guarantees everything would be normal with this child. But I had to be positive about our decision to have another baby and to enjoy it just as much as I enjoyed the other two pregnancies.

At my first prenatal visit to my obstetrician, Dave and I brought Ashley with us. We saw the baby's heartbeat on the monitor and were reassured by the doctor that the fetus looked healthy and normal for the gestational age. We sat down in his office and had a consultation with him. I had had the same consult twice before when I was pregnant with Kacey and Ashley, so we all felt that I had the routine down; that I knew what to expect from the experience. He discussed the prenatal tests I would need to decide to have or not to have in the coming weeks.

We let Ashley wander around his office as we spoke with the doctor. She was becoming a bit whiny and restless. He opened his desk drawer and removed a calculator and handed it to her. Most children would have loved to bang on it and play with it. Ashley did the only thing she knew how—she looked at it, grunted, and turned the other way rejecting his offering. He returned it to his drawer having given it his best shot.

I sat not saying a word about what had just transpired. I was a bit in conflict about whether or not to talk to him at that moment about Ashley's diagnosis. He was the one who brought Ashley into the world. I was a bit unsure how to now tell him that the baby he so carefully monitored for nine months and delicately cut from my abdomen had autism—as if I had failed as a Mother having promised him I'd take great care of her after she was handed to me in the recovery area.

I figured, maybe he wasn't familiar with the autistic spectrum and then where would that lead me? I also feared that he wouldn't have any good statistics to tell me about the probability of my new baby ending up the same way. I kept mum.

I waited until the next visit before I opened up to him about Ashley's condition, this only after he asked, "Do you have any concerns?"

I was surprised and relieved when he actually confided to Dave and me that his older child had also been placed on the autistic spectrum with PDD-NOS. His son didn't have speech issues like Ashley had. He could talk just fine, and he was smart for his age. He had more social interaction issues. He also had motor and vision issues that were being addressed for the past four years in occupational therapy. I now had another person, who I trusted explicitly, and who I could talk with about Ashley's disorder. And although he was a doctor, he talked to me through the eyes of a parent of a child on the spectrum offering me advice and wisdom—something that I needed and welcomed at that point, having since cut myself off from my network of friends.

CHAPTER 7

▼

TESTING, ONE, TWO, THREE

Dave and I returned to Children's Hospital a few months later for Ashley's psychological evaluation. We met with a well-respected psychologist. Dr. Conlon had updated him prior to our arrival about Ashley's recent diagnosis and placement on the autistic spectrum. Dr. Conlon had referred us to this specialist to get his opinion on whether the diagnosis of autistic spectrum disorder was the appropriate one for Ashley—he wanted another professional's opinion.

Having again brought all of Ashley's puzzles to show off her abilities, the doctor didn't ask for them. Ashley sat down at the children's table while the doctor took out many of his own puzzles and examination tools. Ashley quickly gobbled up the puzzles and pegboards he placed in front of her. He remarked at her tremendous visual processing ability—something we already knew.

Although Ashley had started to point to pictures for us at home, she was uncooperative for the psychologist. She was able to feed a doll, something she had just learned at home. But she didn't know what to do with the tissue the doctor handed her in hopes that she would blow the doll's nose. She didn't have that concept down yet.

Her eye contact was reduced with him, although there were some moments of joint attention that he was pleased to see. But he really wanted to see her more engaged with us and enjoying herself. Maybe she wasn't enjoying this, though!

Maybe she was getting kind of tired of this examination routine and didn't want to perform anymore, much like a circus act! We were asking so much of Ashley from all of these tests by specialists. It seemed that everyone, even us, expected her to have an "on" day, every day. She wasn't even two-years-old, and she had so much pressure placed upon her to show her capabilities—or rather, her inabilities, which the specialists focused on more.

The psychologist concluded that she had age appropriate problem solving and memory skills. She performed above age level in color matching and imitating lines on a piece of paper. With respect to speech and language, he felt she had significant delays and social communication weaknesses by not being able to talk or gesture.

He didn't observe any repetitive or perseverative behaviors such as hand flapping or toes walking that day. He seemed very encouraged by Ashley's cognitive skills and thought she could go far in the future such as Dr. Conlon had commented on as well. However, the reduced joint attention and lack of shared enjoyment made him feel that Ashley did, in fact, fall on the autistic spectrum similar to that which Dr. Conlon had diagnosed.

Here was our first confirmation of the diagnosis of autism. Both the neurodevelopmental pediatrician and the psychologist's assessment of her was that she definitely belonged on the autistic spectrum according to their medical and professional opinions.

A few days later I made a call to Dr. Conlon to share with him the good news about Ashley's progress with the brushing and joint compression program. He was delighted that we were seeing some progress with her. His news, however, was not so wonderful. He informed us that the DNA probe and Fragile X test, (which she had blood drawn for a few months earlier), had come back with insufficient data—another sample was required.

Was I surprised? Not really. I knew the day we had the blood drawn that there would come a time when we would have to subject Ashley (and me) to that awful and painful torture again.

But it wasn't just that we had to have the blood drawn again. It meant that the answers to whether she had all of her chromosomes, or if Fragile X played a part in all of this would go unanswered for even more months, until we could obtain sufficient results to indicate these were normal. Not knowing if there was a serious genetic condition at the root of this was unbearable—it was tearing at me.

Dave and I drove to Children's Hospital to have Ashley's blood re-drawn as the technicians would know exactly what tests were needed and how to prepare them for shipping. I was unwilling to go back to our local lab where I had met up with my second nightmare.

We walked into the lab, and I informed the technician of our previous mishap in obtaining Ashley's blood. He assured us he had the expertise to draw blood from little veins—he did it everyday. I gave Dave the job of holding her down while the technician slid the needle into her itty bitty, barely visible vein, all the while Ashley screaming at the top of her lungs. Again, the vein in the first arm came up dry.

"He just told me, he was good at this," I said to myself, cringing with every flinch I saw Ashley make.

He was unable to find just the right spot. Here we go again, I thought! I was told that if he couldn't get the blood in the second arm that we had a mandatory three-day wait before we could try it again. I dropped my head in disbelief.

I stroked Ashley's face as she tried her best to escape Dave's arms.

"Ashley, sweetie. It's okay, just a little bit more," I said, trying to soothe and ease her pain.

The next needle hit the jackpot, and the technician was able to fill all of the tubes successfully. He bandaged her and gave her some stickers. She didn't care for stickers. She didn't know what to do with them. She just wanted out of there. We did too.

We were told the tubes would go out that day to be processed. Again, we had left a lab with Ashley bandaged and bruised, but I felt we could finally relax and didn't have to ever worry about having Ashley siphoned for her blood again.

Not until…I made a call to the doctor nearly a month later wondering where the lab results were. I was a nervous Nelly over not knowing anything, because no one had called with the results.

No one had called me, because…there *were* no results. Apparently there had been a problem at some point in preparing and shipping the blood. By the time the samples had reached their destination, the blood had clotted and was unable to be analyzed. The lab report for the second time had come back with insufficient blood samples to be analyzed.

All right! Was there just not an ounce of luck anywhere to be found in my life? Why was all of this happening to me—to us—to Ashley? All we wanted was to get some test results on some genetic conditions that sounded frightening! Was no one competent enough to draw blood, package it properly, send it off, and have it analyzed without causing such complete and utter horror in our lives? I was near the end of my rope!

It kept me crying. It kept me up at night. It was unfair to us and to Ashley that these answers were still unknown months after we had attempted to do all of the right things. Not knowing any results could mean Ashley may possibly have these conditions.

So, I prepared myself for the worst. I researched Fragile X. And every time I read something about it, I found I was trying to read Ashley into it which was a mistake—one I thought I had learned from a while back researching autism. I guess not!

Dave and I brought Ashley back to Children's Hospital a few days later for what we hoped would be, the last attempt at getting her blood drawn. I think Ashley was becoming familiar with the routine by now and cried as soon as she saw the technician in his lab coat.

Quick, but not painless, the blood was drawn, and I was assured and reassured that there would be no blunders this time. And I was most emphatic that there had better not be. Emotionally, I couldn't go through this one more time, and I wasn't about to subject Ashley to anymore of it—those chromosomal and DNA questions would just have to go unanswered forever, if it meant having to redraw it a fourth time. Her little veins just couldn't take it. She was becoming the victim of laboratory errors, one too many times.

With all of the visits to all of the specialists we had seen thus far, and all of the laboratory testing we had endured, this experience was draining on us, especially Ashley. She had probably been through more dog and pony shows to assess her cognitive, social, emotional, and communicative state than most adults go through in a lifetime. But it still wasn't over!

On top of all the previous testing we had done, we now needed to get a sleep-deprived EEG (a brainwave test) on Ashley to rule out seizure activity—a possible cause for why she wasn't talking. We tried to keep Ashley awake until nearly midnight the night before this test, so her body would ache for sleep during the EEG. I know mine did!

It was almost unbearable to see—Ashley on the examining bed kicking and screaming while the technician glued electrodes to her beautiful blonde locks. I know it was important for the sake of finding out all we could about what was at the root of Ashley's problems, but seeing her on the table so helpless and so innocent was horrifying. I cupped my face with my hands and dropped my head to cry. Dave placed a comforting hand on my back.

Tired from screaming and our cruel punishment of having her burn the midnight oil with us, she had fallen asleep. There was suddenly an eerie calm that swept over her. It was a creepy sight watching her sleep with all of the wires tangled up on her head. I sat down on the bed next to her to monitor her breathing. I constantly tuned into the rise and fall of her tiny chest making sure she was still breathing. She was in such a state of peace at the moment. It was almost like a picture of a parent's bedside vigil with her child in a sick ward.

"What am I doing here? How had it gotten to this point? When will this dream end?" I wondered.

But Ashley, at that point, was the only one dreaming. I knew she was only sleeping, but she was so still. Thoughts went through my mind that something was going to go wrong and that she wouldn't wake up.

"Don't take her from me, now!" I begged whoever above was listening.

I wanted to wake her up right then and hug her and let her know that it would all be okay—that Mommy was here. She was just starting to get to know me.

I got up and took a few steps back from the bed to glance at the computer that captured her brain waves. Not knowing what I was looking at—except many rows of moving lines which simulated a heart rhythm—I was tempted to ask so many questions about what the technician saw. But I just bit my tongue. She wouldn't have told me anyhow, leaving the interpretations to the doctor. The technician signaled for us to wake Ashley. What seemed like an eternity, since the start of the EEG, was now coming to an end.

The technician dismantled Ashley from the helmet of wires in her hair and gave us back our little cutie in a mass of glue and tangles. Ashley was coming to, a bit cranky and quite understandably so. Dave and I put on our coats, and I placed Ashley's Elmo hat on her head. We left the building glad it was over.

It seemed that nothing good ever came out of that building since the day of Ashley's diagnosis. I know it just seemed that way, and that every subsequent trip we made to Children's Hospital was only for Ashley's benefit—to find out all we could about what was going on with her, but it made us so sad every time we left. We never got any good news when we were there. It always seemed to be that Ashley underwent painstaking testing there, and that we always received dismal news as a result of it. She was so innocent in all of this. Why couldn't we just get some good news when we left there for a change?

We stopped for lunch before going back and picking up Kacey. Ashley sat at the table still wearing her Elmo hat that covered the gluey mess on her head. We kept her hat on, not wanting to get glances from patrons sitting at tables around us. Could they ever imagine where we had just been?

P.I.E. In The Eye

Ashley was now fully immersed in speech therapy and OT twice a week, and I was working with her as much as I could at home. She was making some progress, yet ever so slowly. Dr. Conlon recommended I contact the early intervention services in my area for an evaluation. It was called P.I.E.—Parent and Infant Education.

The Individuals with Disabilities Education Act (IDEA) is a federal law which includes provisions for early intervention services for eligible infants and toddlers (ages 0–36 months) with disabilities. As a parent now of a child with a disability, I had the right to an evaluation by the county to determine Ashley's eligibility to receive such services.

Dave and I walked into the county building with Ashley. We were greeted by a service coordinator and were taken back to one of the examination rooms. We made our introductions to the speech therapist and special educator who were conducting the test that day and joined them on the floor amongst an array of toys and testing material. They told us in order to be eligible for services from the county, Ashley needed to present with at least a 25% developmental delay in cognitive, expressive communication, receptive communication, gross motor skills, fine motor skills, social, emotional, or self-help skills.

The two-person team each gathered a little bit of data upon observing Ashley and asked her to do various tasks. Ashley showed good attention span, but on her own terms. When it came to introducing something new to her, at times, she would tantrum at their directions as well as when they asked her to sit and participate in a game. She mouthed most of the objects they gave her. She showed an inability to participate in turn-taking activities.

Ashley had good problem-solving skills, but her symbolic play skills lacked pretend play and imitation. Her self-help skills were average as she was beginning to help out with dressing herself (although I still tended to dominate), but she still didn't use utensils to eat with and couldn't drink well from a cup.

Her expressive language was noted to be below average, but she was beginning to use simple words. Her receptive language was a bit stronger.

Her oral motor skills indicated a possible decreased awareness in her mouth, putting a lot of food in her mouth at one time and preferring only crunchy foods.

Although previous speech therapists clearly felt she had delays in both expressive and receptive language, the county therapists found Ashley eligible only for delays in her expressive language, which fell into the 12 to15-month range; Ashley was now 22-months-old.

Dave and I attended a meeting to write Ashley's IEP. This is an "Individual-ized Education Program" developed by the parent and the school personnel out-lining the intervention services specifically designed to meet the needs of a child with a disability.

Dave and I mapped out the goals we wanted to see Ashley attain within that given school year. Just communicating her basic needs was our long-term goal. Her short-term goals were to include her being able to say a simple Mama and Dada and the names of her other family members. The therapists wrote goals of their own such as wanting Ashley to produce basic word approximations, use functional actions with play, and use more gestures. These goals were to get her started, and she had various target dates for attaining each.

We started receiving services from the county twice a week. Lindsey was our special educator and was exceptionally good at her job. Lindsey came to our house with a bag full of toys and games hoping to elicit a response from Ashley—a glance, a smile, a laugh, and hopefully teach her a new word or two.

Ashley and I (and sometimes Kacey) would always wait at the front door and watch Lindsey collect her gear from her car and walk up the steps to our porch. Although Ashley couldn't say her greetings back to Lindsey as they were said to her, Ashley always sped out of the foyer into the den and sat down on the floor waiting for Lindsey to open her bag of goodies. I could tell that Ashley enjoyed her time with Lindsey.

I found Lindsey to be quite engaging and ever so patient with Ashley. At times, Ashley would retreat back a bit and not want to do something. But Lind-sey knew all the tactics to keep her attention and to keep it fun, enjoyable and most of all productive. To Ashley it was playtime. She was too young to under-stand the real reason for Lindsey coming to our house and playing with her—that of early intervention.

After what seemed like hundreds of tries and many weeks of visits, and games and doll houses later, I got yet another surprise from Ashley.

"Ashley, eyes!" Lindsey would say, trying to get Ashley to look at her. "What do you want, Ashley? Use your words. Do you need help? Say, 'help me'."

Trying with all her might to push down on the button of the doorbell on the doll house, Ashley's little fingers and weak forearms just couldn't make it ring. Lindsey placed her hand over Ashley's to assist her.

"What do you want, Ashley? Tell me. Say 'help me Lindsey!'"

"Heh meh," Ashley said, looking straight into Lindsey's eyes.

It didn't faze Ashley what she had just said. All she knew was that she needed help with a toy. But a very purposeful command, full of intent, had just crossed

Ashley's beautiful pink lips. The words glided through the air and resonated off the wall of the den and took up residence right there in my ear.

"Did I hear what I think I heard?" I asked myself.

I did a double take, because I wasn't quite sure. But I looked at Lindsey in total shock as I threw my hands up and leaped off of the couch.

"Oh, my gosh! She said it! She said it!" I yelled.

Lindsey and I smiled back at each other. Lindsey repeated the words many times after that to keep Ashley focused—Lindsey was a goddess to me. The image of Ashley looking up at Lindsey remains glued in my mind—a moment that may have been one of the turning points for Ashley early on—more hope on my part that things were going to turn out right for Ashley.

Lindsey was *my* educator too. I studied her methods, like I did with our occupational therapist, and watched her carefully during each visit. I purchased toys, dolls, and games to replicate what she was doing with Ashley to mock her visits when she wasn't there. I wanted to keep Ashley as comfortable as possible with the same material she was used to—change was extremely difficult for Ashley.

Lindsey often gave me reading material and great ideas to increase my knowledge of educating a child with special needs. After every visit, she left me with home activity suggestions. Some of the activities were to structure Ashley's environment so that there were out-of-the ordinary experiences that could evoke a reaction from her and subsequent interaction with me. For example, I was to add some pieces of a different puzzle into the puzzle Ashley was currently working on and act surprised when we came upon them and they wouldn't fit.

"Look Ashley, this piece won't fit! What should we do?"

I was expecting from Ashley a look that something wasn't right, a tug on my arm to throw the piece aside to show me that it didn't belong there—just some kind of interaction with me was enough of a response.

Putting two socks on one foot or putting the wrong shoe on her foot and having her figure out that it didn't belong there would also be creating moments of shared enjoyment and interaction.

I was to build as many interactive scenarios with Ashley as I possibly could throughout the day. Something I always had a hard time doing. I was always instructed by Lindsey to wait Ashley out—to give her time to respond to me and not try to predict her needs. I was incredibly astute at doing that—*to a fault*!

Ashley was meeting her goals, and all of her specialists were thrilled. Learning from Lindsey was really paying off. The school year was coming to an end. Dave and I were informed by the director of the P.I.E. program that we had some choices to make with respect to Ashley's therapy for the coming school year in the fall. I could leave her in the P.I.E. program with Lindsey until she turned three, the age at which every child (in my county) is then transferred into the public school system's early intervention program called Child Find. The other option I had was to transfer her to the Child Find program while she was still two, as long as she would be turning three in that school year which she would. Transferring Ashley to the Child Find program meant the county would pick up the tab for the early intervention program, since it was through the public school system, whereas I was paying for P.I.E. out-of-pocket—and P.I.E. did not come cheap. The county had to provide services for my child under the law. But under the age of three (in my county), they didn't have to pay for it—somewhat paradoxical to me!

So I was faced with the decision of leaving P.I.E. and Lindsey behind—someone who I had come to adore and found to be top-notch in her way of educating a child with special needs—or transferring Ashley into Child Find to reduce the financial burden of this journey. The latter meant subjecting Ashley to "square one" by meeting a new educator and starting to feel comfortable around that person so she can continue on the path laid out by Lindsey. It was not Ashley's strength by any means to be adaptive when the pot was stirred. I didn't want to cause Ashley any regression or aggression with respect to bringing in a new educator. We had just taken a monumental step with her and Lindsey, and I believed we were starting to break through with Ashley.

I agonized for weeks about which way to go with my decision. I needed to do the best thing for Ashley, but I also needed to work within our budget. It hurt a lot, but I chose the route of transferring Ashley to Child Find opting not to pay for services at the expense of leaving the greatest person yet, to date, who seemed to be able to reach Ashley. It was a gamble, but financially I felt I must.

But Lindsey and I didn't part without me first begging her to get a job with Child Find so that I could keep her and Ashley together. However, Lindsey preferred working with the younger children in the P.I.E. program, and that was most respectable to me—she was awesome at it. So it made our departure less heart wrenching, and we both respected what each of us needed and wanted to do.

I thought Lindsey's shoes would be hard to fill, but then we found Diana. Diana came highly recommended by the program's coordinator, and I immediately sensed she was a great match for Ashley. She too, had wonderful ideas. At every visit, Diana brought a small television tray and had Ashley sit on the floor "at her desk." She commanded Ashley's attention beautifully with her activities, all the while, Ashley staying seated (for the most part) behind her desk.

Diana was great with reinforcing Ashley with compliments.

"Good talking, Ashley. I liked how you said that!" Diana praised.

Just when I thought I had learned it all from these specialists, I hadn't. I kept learning.

Diana made a "choice board" for Ashley. A choice board was a notebook full of small, laminated pictures of games or toys with Velcro strips on the back of each picture. Diana would remove three pictures from the notebook and stick them on the Velcro pad in front of the book.

There was a picture of a girl pointing to herself that represented Ashley ("I want") and three other pictures of various activities.

"Ashley, I want music? I want feely box? I want bubbles?" Diana would ask Ashley, as she pointed to the picture of the person ("I want") each time before combining it with the other picture choices.

"Bubbo!" Ashley would say, delighting herself and jumping up from behind her desk to pop the bubbles Diana blew at her. Diana always gave Ashley a turn at blowing the bubbles, but Ashley's muscles in her mouth were just too weak, and she didn't understand the puckering that it took to push out a bubble. But she tried and tried.

When the bubble activity was done, Diana pulled off the bubble picture and replaced it with another picture choice.

"Ashley, I want music? I want feely box? I want lotion? After Ashley made her choice of the lotion, Diana took the lotion out of her bag and dabbed a drop into Ashley's hand, prompting her to rub her hands together. Ashley still had some tactile sensitivities, so sometimes the lotion activity brought out a few whines. But with persistence and keeping her engaged, Diana tried to move past those sensitivities and got Ashley to respond to the texture and become aware of the smell of the lotion.

Diana had so many wonderful activities that helped Ashley to work on her social skills, her communication, and her sensory integration issues. Similar to Lindsey, Diana was teaching me as well. I put in as many hours a day on Ashley's home program as our family schedule and demands would allow. As Kacey got older, I recruited her efforts. Kacey would watch and even participate in the session when Diana came to the house, so she became my assistant. It was like school to Kacey, she loved being the teacher. Kacey was a natural, a born teacher, and she helped her little sister become more verbal and interactive.

The choice board was a terrific way of getting Ashley to communicate her wants and needs. Making it mandatory for her to look at Diana prior to getting what she wanted was the underlying message, and a way to sustain the eye contact. So I replicated the choice board as I did with so many of our therapists' activities to use with our in-home therapy program. I must have been doing a great job with it. I was in the den working with Ashley and the choice board one evening. I always followed Diana's directions of praising Ashley for a job well done.

"Nice tawking, Ashley!" I said, recognizing the great job she did.

Dave, who was in the kitchen cleaning up at the time, looked over at me.

"I thought Diana was here for a second," he said, confused by the voice.

I guess Diana's knowledge wasn't the only thing that rubbed off on me. Now, I was starting to talk in her northern accent too!

CHAPTER 8

▼

GUT FEELINGS

As my pregnancy progressed into the later months, Ashley progressed as well. She was almost two-and-a-half-years-old and was meeting her speech and OT goals consistently. Her words were beginning to emerge. Her special education goals were being revised as well.

Her interactions with all of us were beginning to surface, and we understood her wants and needs better through the choice board. I made a similar board on the side of our kitchen counter island and put pictures of food items there so she could pull off a picture to tell us what she wanted to eat. My kitchen soon became plastered with pictures and teaching tools to get her to communicate with us.

We finally got Ashley's lab results and were relieved her Fragile X test came back negative. I closed the book I had checked out of the library on Fragile X and put it in the return slot. Her chromosome results came back normal as well—46 beautiful chromosomes. There was nothing to suggest a metabolic condition, and her EEG had since been read as normal. Finally, some good news was starting to come our way!

I felt like the past ten months had finally brought me to a place where I was comfortable talking about Ashley's disorder. At the suggestion of my sister when she first heard about Ashley's diagnosis, I called my brother-in-law's cousin, Kathy, who had a son on the autistic spectrum. I was ready to hear another Mom's perspective on all of this as well as any insight she could offer.

The first thing Kathy mentioned was her son's diet. She had put him on a gluten-free/casein-free (GFCF) diet. Gluten is a protein broken down from wheat, barley, oats, and rye, and casein is a protein broken down from dairy products. By removing these from the diet, many children on the spectrum have had success in alleviating, and at times eliminating, the symptoms of autism.

I didn't know anything about the diet until Kathy introduced it to me. But she explained how sometimes children on the spectrum have allergies to foods and they reveal themselves not in a rash form, but rather in the form of behavior. The antibiotics that children are exposed to for ear infections or other ailments can destroy the good bacteria in the gut and cause yeast to overgrow, leaving an imbalance in the intestinal flora. The membrane of the stomach is then compromised and is more permeable to nutrients or toxins that leak out of it. This is considered a "leaky gut." The result of proteins leaking out of the gastrointestinal wall can result in developmental, behavioral, and learning problems.

When gluten and casein are not able to be fully broken down by normal means, their structures are very similar to that of opioids (such as morphine). These proteins seep out of the gut and enter the bloodstream and travel up through the blood/brain barrier and attach themselves to opioid receptors on the brain. This is what is called "the opioid effect" and puts the child in a drug-induced state, dulling the mental processes.

I didn't realize at that time that foods could do all that. My biggest problem was just trying to get Ashley to eat *anything*! I couldn't imagine that the little bit she was consuming could be harming her. But I was game to try the diet and thought it seemed safe. I did further research, and found that there were just scores of children out there on this elimination diet. For some it seemed to be working. For others, it seemed to be a slow ride.

The literature indicated that to be successful, both gluten and casein had to be eliminated from the diet and done so gradually to avoid a withdrawal effect. I learned that gluten was everywhere! It encompassed pretty much everything considered a "baked good." And casein comes from everything considered a dairy product (cheese, yogurt, milk, etc). That really left only rice, corn, and water, I felt. I knew the rice and corn part were going to be difficult to get in her. Ashley didn't eat them. I thought I might be able to get water in her.

"Wow, okay, where do I begin?" feeling clueless as to what to feed her.

I started to glance at food labels thinking "gluten" would just jump out at me as an ingredient. It didn't. It is a protein that is broken down from grains. I really had to immerse myself in the labels, not just skim the ingredients.

I served Ashley kosher hot dogs, cooked chicken, rice crackers, and rice milk. She touched very little of it. But this was a start, as I was still learning about the diet. Some things unintentionally slipped through the cracks. The rice milk contained a speck of barley, maybe to maintain its consistency, but a speck nonetheless. So, I was really serving her gluten when I thought it was gluten-free. There was a learning curve here.

"I've contaminated her! All along I thought I was doing the right thing, and come to find out, I've been feeding her poison," I exclaimed to Dave.

"Sharon, I think it's okay, she's fine. Don't be so hard on yourself!" Dave said, thinking I was over-dramatizing the rice milk issue.

But only two days into stopping the milk, we immediately noticed Ashley's speech had doubled.

"This was a very good session," Shelly remarked on her progress note at Ashley's following speech therapy session.

The week before, Ashley was having pretty good sessions and saying about ten words. I thought ten words were wonderful after ten months of trying. A week after stopping the milk and gluten, Ashley had about tripled the word count in her session. They weren't totally clear words, they were more like approximations, but they were definite attempts at language, more so than we were seeing before we had implemented the diet.

"This was an outstanding session," Shelly remarked a few sessions later.

Ashley's great remarks kept coming in speech therapy. I was completely stunned by it all. Shelly and now Tina, the new occupational therapist, were stunned as well. I had completely blinded them to the diet. I decided not to tell them about it, I just wanted to see its magic at work. And I did.

"What have you been doing to Ashley? This was a great session with lots of eye contact and good attention span. She's trying to repeat more words," Shelly beamed with excitement.

"I know! We're seeing really good stuff at home too!" I said, still blinding her to Ashley's diet.

I eventually had to tell them both about the diet after I found Tina had given Ashley some non-allowed food items in the OT sessions to work on her oral sensitivities to textures. Shelly and Tina had not heard of the GFCF diet before, so Ashley was their guinea pig. And, I was their educator. As much as I had learned speech and OT techniques from them, I now found myself in the role of teacher, enlightening them about this powerful diet. We thought Ashley was responding beautifully to it. They too, agreed the diet was playing a positive role in her rehabilitation.

Needing some advice where Ashley's diet and nutrition were concerned, Dave and I met with Kelly Dorfman, a nutritional consultant and health program planner who Kathy had recommended to us. We discussed with Kelly, Ashley's limitation with many textures and her runny, odorous stools. Having stopped all dairy products, we were concerned about Ashley not getting the daily allowance of calcium she needed. She also had constant diarrhea, and we couldn't figure out why.

I mentioned to Kelly that ever since starting Ashley on the GFCF diet about a month earlier, I had seen immediate effects with her language and was I just imagining it, or was it true that the diet really works? She agreed that the diet does help children on the spectrum. In particular, those who are so very intolerant to gluten and dairy respond to it the most. We were definitely seeing this great change in Ashley.

Kelly thought we were on the right track with all of Ashley's therapies, but acknowledged we needed to get a handle on her stool problem. Kelly recommended a comprehensive stool analysis with a parasitology report to analyze the flora in the intestinal tract and assess how it was functioning. We sent a stool sample to a lab suggested by Kelly, and the results came back and showed Ashley had no "good bacteria" in her system. She also had a slight overgrowth of yeast. Beneficial bacteria normally live in the intestinal tract and are needed for proper metabolism. They aid in digestion, break down vitamins, eliminate toxins and prevent the formations of carcinogens (cancer causing agents). The fact that Ashley's system contained none of the beneficial flora meant her gut was not functioning optimally and wasn't combating the overgrowth of yeast.

"It's a barren garden with poor soil—not even weeds can grow," Kelly remarked.

Ashley's gut was in such horrible condition, that not only couldn't the beneficial bacteria grow, but even the bad bacteria had backed off! She also had a very high level of fecal secretory IgA (sIgA). Immunological activity in the gastrointestinal tract can be assessed using this marker. sIgA plays an important role in controlling the intestinal environment that is constantly presented with potentially harmful antigens such as pathogenic micro-organisms. Some type of allergenic protein was causing this abnormal value. It was seven times the upper limit of normal.

Kelly talked to us about the need to restore Ashley's good bacteria with probiotics, to get her digestive tract back on track. It became a daily regimen, adding back the beneficial flora that a history of antibiotics had destroyed.

Dave and I took away many recommendations from our consult with Kelly. We cut Ashley's juice amounts down to one cup a day, splitting it with water at each offering. The sugars could've been the culprit for her bowel problems, so we started there. Every morning and evening, we hid the good bacteria—a white powder from a capsule—in her sippy cup along with a calcium supplement and fish oils for brain development. It was our version of a "cocktail" for Ashley. She didn't mind a bit. She drank it down just fine.

We worked even harder on her oral program to get her to be less defensive to textures. We gave her nitrate-free foods, since nitrates can play a role in stomach cancer according to Kelly Dorfman. We inspected every diaper for firmer, less odorous stools. We waited and waited, and gagged and gagged at the odor. We played around with the dosage, but the noxious odor of her stools was still there. The beneficial bacteria were not growing as we had hoped. Something was irritating Ashley's system.

At our next consult with Kelly, she recommended that we test Ashley for food allergies. We knew she was most likely sensitive to gluten and dairy products, but we wondered if there was anything else that may have caused such a high level of immune response as the results of her sIgA showed.

I received a kit from a laboratory specializing in food testing. The test required only a finger prick and a few drops of blood. This seemed much easier than trying to get it from her vein that previously had proven to be sheer torture on Ashley. With all she had gone through trying to squeeze blood out of her for various laboratory tests, I still was uneasy about subjecting her to yet another test. But I thought a finger prick would minimize a lot of the guilt on my part and intolerance on hers.

Set up at the kitchen counter, I read and re-read the instructions to draw the blood. I made sure I knew just what I was supposed to do. I had all of the material spread out and tubes at my fingertips to collect, package and ship the blood sample so that there would be no errors. This time any errors would be my fault!

As Dave held Ashley as tightly as he could, and with a scream from her that did not help my frame of mind, I gave it my best shot. I put the lance to her tiny finger and pressed. Wanting to spare her the pain, I barely nicked her. This was probably worse than if I had been more accurate and caused her pain, because I had to milk her finger pretty long to get enough blood to fill only a thimble. I tried not to cause her pain, but I didn't do a very good job. The kicking and flailing really made me feel guilty.

I felt like I was back in the laboratory, where I had been nearly 15 years before doing research on rats. Back then, I used to put the rats in a guillotine, decapitate them, drain their blood and then take out their livers for further analysis. I didn't really feel badly for those rats—I was a scientist, it was all in the name of science—cholesterol research. Yet this time, it was my own flesh and blood I had to inflict pain upon. I just felt slightly haunted by every rat whose life I had taken back then. They were somehow getting their revenge against me from wherever it was they had gone.

But I managed to fill the vial to the line and come away feeling, although like I was torturing her, that I had done it for the sake of finding out what was going on in her gut. I sent the blood sample off through the mail.

A rather thick packet arrived from the lab a few weeks later. I was surprised at what the results revealed. Ashley was intolerant to more than just gluten and dairy. The results were broken up into "foods to avoid," "foods to rotate," and "foods with no reaction." Ashley reacted positive (foods to "avoid") to soybean, garlic, coconut, and egg whites—especially egg whites. Soybean surprised me. Well, they all surprised me, but one of the substitutes on a GFCF diet was soy. Now that was out. The garlic threw us for a loop, but then again, when she had started to eat hot dogs she really seemed to like them, almost crave them. But I never realized that garlic was an ingredient until I went back and checked the label. It made sense though. Her body craved what it shouldn't have. So the hot dogs and garlic rice crackers, which she had come to enjoy, where thrown out without haste. No wonder she had runny stools! I suspect the whole stick of pepperoni she ate for dinner one night wasn't helping matters, either. She wouldn't eat much, but she loved the nitrate-free pepperoni. After we gave it to her, she gave it back to us! Her stomach nearly imploded. Not only did she have runny stools, they ran everywhere—down her leg, to her shoes, onto my white carpet. The trail of those events stayed with us for a few days after.

Ashley had recently begun to eat eggs. I was thrilled with this. Great, I thought, a source of protein! I even bought a very expensive jar of egg whites at a specialty store and made her egg white omelets. She ate them! So I gave her more. But the test revealed that egg whites were very unfriendly to her system, even more so than soy or garlic!

I just held my head in disbelief! I was the one putting toxins in her body just when she was coming around and trying new foods. I really felt miserable—but I didn't know!

The foods to "rotate" were oranges, corn, wheat, buckwheat, gluten, and cow's milk. It was my hunch that the gluten and casein had shown up as "to be rotated" and not "to be avoided," because we had taken her off of these months earlier, but there still seemed to be traces of these in her system—at least enough to show up on the test. Had we tested her prior to the start of her GFCF diet, I'm most certain these would be in the "to be avoided" column. We had been giving her GFCF waffles, yet had recently tried some made of buckwheat. Now all of a sudden her test revealed this was an irritant to her as well. We were just batting a thousand! She had just been introduced to oranges and took a few bites one day. Finally a fruit I could get in her! Now it was to be avoided!

So now there was a very long list of foods we couldn't give her. There seemed little left that she could eat—or so it seemed. I had mentioned to our friends that Ashley was on a restricted diet that helped her speech difficulties, but I still hadn't mentioned autism to them. I tried to teach our friends and families about the diet and why it was necessary. I know I made their heads swirl. As hard as it was for me, Mrs. Biology, to understand it, it was completely out in left field to them.

"What is there left to eat?" they'd ask me.

Early on it seemed that way to me as well.

"What *do* I feed my child?" I wondered.

I was so new at this. I knew it served Ashley well to be on the diet, but I just needed to dig my heels in deeper. There was so much information on the diet out there. It was just a matter of me needing to become more familiar with its implementation and getting better at cooking with the foods she could have. I didn't want to feel as though her dietary requirements were a hindrance to our daily life. I had to adjust things for Ashley and do it as if it were like any other part of our life, which it had now become.

I became fastidious in reading labels. To be honest, I never read one prior to this diet. Did I need to? Ashley's diet tuned me into a whole new aspect of life—food processing. And frankly, it woke me up! I was taken aback by some of the ingredients in our food. To my surprise, some canned tunas have casein in them. Thinking I could give Ashley tuna, a nutritious fish, I found out the brand I bought was off limits. My father-in-law didn't believe it until I put him to the test and made him get a can of tuna from his pantry. There it was, right on the label—casein! Why would casein, a milk protein, end up in tuna? Some plain spaghetti sauces (without cheese and garlic listed on the front label) may actually have them listed as ingredients on the back label. Clearly, I had to be a more conscientious consumer.

I made many mistakes early on by not taking the time to thoroughly educate myself in all aspects of the diet. But I learned from them fast. I kicked myself every time I thought I was doing the right thing for Ashley, when really I was contaminating her.

I was pretty much alone in figuring out what foods to feed Ashley on this diet. Food shopping was taken to a whole new level. There was very little I could buy at the grocery stores where I regularly shopped. There were few gluten-free or casein-free foods she could eat, except for fruits and vegetables, which she didn't like. I even spoke with the manager of the store and told him about my daughter's special food needs. I educated him about all of this. He must have thought I was Einstein, because I wowed him with all my knowledge. He was not familiar with any of it. In the end, there was nothing he could do for me. I had to travel 20 miles to a specialty store to find some of the things Ashley could have such as pastas made from brown rice, sodium nitrate-free deli meats, tomato sauces made only from tomatoes (without the added surprises), rice cereals and other assorted products.

But as time went on, I found solace again on the Internet. I visited online stores that catered to people on the GFCF diet and made purchases from them. I found cookbooks that were written especially for children with special diet needs. I felt somewhat more at ease knowing there were just bunches of us parents out there who were in the same situation, and who needed guidance to give our children something to eat. It still left Ashley with a plausible diet. She just seemed so limited due to her pickiness and her oral sensitivities.

It was really amazing how much there really was out there for those on the GFCF diet and how someone had figured all of this out—how to cook no longer using the usual ingredients. It was now a game of substitution. It didn't seem like such a jail sentence any longer when I really started to educate myself about how to cook foods required on this diet.

After purchasing what seemed like a pantry full of GFCF ingredients and foods, my early attempts at cooking with these products were just comical. Forget about all the years I spent watching my mother make all the family traditions and learning from her—as proud as she is of me today. This was so different! This was hard, almost impossible at first. If reading labels and shopping for food was now being taken to a whole new level, cooking was right up there with them. I was somewhat more at a disadvantage than the average person cooking gluten/casein-free. Now I was cooking gluten/casein/egg/corn/garlic/soy-free.

"Is there anything left to mix in the bowl?" I asked myself. A lot of recipes just don't work well without real eggs and milk. For real egg, I substituted a powdered egg replacer that is mixed with water. I had no milk to cook with, since I had taken her off of the rice milk. I found the recipes I baked crumbled more. Or maybe I was just doing something wrong. I was not good at this *at all!* I just had to be witty enough to put my crumbled baked goods back into a shape that looked somewhat pleasing to Ashley so that she'd ask for it—or better yet, eat it!

But with practice and learning about prepared foods or milk substitutes offered by online stores, I was becoming more knowledgeable and could prepare Ashley's meals similar to those that we all ate. I was now able to make her a ham sandwich with GFCF bread and nitrate-free meat. I made her pancakes, waffles, empanadas (meat filled dough turnovers), muffins, cakes, and cookies. I made tomato sauce and hid vegetables in it and served it over rice pasta. It went over great with Ashley.

All of her meals were gluten-free, casein-free, soy-free, corn-free and egg-free. I hoped it wasn't taste-free—I was trying really hard to learn this stuff. Ashley was still limited in her likes and dislikes, though. At least I was now armed with foods she was *allowed* to eat. It took some time to get her used to the diet, but she was making progress. She was eating and subsequently gaining weight—and making gains in her behavior, eye contact and verbalization, as well.

CHAPTER 9

▼

PLAYFULLY OBSTRUCTIVE

The beneficial bacteria in Ashley's gut may not have been growing, but our therapy team, however, was. Dave and I had now brought on board a speech therapist, an occupational therapist, a neurodevelopmental pediatrician, a psychologist, a special educator from the county and a nutritionist—and I was becoming educated in my own right, as I caught on fast to the world of autism through research and therapy.

Ashley's schedule was overflowing with seeing specialists and participating in therapy sessions. We were seeing some progress, albeit, slow. But I felt Ashley was getting somewhere—that we were on our way down the right path with the right people. We marveled at each new word she attempted to say and each new nibble she took, much the same way a new parent glows with excitement over their child's first smile or first gurgle.

To an outsider, Ashley's strides probably weren't much to shout about. Any other neighbor's child would have already mastered two-word phrases, jumping down from the bottom step of the stairs, eating with a spoon or setting out playtime teacups for a teddy bear. But to us, Ashley's achievements were worth ten of another child's. She had obstacles in her way that other children would never know in their lifetime. And Ashley's achievements on a given day gave us hope for more tomorrow. But no one was prepared for what tomorrow was about to bring.

Dave had dropped Kacey off at school and was making his way up to speech and occupational therapy with Ashley. I packed for the hospital. My delivery date was the following day. I had made the decision a few months earlier to deliver the baby by C-section.

I turned on the television to watch a morning talk show. What I found on in its place was a breaking news story of a horrifying disaster. I stood in disbelief at what I saw. I watched as the World Trade Center billowed with smoke. I heard reports that a plane had flown into one of the Twin Towers. Some reports speculated it was an "accident." But as another plane headed straight for the second tower, reports hinted at "terrorism."

"Oh, my God!" I screamed at the television, watching with a frozen look on my face. I ran to the phone. I picked up the receiver and could barely hit the numbers on the phone—my hands were shaking terribly. My mind all of a sudden went blank.

"What's his number? What's his number?" I begged my brain to retrieve it.

But it seemed to be in tangles. I couldn't recall my brother's number like I could do at any other time in my life. His office was not too far from the burning devastation. I felt the baby jolt my ribs as if to say, "Hey what's going on out there? Keep it down!" I had awakened the baby from a deep slumber with my sudden outburst. Or maybe it was my racing heartbeat, which probably sounded like a heavy metal rock band on its opening song.

I kept dialing the number I thought certain to be my brother's. All I heard was an "all circuits are busy now," message. I tried repeatedly. I managed to get through to him after several minutes of trying.

"Hi. I'm watching the World Trade Center. It's on fire! What's going on there? Are you okay?"

"Yes, I'm okay, Sharon. We may get disconnected, though. The communication towers are on the World Trade Center. Call Mom and Dad and tell them I'm fine."

"Okay, I will."

"Sharon, did something happen at the Pentagon?"

"The Pentagon? I don't know. Let me listen."

I looked up at the television. I thought I had heard the Pentagon being talked about, but pictures of the World Trade Center shooting flames toward the sky were all that filled the screen.

"Where are the girls? Where's Dave?" he asked.

"Dave took Kacey to school and Ashley to speech and OT. Wait, let me hear this," I turned to listen to the report.

"A plane did crash…into the Pentagon! Dave's driving straight in that direction!"

The rehabilitative center was only a few exits from the Pentagon. I was getting lightheaded and panicky. I kept my brother on the line, while I tried to reach Dave on the cell phone.

"Hi, Hun. What's up? Are you feeling okay?" he asked me.

"Dave, a plane just hit the Pentagon! It's on fire! The Twin Towers in New York are on fire too!" I said with panic in my voice.

I held a phone up to each ear, still watching the television.

"I just saw a plane fly in that direction," he said.

"Maybe that was the one that just crashed! Dave, come home, NOW! Go pick up Kacey and come home! I'm hearing things on the news about terrorism. They don't think these were accidents! Come home, please! I'll call the therapists and let them know you're not coming. My brother's on the other phone. Let me finish talking to him. I'll call you back. He's okay."

"I'll turn around. Traffic's getting really bad now. I'll do my best to get there soon. Bye, hun—love you."

No sooner did I hang up with both of them, an operating room nurse called to inform me that I was on standby for my C-section the next morning—that they were going to need all of their operating rooms for casualties from the Pentagon. She said she would keep me posted throughout the day.

The delivery of my baby was hanging with uncertainty. I was bursting at the seams. I was aching for my baby to be born and hold it close—more so now than ever. But I didn't know if I'd get the chance to meet my baby tomorrow, or even the day after that. My impending delivery was now on hold.

Dave arrived home safely with both girls. The traffic had stalled him for quite a while. I felt much better knowing my family was at home. At Kacey's school, the halls were filled with crying parents and unsuspecting children. Many of her schoolmates had parents who worked at the Pentagon. It was hitting too close to home.

I couldn't believe this was happening. And now, I was about to bring a new baby into the world while the aftermath of one of the attacks burned a few miles up the road. As I watched the television, I couldn't get the pictures out of my mind of the times I rode the elevator to the observation deck of the South Tower of World Trade Center—an ascent 107 stories into the sky making me queasy as we passed every floor. But the ride was worth the view. I just couldn't fathom now that these gigantic buildings had plummeted to the ground—taking with them a nation in tears.

But in the wake of September 11th, there was a bright light. We named her Sydney, and she arrived early the next morning—her delivery having been put back on the schedule in the operating room. I was overjoyed and finally able to hold her close to forget about the tragedy that had just befallen on our area.

Nearly every half hour that day I could hear helicopters land on the hospital's helipad. Along with the emergency codes that echoed the halls continuously, both were reminders that outside my window of the maternity ward, the world had changed forever—without forewarning any of us.

But my part as educator and advocator for Ashley was still a role that didn't change in the days following the country's horrific events. Even with the added responsibilities I now shouldered having had another child, peppered with the new-found fear and concerns for our safety hovering over the nation, it was still my mission to bring the best therapeutic interventions I could bear to Ashley's recovery process. And all of those events slowed me down little toward that end. I remained committed to fighting Ashley's battle in her ongoing struggle to master motor coordination and social communication.

Two weeks after baby Sydney arrived, I decided to look into another child psychologist recommended to me by my brother-in-law's cousin, Kathy, who has a son on the autistic spectrum. I was looking for a third opinion regarding the diagnosis of PDD-NOS that we had received nine months earlier.

Dr. Wieder is a clinical psychologist who specializes in diagnosing and treating infants and young children with developmental problems. We drove to Dr. Wieder's in-home practice a state away. She greeted us, and Dave and I played with Ashley for a few minutes. Dr. Wieder observed our interactions with Ashley. She watched to see how we captured and sustained Ashley's attention. She watched to see how Ashley used her emotions, her wants and desires to guide her behavior and thoughts. When Ashley wanted something, how was she going about letting us know that? More importantly, how did we respond to her wishes?

Ashley found a toy piano among the elaborate collection of playthings on the shelves. She got into her "W" sitting position on the floor and played with the piano.

Each time she hit a colored piano key, a picture of an animal popped up from the piano top.

"Bunny!" I said to her.

She hit another button.

"Is that a bear?" I asked.

"Ashley, where's yellow?"

She hit the yellow key. A cat popped up.

"Where's purple?"

She found it. A lion surprised her.

"Where's red?"

She knew that one, too.

"Is that a dog?" I said, as the dog popped up after she hit the key.

"What's a dog say, Ashley?"

"Woof, woof" she replied.

"Good talking, Ashley. What's a pig say. Oink, oink?" I answered for her when the pig appeared.

I migrated to the toys that had colors or numbers I felt Ashley could respond to—all the visuals. I wanted Dr. Wieder to see that Ashley came to her with some expressive and receptive language that had emerged from a year of speech and occupational therapy.

Ashley placed both hands across the key board so each finger found a key, as if she were a classical pianist. She tried to open all of the keys at once to pop up all the animals.

"She's very good with her hands; more so than on her feet. She's very wobbly," Dr. Wieder remarked, noting her reduced muscle tone.

"She can actually hold up the correct number of fingers if you ask her," Dave told Dr. Wieder still amazed Ashley could do this.

"Ashley, how old are you? Are you two?" Dave asked.

Ashley put up two fingers, while she hunted for another toy.

"Where's three?" he quizzed her again.

She held up three fingers, still without looking at him.

Ashley eyed a toy and reached for it. She grunted to cue me to get it down.

"What do you want? Do you want the house?" I asked her.

"I…want…" I started the sentence for her.

"Howt!" she said, helping me carry the doll house to the floor.

"Good talking, Ashley," Dave and I praised her.

It was the same doll house Lindsey brought on her visits; the one Ashley played with when she approximated the words, "Help me."

It was as if Ashley had picked up where she left off from Lindsey's visit. She pulled on Dave's hand and placed it over the doorbell.

"Do you need help?" Dave asked.

He helped her push the button.

"Ding dong!" I provided the sound effects.

"More?" he asked, as they pushed it again.

She placed a small doll in the chimney of the house, and it fell down.

"Bye, bye doll," I said, watching it fall.

"Open door," I said, as Ashley pulled on the door to retrieve the doll inside.

"Close door," I prompted her.

"Is this pretty typical of her play?" Dr. Wieder asked, beginning her critique.

"Yes," we both answered and looked up at her.

"So, what do you think is the missing piece?" Dr. Wieder asked.

"She's just not connecting," I answered.

"Right. She is not engaged. She doesn't look up or attend to you. She doesn't really take pleasure in it with you. She has a plan. She's very purposeful. She wants to put the doll in; she wants to take it out. Even when you prompt her with the language, she answers maybe only a quarter of the time," Dr. Wieder explained.

"Our goal is to make you become much more compelling with her. Her challenge is not playing with the toys; she can do that very well. But she does it in a very self-absorbed way. All we want her to do is relate to you. Maybe it's with a look of 'that's mine,' or 'give it back,' but we need to have her make that connection with you."

"For the most part, children with auditory processing problems are self-absorbed—they turn in. Their connectedness is very in and out. In this brief play session, she has never looked up. She's more engaged with the toy than with you. We have to make you more compelling than the toy. You have to start getting more playful with her. Your goal is not to just prompt her like a speech therapist, 'What's this?' or 'What's that?' You can do some of that, because obviously, we want to encourage her to talk. She's a very good problem solver, and you're going to be her problem—but in a positive, playful kind of way.

"You have to get her to deal with you, to relate to you. You need to entice her and say, 'I want that one!' and reach out, and see how she responds. You can also do something that makes her solve a problem, because we know she can. If she's going to the chimney to put the doll down, put your hand over the chimney playfully so that she has to interact with you—just little things to make it necessary to look up and notice you or reciprocate with you. Get her interacting with you on that level of shared problem solving. She does look up, but only when you break into her self-absorbed world, or if you have something she wants. So we need to entice and get the eye contact going as you woo her with the object she wants; but she must first acknowledge you. Try it with her," she said to us.

"Do you want the boy?" Dave asked, holding up a boy doll for her to reach.

Ashley tried to pry it out of his hands without responding to him. Dave didn't give the doll to her.

"I want boy," Dave prompted her to say.

"Boooy," Ashley replied, in a slow, drawn out voice.

"There you go. She gave you half a look. And she used her natural language. Now give the doll to her. You want to be playfully obstructive and enticing using your warmth, your voice, as well as what she desires, but she's to "win" in the end. Because, if she doesn't get what she wants, she'll go on to something else, and you'll lose the connection with her—remember, she has her own resources and solutions," Dr. Wieder suggested.

"But don't use direct prompts with her, like 'say this', or 'say that.' Let it come from her intent, her desire. She has to connect her words with her wish to communicate. If we prompt her, all we end up doing is teaching her to talk or use words when you tell her to."

This was such a new way of playing with our child. I found out I wasn't very good at it. Ashley needed much more interaction and assistance with language than Kacey ever did. Dr. Wieder remarked that Ashley was very bright and had some great skills, but we were working way below Ashley's level—we asked her things she already knew. She wasn't challenged from our interactions with her.

"What do you want, Ashley? You want the dolly?"

I found out that I didn't always give her time to answer me, and I tended to comment on the appearance of the toys.

"Oh, Ashley, look at the dolly's pretty dress," I said, trying to engage her and increase my emotion.

There was nothing in that sentence Ashley could reply to. I was doing it all wrong.

"Where is the dolly going?" Dr. Wieder interjected.

"Ask a question she can answer," she reminded me.

"Ashley, where is the dolly going?" I asked, putting the doll in the toy car.

"If she doesn't answer you, give her a choice," Dr. Wieder suggested.

"Ashley, is the dolly going to the park, or to the store?"

But, Ashley still didn't answer. I couldn't engage her.

She wandered over to a toy pirate ship.

"Go, follow her, Mom," Dr. Wieder advised.

I scooted to the ship. It seemed more like a toy for little boys. I couldn't imagine she was interested in it. But something about the ship appealed to her.

"That's a pirate," I told her, as she picked up the pirate doll.

"Pie," she said back.

Dr. Wieder was amused that Ashley took to such an advanced toy.

"Hey, what's this?" Dave asked, finding the pirate's hat.

"Create a problem for her, Dad," Dr. Wieder instructed Dave, now having captured Ashley's attention.

"I can't get it on his head. Can you help me? It's stuck," Dave said, pretending he needed help.

"Haaat," Ashley said with her soft voice.

She fit the hat on the pirate's head.

Dave found a plastic cannon ball and put it in the cannon. He pressed the button.

Pop! Out it came and hit her in the tummy!

Ashley laughed. It was one of her first moments of enjoyment during this visit.

"Keep it going. You've got her," Dr. Wieder said.

"One, two, three!" Dave said, shooting the ball out of the cannon again.

Ashley was engaged. She wanted to try. She put the ball in the cannon.

"Ready, aim, fire!" Dr. Wieder said, having fun with us as well.

Ashley kept laughing and started to look at us.

Of all the toys in Dr. Wieder's office, I certainly didn't think a pirate ship would ignite Ashley. But it did. She loved it. Dave captured her attention and sustained it for several minutes.

"One…two…" Dave paused.

Ashley looked at him waiting for the next count.

"Three!" he said, and shot the ball out.

Ashley was left in giggles.

"Great! Now create a problem for her. Get the ball stuck," Dr. Wieder suggested.

"Oh, no it's stuck, Ashley. What should I do?" Dave asked her.

"One…" he waited to get her attention.

She looked at him.

"Two…" said Dr. Wieder, joining in.

Ashley looked at Dr. Wieder—the first time during this session.

"What should we do, Ashley?" I asked her.

Dave struggled with the button to show her the ball was stuck.

"Puh," Ashley said, and pushed the button making the ball pop out.

"Three!" we all said, and the ball shot out.

Ashley was delighted.

"That…right there…is what we want—the anticipation, the looking, the fun." Dr. Wieder congratulated us.

Ashley was certainly not ready for symbolic play with pirates, but she was overjoyed to play with us. The pleasure or "fun" created a continuous flow of interaction where we were all connected and engaged.

What Dr. Wieder taught us that day was the beginning of "Floor Time and the Developmental, Individual-Difference, Relationship-Based (DIR™) Model." Dr. Stanley Greenspan, a nationally recognized child psychologist and Dr. Wieder's colleague, had developed it. It is a one-on-one approach where the parent or therapist follows the child's lead and his or her interests with just good old-fashioned toys they love to play with down on the floor.

By following Ashley's lead during Floor Time sessions, and interactions during other parts of her life, we could help her develop the six functional, emotional capacities which would become the building blocks for her development. It was already clear we had to get shared attention and engagement with two-way communication. Then we could develop the next three capacities of social problem solving, creating symbolic ideas and logical abstract thinking. Ashley already loved toys which could become elaborate roles and fantasies if we just learned to really play together.

This teaching method taught us how to better relate to Ashley so she could make her wants and needs known by creating situations to have repeated interactions with her. These interactions were called "circles of communication." A circle of communication was opened by Ashley when she showed interest in someone or something, we responded with a gesture or a question to sustain her attention, and the circle was closed with Ashley's verbal or symbolical response. Once Ashley responded using gestures or words, she completed the circle of communication. I responded again to what she said with another question or action, and when she responded back, she closed the next circle. In this way, a continuous flow of interaction kept us connected, "on topic" and allowed us to elaborate on her initiated interests and purpose.

Our job was to keep following her lead. We were to play with her on her terms and then move the play along so we could get, if not words, then hopefully more eye contact or gestures—some sort of indication to let us know that she acknowledged us. We were to open and close as many circles of communication as possible in a play period.

Dr. Wieder commented that Ashley was perfectly capable of giving us an answer, when she wanted. We just had to captivate her a little more with our emotions—our "affect," using our voices and gestures to woo and engage her.

A few minutes later Ashley dropped a doll she was holding.

"Oh, no, the dolly fell down! What should we do? She has a boo boo," Dr. Wieder said, attracting and engaging Ashley with her tone of voice and sympathetic look.

"Can you kiss her boo boo?" I asked.

Ashley leaned over and gave the doll a kiss.

But the imaginary play, we learned, could be taken to greater levels than just a kiss on the boo boo ending the interaction. We had to help Ashley elaborate and here was the opportunity to work with her emotions.

"Dad, get the doctor's kit over there," Dr. Wieder cued, motioning to the shelf.

By incorporating a doctor's kit, we could sustain Ashley's interest by listening to the doll's heartbeat, bandaging the boo boo, and taking the doll's temperature. It was taking play to the next level and re-enacting a real life situation, which she had experienced many times. This expanded her attention and encouraged more symbolic elaboration by "deepening the plot" a bit more.

Dr. Wieder made it all look easy, especially by her being there to prompt us every step of the way. But it was really quite a difficult and different way of playing with a child. Dr. Wieder recommended, *The Child with Special Needs: Encouraging Intellectual and Emotional Growth,* the book Dr. Greenspan and she had written to explain Floor Time and the developmental growth of children with special needs.

Dr. Wieder concluded that Ashley seemed to have more of a regulatory disorder. It was clear to Dr. Wieder that Ashley had problems with auditory processing. This inhibited Ashley from communicating with people as effectively as a child without this deficit.

Ashley had come a long way since the day of her initial diagnosis. She played with toys without continuously mouthing them. She used a few words and answered simple questions about her numbers, letters, and colors. But she still lacked the imaginary play, the two-way communication, and most of all, the spontaneity. These were never there.

We felt Dr. Wielder was impressed with Ashley's potential and with consistent and continued work at the new Floor Time Model, Ashley would learn to become more focused, able to role play, and move up the ladder of emotional and social development and become more of an abstract thinker. Dr. Wieder recommended (if possible) eight 20-minute sessions of Floor Time each day. That was asking a big chunk from our day, which was already spilling over with other therapies. Dr. Wieder made it clear that Floor Time was the most important component of the overall DIR^{TM} Model, which is a comprehensive intervention approach and includes day to day social problem solving interactions, semi-structured learning, play dates and relevant therapies. We were doing some of these elements already, but we agreed to do as much as our schedules allowed. It was in Ashley's best interest to find the time.

At the conclusion of our session, Dr. Wieder talked to us more about Ashley's individual differences, particularly her auditory processing difficulties. She wrote down two websites and suggested that I visit them—that they could be very beneficial to Ashley.

CHAPTER 10

▼

AN EARFUL OF THERAPY

From the discussion with Dr. Wieder, Ashley's underlying issue was auditory processing—she was not able to understand, or process, what anyone said. Children who don't process sounds properly have difficulty learning language and, therefore, don't respond to verbal cues. This means they have trouble with opening and closing circles of communication and, subsequently, don't attempt to communicate. Now, I understood better why Ashley shut down and protected herself from, what she viewed, as being a most complicated act—interacting and making that social connection with others.

I read a book when Ashley was first diagnosed called, *The Sound of a Miracle: Triumph over Autism,* by Annabel Stehli. The title alone made me open the book. I liked the fact it expressed someone was victorious over this disorder.

Annabel's daughter, Georgie, was thought to be functionally retarded. She was diagnosed with autism and institutionalized. The doctors did not know what else to do for her. But a French doctor, Guy Berard, realized that her behavioral and communication problems stemmed from a hypersensitivity to sound. With his form of auditory training—now referred to as the Berard Method—he desensitized Georgie's ears to the frequencies that were particularly painful to her. After this treatment program, Georgie could process the sounds around her better and not feel so overwhelmed by them. She no longer retreated from everyone. She started to communicate and emerge from her diagnosis of autism. Georgie recovered! She not only learned to talk, both in English and in a foreign language, but she excelled academically and was very gifted.

This was one of many books I had read to learn more about Ashley's newly-diagnosed condition. But Georgie was treated in France.

"How would I ever have access to such an incredible therapy?" I wondered.

Though it was a non-fiction book (and a really good one), it seemed like a fantasy to me—a therapy too far out of my reach.

But now, Dr. Wieder informed us of an auditory training center in our area that she believed could benefit Ashley and her auditory processing difficulties. If there was a promising treatment, (such as the one touted in that book), and I didn't have to travel to France to get it, then I wanted in on it! I felt like I was pretty much at the end of my rope—this was my last resort.

Granted, I had only read about this treatment in a book, but the book moved me! I sobbed for pages. I identified with having a child who was out of touch. I would have no reservations in considering such therapy. The treatment didn't only sound like a miracle, but my hopes of having the same success shot up real high, real fast!

Upon our arrival home from Dr. Wieder's, I went to one of the websites she gave me—Tomatis.com. I took the tour of the website and read every word. I had to re-read the complex and technical information a couple of times to really understand.

I was learning about a form of auditory training known as the "Tomatis Method." It was slightly different than the Berard Method described in *The Sound of a Miracle* that treated sensitivities to *hearing* certain frequencies. The Tomatis Method improves the functioning of the ear and its ability to *listen*.

I read that hearing and listening were totally different processes. Hearing is a *passive* process just having the sounds taken in by the ear. Listening, however, is an *active* process and involves the brain to interpret and understand what is being heard. One can hear perfectly but be a poor listener. To my surprise, I learned that many learning disabilities are really listening disabilities.[3]

Dr. Alfred Tomatis was a French ear, nose and throat specialist who spent his career studying the role of the ear and its connection with the brain. His extensive research showed how good listening can positively influence our health and well being, and how poor listening can adversely affect it. The ear, he believed, was responsible for more than just taking in sounds. The ears control balance, coordination, muscle tone and the muscles of our eyes. Our ears analyze sounds. Our

---

3. Pierre Sollier, Overview, "Summary," http://www.Tomatis.com.

ears relay all sensory information to the brain. Our ears give us energy.[4] Dr. Tomatis discovered through his experimentations with subjects that: *When our ears cannot hear certain frequencies, our voice does not contain them either.*"[5] This is known today as the "Tomatis Effect." When he blocked the ears of singers from hearing certain frequencies, their voices deteriorated—the blocked frequencies were no longer present in their voices. His second law was born: "*If we modify the hearing, the voice changes immediately.*"[6] Realizing that sounds could enter the ear more easily if the tiny muscles in them were in shape, gave Dr. Tomatis his third law: "*One could restore someone's hearing (and thus their voice), by retraining these muscles.*"[7] Through exercising the ear muscles of his subjects, he found the muscles became stronger and were better able to perceive the spectrum of sound. The voices of his subjects were re-united with the frequencies they had lost.

The foundation for Dr. Tomatis' method of sound stimulation is patterned after the way a fetus hears sounds in-utero. As the mother speaks, only the high frequencies in her voice are rapidly channeled through her skeletal system to the fetus. This is hearing through bone conduction. It is the only way a fetus can hear its mother's voice. The high frequencies carry consonants such as (f/s/p/t/) and consonant blends such as (sh/th/ch/). Being able to hear these high-frequency sounds, in essence, wires the fetus for language and prepares it to hear and attach meaning to language outside the womb, when it is born. It also sets the stage for bonding. When a fetus hears the mother's voice in-utero, it becomes emotionally attached to it.

In the absence of a "mother" for his experiments, Dr. Tomatis re-created the mother's voice for his subjects by using Mozart music. Mozart is naturally very rich in the higher frequencies, those above 8000 hertz. These higher frequencies stimulated the brain and were what Dr. Tomatis dubbed "charging sounds."[8] Therefore, he removed (filtered) all of the lower frequencies, those below 8000 hertz, leaving just the higher frequencies. When subjects received the higher fre-

4. Pierre Sollier, Dr. Tomatis, "How We Listen, More Than Hearing," http://www.Tomatis.com.

5. Pierre Sollier, Dr. Tomatis, "Biography," The Three Laws of Tomatis, http://www.Tomatis.com.

6. Pierre Sollier, Dr. Tomatis, "Biography," The Three Laws of Tomatis, http://www.Tomatis.com.

7. Pierre Sollier, Dr. Tomatis, "Biography," The Three Laws of Tomatis, http://www.Tomatis.com.

8. Pierre Sollier, Dr. Tomatis, "How We Listen, More Than Hearing," http://www.Tomatis.com.

quencies, their speech, language, even coordination, posture and energy level improved. The lower frequencies were considered energy-draining. Listening only to low frequencies gave subjects a monotone, as well as put them in a state of depression.

Because of its high frequency properties, Dr. Tomatis found the music of Mozart to be the best suited for simulating the developmental period of listening in the womb. The classical music of other composers does not have as many of the high frequencies (above 8000 hertz) left to its arrangements after a filtering process, which leaves little in the way of charging sounds needed to nourish the brain and induce a state of alertness and attention—one primed for learning.

Dr. Tomatis also believed there was a dominant ear, the right ear, which was characteristic of good learners.[9] Good learners can easily distinguish between various frequencies that make up speech. Right-ear dominant persons can filter out much of the noise around them that is irrelevant, while focusing on those sounds important to them and making sense out of the information. Those who are left-ear dominant have difficulty with the spectrum of frequencies, and hence, are poor learners. Left-ear dominant persons cannot easily filter out the surrounding noises to tune in and focus on the important sounds—they are constantly being bombarded with stimuli. These differences are due to the connection each ear has with the hemispheres of the brain.

The right ear makes a contra-lateral (crisscross) connection with the left brain, where language is processed. This is a fast connection without incurring delays. Having no place to process language in the right brain, which makes its connection with the left ear, sounds must then travel to the left brain to be interpreted. This creates delays in processing, albeit in milliseconds, but sounds can be omitted or misinterpreted by the time they get to the left brain to be processed. Left-ear dominant listeners, therefore, are always trying to catch up to what has been said to them. Finding that difficult to do, they often just shut down and avoid interacting. The Tomatis Method also promotes more of a right-ear-dominance for just these reasons.

By exercising the ear muscles using various frequencies of music, the ear muscles are forced to stretch and relax. That is how they are strengthened. Strengthening the ear muscles makes it possible for the ears to become better filters. When the ears filter sounds efficiently, the body can modulate itself better, and not become over-stimulated or overwhelmed with unnecessary sounds. Dr. Tomatis

9. Pierre Sollier, Dr. Tomatis, "How We Listen, The Learning Ear," http://www.Tomatis.com.

believed that some children don't have effective filtering mechanisms and tend to take in every sound they hear. As a result, they receive a barrage of unfiltered sounds that are sometimes painful or distracting. As is the case with autism or Attention Deficit Disorder (ADD) and Attention Deficit Hyperactivity Disorder (ADHD), these children are often frustrated and full of anxiety and aggression that can promote learning disabilities. Correcting for these listening problems creates a calmer, more organized listener who is then able to learn and be more on task. Good learners are good listeners.[10]

I read the Tomatis Method addressed not just the spectrum of developmental disorders affecting children, but that this sound stimulation therapy has also been credited with combating depression in adults, helping people to learn foreign languages, assisting in developing better public speaking skills, and aiding in honing the skills of musicians, singers, and actors.

"Wow, it can do all that?" I said aloud, beginning to understand the miracle that might be contained within this technology.

"This is amazing! Dave, come here! You've got to read this!" I shouted to him from the office.

"Read this about Tomatis. It's the auditory training program that Dr. Wieder told us about. It sounds fantastic. I think it's just what Ashley needs!"

I got up out of the chair and let him sit down to read what I had just marveled at.

"They can retrain her ears, so she can learn to talk!" I said, interrupting his reading to give him the *Reader's Digest* condensed version.

"It almost sounds too good to be true! What do you think? Should we try it? Dr. Wieder thinks it could help her," I said, enthusiastically.

"Sharon, we're already doing so much with Ashley. Do we have time for this? We have a newborn, don't forget!"

"I'll make time. Sydney's easy. I'll tote her around with me. I want to try it! We have to do this!" I said, pleading my case.

"Remember what Shelly said? There's just something blocking Ashley from really connecting. Maybe this is it! Maybe this can help her! It's not just about her ears, it's about her brain!" I exclaimed.

Dave got up from the chair and looked at me like I was crazy. He knew I was already stressed from a whole year's worth of a diagnosis, labs gone awry, doctors, therapists and slow progress—maybe even a tad bit of post-partum depression. He thought I was setting myself up for major disappointment. He was always

---

10. Pierre Sollier, Overview, "Summary," http://www.Tomatis.com.

protective of me like that. And he was quite cautious when it came to "schedule overload," especially now with our three daughters under four years of age. But he could see the hope in my eyes and my newly-acquired enthusiasm about this treatment.

I went to SpectrumCenter.com and clicked on the numerous links to read more about how the Spectrum Center uses the Tomatis Method combined with sensory integration techniques to organize the central nervous system, open up the channels of communication and enhance learning. It sounded more and more like that miracle I was in search of. I had to make the call.

I spoke with a secretary at the Spectrum Center who explained the auditory training program. It consisted of three "loops." The first loop lasted 15 days, then a break of about a month. The second loop lasted eight days, then another break for about a month. The third loop also lasted eight days. Each day consisted of two hours of listening therapy combined with sensory integration activities. The three-loop program entailed 62 hours of listening, continuous parent/staff consults, daily feedback logs and periodic testing. Each child's program was individualized based on the results of an initial assessment.

The Spectrum Center is under the direction of Valerie Dejean, an occupational therapist and trained Tomatis consultant who studied under Dr. Tomatis in France. Her unique method of incorporating sensory integration techniques with the Tomatis Method improves how the brain takes in, sorts out, and responds to information.[11] The staff consists of licensed occupational therapists, audiologists, as well as listening therapists, who work directly with the children and implement the treatment plans. They are a well-respected auditory training facility, having nearly ten years in the business and the only one in the Mid-Atlantic States.

However, they were filled to capacity with patients already, and I was told there was a two-month waiting period. I didn't want to wait that long to have Ashley evaluated for such a hopeful therapy. I was excited about the program just by what I read on the website. I wanted in, *now!* But I had no choice. Like every other specialist we saw, there was a line in front of us a few months long. I had the secretary send me information and history forms to get the process rolling.

A large packet from the Spectrum Center arrived in the mailbox a few days later, and I ripped the envelope open! The 14-page questionnaire required me to

---

11. Valerie Dejean, "What is Sensory Integration?" http://
www.motorplanning.com/sensor3.html.

capture every bit of information from my pregnancy and Ashley's infancy, to her motor, sensory and speech and language development.

I spent days completing it thumbing through pages of Ashley's scrapbook and reading the notes I made on her milestone achievements. I copied the timeframes down—when she rolled over, when she sat, when she crawled, when she walked. The questionnaire asked for details about her behavioral characteristics, what her interests were, and how she got along with peers and adults. It requested information on our previous professional interventions. I listed them one by one. I didn't realize how much we were doing with Ashley—how many specialists we had seen thus far—until I itemized them on paper. I was fastidious about capturing it all!

Why did I think this might be the one therapy that would bring Ashley back to us? Because it seemed to be describing Ashley as having the characteristics of being a poor listener—she certainly didn't listen to us! The Tomatis Method claimed to be able to improve upon this and help her language emerge. The site listed some reasons why Ashley was perhaps a poor listener[12]:

- Her developmental history—which could reveal reasons for listening trouble—showed delays in motor skills, delays in language acquisition, and recurrent ear infections.

- With respect to her receptive listening—that which keeps us in tune to the world around us—she had a short attention span, an inability to follow sequential instructions, was very distractible, and confused similar sounding words.

- Her expressive listening—that which we use to control our voice when we speak or sing—showed weak vocabulary, confusion or reversal of letters, and a flat voice.

- Her motor skills—anchored by the vestibule in the ear, which controls balance, coordination and body image—showed clumsy and uncoordinated movements. She had poor rhythm, difficulty with organization and structure, a mixed dominance (use of left and right hand equally) and poor sports skills.

- Her energy level was poor, and she had difficulty upon wakening—throwing uncontrollable tantrums. She always seemed tired and sluggish

---

12. Paul Madaule, "Listening Checklist," adapted from Appendix B in *When Listening comes Alive*, (Norval, Ontario: Moulin, 1993), 191–192.

suggesting that maybe she could only hear the low, draining frequencies, not the high energizing ones.

- With respect to her behavior and social adjustment, she was shy, had difficulty making friends, tended to withdraw and avoid others, was irritable, immature with low motivation, and had little interest in learning.

Ashley pretty much fit the bill of being a poor listener according to Dr. Tomatis! I agreed with everything I read—I saw Ashley in every one of them. As much as I had read a year earlier about autism and how Ashley fit that definition, much to my denial of it, the listening checklist described Ashley's listening deficiencies to a "T." I couldn't help but feel completely elated that this could be the missing link!

Ashley's Candidacy

The day we had been waiting for had arrived—her auditory training assessment was upon us. The previous months' wait had taunted me with hope. I was nervous and anxious—my emotions all wrapped up into one. I hoped I wasn't setting myself up for disappointment like Dave had warned me I may do. I looked forward to the therapist's analysis of Ashley and her candidacy for the program.

We dropped Kacey off with Dave's parents and headed to the Spectrum Center in Bethesda, Maryland. (Grandparents' Day at Kacey's school was the next day. So timing was great. Kacey could stay with them and have a sleepover. Her grandparents would take her to school the following day and participate in her classroom activities.)

If all went well, (and I was optimistic it would), Ashley was scheduled to start her first loop after the assessment that afternoon. I scheduled her second session for the next day at 7:45 a.m—too early for us to get to the center in morning rush hour traffic, so Dave and I made the decision to stay the night in Bethesda.

We checked into the hotel and got organized before going down the street to the Spectrum Center. We found our way up to the offices and waited with nervous energy in the reception area. We were called and taken downstairs to one of the therapy rooms. We met two women, Rochelle, an occupational therapist and Alicia, an audiologist. They immediately took a liking to Ashley.

"Hi, Ashley! We knew you were going to be a cutie. We get a lot of boys here and reviewing Ashley's chart, we knew she was just going to be a cute, little girl. We are so excited to finally get one (girl)!" Alicia said, wearing a broad smile.

Dave and I sat on an exercise mat on the floor. Rochelle played with Ashley and observed her at play while Alicia talked to us about Ashley's history, the therapy program, and to see if she was a good fit. I watched as Rochelle playfully tested Ashley on different skills. She gave Ashley a crayon and observed how she held it. Ashley scribbled some lines on paper. Rochelle then tried to get Ashley to throw a ball—she wasn't so good at it. She watched Ashley walk around the room—she toddled gingerly and was unsure of herself. Rochelle asked her questions to see if she could respond—she didn't always. Rochelle tested Ashley's vestibular system by putting her in a swing and spinning her lightly ten times in 20 seconds. She looked to see if Ashley's eyes twitched back and forth upon stopping her, which they should have done—Ashley's did not!

After about 30 minutes, Rochelle and Alicia put together their opinions of what Ashley's issues were and formally discussed them with us. From a postural perspective, Ashley appeared clumsy. She had very loose ligaments in her wrist and fingers. She also "W" sat. They explained to us that she sat this way, because it gave her a wider base of support, so she wouldn't fall over. They also said this sitting position was not unusual for children with low muscle tone.

With respect to Ashley's eyes not twitching back and forth after she had been spun around, this indicated a depressed nystagmus—an involuntary spasm of the eyeball. It correlated with depressed processing within the vestibular system—the inner ear.

With respect to tactile issues, Ashley's defensiveness with gooey textures was still evident, but it had been reduced somewhat, being addressed by our private occupational therapist. Ashley had a lot of oral defensiveness, like not allowing us to put a toothbrush in her mouth to brush her teeth. She was also still quite limited in the food textures she preferred.

Dave and I knew Ashley's strongest sense was her vision. Alicia and Rochelle agreed. She didn't disappoint them when they asked her to identify some shapes and colors. Ashley made good eye contact with both of the therapists that day. The fact that she had a history of using her peripheral vision for watching television suggested to them, that although this was her strongest learning channel, it wasn't functioning adequately. It was lacking the sensory support from the other systems, most notably the vestibular system. They indicated to us that she was using her peripheral vision to compensate for depressed processing from the other senses.

From an auditory perspective—because Ashley often mixed up her consonants such as "p" and "m," in addition to needing repeated instructions to carry out a direction—it suggested to them that she didn't perceive or register auditory information accurately. She was, therefore, unable to discriminate and sequence sounds appropriately for higher level language skills. Perhaps, they surmised, this was a result of repeated ear infections when she was younger.

With respect to her motor planning—the brain's ability to conceive, organize, and carry out a sequence of unfamiliar actions—there were obvious problems with her motor skills, self-help skills and play skills. Having poor motor planning meant Ashley had a reduced ability to execute a task. Rochelle explained to us that there were three components to motor planning. The first one was the ability to *ideate*, or envision what one wants to do. The second component was the *sequencing of the actions* required to accomplish the task. The third component was having the motor control to *execute* the task.

The fact that Ashley had difficulties with motor planning translated to oral motor planning, which was important for speech articulation and speech development. Her motor planning difficulties spread to her inability to acquire symbolic play, since it is dependent on the ability to ideate and develop concepts needed to be communicative. It's easy to see how Ashley's imaginary play never developed due to poor motor planning.

Ashley still didn't display the elaborate gestural communication that would be expected for a child her age, but it had been improving in the past few months. She started to use a fork, but she hadn't begun using a spoon. This is due to the fact that foods which required using a spoon weren't part of her diet, yet. She still wasn't able to undress herself and was unable to execute simple tasks such as pulling off her socks.

Their overall opinion was Ashley had an underlying sensory integration and listening disorder that resulted in atypical processing of the vestibular system which detects motion and gravity and provides us with our sense of balance. She had a motor planning disorder resulting in her inability to perform tasks and play appropriately. She had an auditory processing disorder that resulted in abnormal perception of sound.

Rochelle explained to us that the vestibular system develops early in-utero. Through its many connections with the rest of the brain, it is believed to provide the foundation for many other functions. When the influences of vestibular stimuli fail to reach their destination, they cannot adequately contribute to sensory integration. Depressed vestibular processing is often associated with and can contribute to low muscle tone, or hypotonia. If muscle tone is decreased, it is more difficult to initiate movement or to maintain muscle tension during movement. Muscle tone is necessary for stability. A lack of sufficient postural support can contribute significantly to difficulties in fine and gross motor skills and oral motor coordination. All movements of the extremities and head are dependent on an adequate base of muscle tone to provide postural support. Ashley certainly showed deficiencies in this area.

Alicia explained that Ashley's motor planning difficulties translated into auditory processing difficulties, because motor planning and sequence skills are combined for the ability to follow directions. First, one has to process the instructions given to them (auditory), and then one has to organize and sequence how they will go about doing them (motor planning). Ashley's motor planning difficulties were also impacting her ability to organize her thoughts and thus, verbal expressions. In order for her to develop language, it was necessary for her to process complex information through the auditory system that is responsible for separating the speech stream into meaningful auditory units. This is usually all done in the setting of rapid-fire conversation. Without the ability to process speech in this fashion, it was difficult for Ashley to develop normal processing skills, and even more difficult to develop normal two-way conversational skills.

The ability to listen, Alicia explained, is based on the ear's ability to analyze sound accurately. With the auditory processing deficiencies that Ashley possessed, the major portion of her expressive and receptive language had been affected. These weaknesses in auditory processing had contributed to her social difficulties, with her being less able to carry on back and forth conversations.

So how was all of this going to be addressed by their program?

They explained they were going to exercise the tiny muscles in her ears using Dr. Tomatis' technology, the Electronic Ear. Different frequencies would be passed from the machine to the ear muscles strengthening them and training the ear to listen more effectively. Mozart music would initially be used to do this, as well as my voice later on in the program. The high-frequencies from both of these sources would be used to simulate the developmental period, re-creating the environment for how a fetus would hear in-utero[13].

The Tomatis Method, together with sensory integration therapy, would focus treatment on the inner ear. The combination of these therapies would work on addressing Ashley's auditory processing (issues of attention, concentration and communication); her motor planning (issues of coordination, fine and gross motor skills); and her sensory integration dysfunction (issues of tactile defensiveness and hyper/hypo sensitivities).

---

13. Valerie Dejean, "The Tomatis Method of Auditory Stimulation-An Overview," 2002.

The reasons for her delays were becoming understandable when presented like this. It all sounded treatable—at least, that's what I was banking on!

CHAPTER 11

▼

AWAKENING ASHLEY

The possibility of Ashley getting better using this technology was still difficult to envision and understand—but I was ready for results. The therapists were very optimistic that Ashley would do well in the program, since she had the classic signs and symptoms that their therapy seemed to address. They were looking forward to having this cute, little girl in pigtails around their offices for the next few months.

With Ashley's evaluation under our belt, Dave and I took a brief tour of one of the listening rooms. It was a large room with many OT-type toys, equipment and mats. There was a side room that housed the audio equipment. The wires of the headphones fed through holes in the bottom of the floor to reach out into the therapy rooms. The children walked around with the long headphone cords wagging behind them. It seemed like a great atmosphere for learning...and listening.

With nothing to lose, and hopefully everything to gain, we hugged and squeezed our little Ashley, said our good-byes and relinquished her into the therapists' very knowledgeable and capable hands.

"Just get her better," I said under my breath. "Just get her better."

My eyes began to tear with hope and a tad bit of fear of the unknown. The door of the listening room closed. It was all in their hands now. I was already missing her.

Music to Her Ears—Loop One

We took the elevator to the waiting room. For the first day, we preferred to stay in the building to feel somewhat closer to Ashley. She was only a floor away, but just in case they needed us, we stayed and passed the time there. I listened to the other mothers. It was informative to hear them talk about the issues they were facing with their children—some had autism—both mild and severe; some had dyslexia, some had other learning difficulties. But most of them had traveled a significant distance to be there. Some drove upward of 11 hours, others flew from the Midwest and beyond. It was unbelievable that they made the distance for this therapy. But who wouldn't have with such potential that it held to help our children?

They talked about the other specialists they were seeing. Some of the names were those that we were seeing too, or had appointments to see in the future. There seemed to be a network of specialists in our area who saw many of the autistic children seen at the Spectrum Center. When these parents came for their loops, they packed in visits to all of these specialists while they were in town. It made me feel good to know that I was at least in the ballpark when it came to seeing the right people for Ashley. I made notes of additional specialists' names, and chimed in on occasion to learn either more about a particular specialist or to get information on anything more I could be doing for Ashley.

Two hours had passed quickly, and it had turned dark outside. I looked out of the office window into the hall and saw the elevator door open. The children came running out screaming. A large boy, who looked in his teens, pushed his way passed Ashley to open the door to the office. As Ashley tried to make her way past him, he nearly trampled her on his way over to me, thinking I was his mother. About to plant a kiss on me, his mother quickly tugged on his arm and re-directed him to where she was sitting.

At that point, Ashley appeared out from under his legs and greeted us. We hugged her and planted our own kisses on her. I was amazed to see her so full of smiles. I thought she was going to probably sit in a corner down in the therapy room and suck her thumb not getting anything out of the session. I was totally wrong!

"Hi, I'm one of the listening therapists. I worked with Ashley today," a young woman crouched down to talk to me.

"So, how did she do?" I asked, nervously.

"She did awesome! Oh, my gosh, she is sooo cute! She manipulated Play Dough briefly. She swung and straddled the bolster swing with fair balance. She independently strung large beads. She enjoyed drawing on the dry-erase board. She bounced standing on the therapy ball with good extension. She completed a peg puzzle independently and needed minimal assistance for an eight-piece puzzle. We played a nose-matching game, and she did a good job of matching the correct nose to the animal," she said, summarizing Ashley's first session.

"Wow, what a great report," I said, hugging Ashley.

I was stunned that she had enjoyed it so much. She looked happy!

"She didn't have any tantrums?"

"No. She did great!" the therapist said.

"She kept the headphones on?"

"Yes, for the most part. We just put them back on if the children take them off. We keep them on with a headband," she told us.

"Bye, Ashley. I'll see you tomorrow," the therapist said, and moved on to brief another child's parent.

Dave scooped her up, and I collected our bags and baby Sydney. We headed back to the hotel for the evening. Ashley didn't have any trouble falling asleep. Her first therapy session seemed to have knocked her right out. We watched her sleep, as we ate our dinner—delivered by room service—and played with Sydney.

The next morning we arrived for Ashley's second visit at 7:45 a.m. The waiting room was filled with children shouting and running amuck. Ashley spent some of the time spinning around and rolling on the floor. The listening therapists entered the room and collected all the children to go downstairs. We said good-bye to Ashley and watched her get on the elevator. I blew her a kiss. The elevator door closed. She was gone.

We took Sydney back to the hotel and checked out. We returned two hours later to wait for Ashley to come up from therapy. Ashley spilled out of the elevator with the crowd of children, and the office door flew open. They each ran to their respective Moms and Dads. Ashley was full of life and showed that sparkling smile. The listening therapist came over to summarize her second session.

"Ashley did a great job again, today. She worked with Play Dough and shape cutters to strengthen her hands. She swung on the platform swing and had fair-to-good balance. She strung small beads, but had difficulty with motor planning to get the beads to the bottom of the string. She completed an eight-piece puzzle with minimal assistance. We did high fives across the body to get her to cross the mid-line. She tried to blow bubbles, but could only form the lip shape. She had difficulty with the oral motor control for actually blowing the bubbles. We'll work on using a sensory brush in her mouth, if she lets us."

Another great report! I was so pleased that it was all working out. Ashley seemed to like being there, and the listening therapists certainly adored Ashley. I felt very comfortable with that! I was just hoping that this was going to be the jump-start that Ashley needed, and that the high regard in which I held this therapy would not let me down. I was really putting all my eggs in this basket. I was hoping for a miracle—just like Annabel's.

We walked to the parking deck and buckled Ashley and Sydney into their car seats. We made our way onto the Beltway toward home. Dave and I were taking, when all of a sudden from the back seat, a voice rang out.

"I want cookie!"

I looked at Dave, and he nearly drove off the road.

"What did she just say? Did she just ask us for a cookie?" I turned to Dave in disbelief.

Sydney was only eight-weeks-old. I figured it hadn't come from her. I was totally caught off guard by that one, but I fumbled around for one of Ashley's gluten-free cookies in my bag and found one.

"Yes, yes, cookie! Here you go!" I said, tossing a cookie to the backseat.

It landed in her lap.

"Good talking, Ashley!" I said, beaming with joy.

Wow! Something was happening here.

She had never spoken a spontaneous sentence! It had all been with prompting up until now. This was clear as day. We were just shocked!

"Could this be the therapy already?" I wondered.

It was only day two of our first loop! I was hoping for a miracle. But I didn't know it was coming on day two!

This was unbelievable to us! It wasn't just a sentence, but it was logical, expressing her wants and needs. And it was a 24 to 29 month expressive skill that she had previously lacked on her speech evaluation form that Shelly kept updating during her sessions with Ashley. I noted this finding—this glorious finding—on our daily parent observation form the next day at the Spectrum Center. Everyone was thrilled!

During the mid-loop consult, I learned more about what the Tomatis Method was actually doing for Ashley. Since Ashley was young they didn't want to shock her system with the higher frequencies immediately, so she listened to Mozart music that contained more of the lower frequencies. These were the vestibular-based frequencies that worked on her body. About eight days into the program, the filtering process began. The lower frequencies were gradually removed during a period of many days leaving just the higher, more energizing frequencies.

This first loop was the *passive* phase of the program. There was no real work for Ashley to do in terms of listening. She did her sensory integration activities of swinging, bouncing and fine motor skills, but she didn't need to concentrate on the sounds in her headphones. The special headphones clicked on and off from different frequency channels at different times to exercise her ears and to convert her to more of a right-ear listener. Ashley, at that point, listened more with her left ear—classic of poor learners.

I was told that I would be making a recording of my voice near the end of the first loop to be used throughout Ashley's treatment program. They were going to take my voice and alter it by removing the low frequencies—leaving just the high frequencies—and then feed it through Ashley's headphones. What Ashley would hear would be a high frequency chirping noise similar to how a fetus would hear in-utero.

Dr. Tomatis' technology goes back to the in-utero environment, because that is the foundation for learning. Correcting for learning problems and stimulating the brain's pathways again are achieved by basically starting over—back in the womb—back where a fetus first learns to listen and develop language.

The nervous system's pathways in Ashley were dormant and needed to be re-stimulated to start making connections that it should have been making all along. Babies go through a period of sensory motor development and absorb sensory information like a sponge. By the time a baby reaches around 18-months and is more purposeful and operational in its abilities, it has a wealth of stimulation from these connections, which become the foundation of how they interact and communicate with their environment.[14]

The Tomatis Method re-establishes these connections through the inner ear. Sensory integration therapy is also applied, in addition to the Tomatis Method, to stimulate the body. The Spectrum Center is unique in that it doesn't just provide the Tomatis Method for the ear, but incorporates Jean Ayres' theory about sensory integration. Jean Ayres, an occupational therapist, asserted the primary building blocks of the central nervous system are the senses, particularly the special senses (vestibular, tactile, and proprioceptive). All other skills are complex processes based on a strong foundation of sensory integration[15].

14. Valerie Dejean and Alex Freer, "What is Sensory Integration?" 2002.
15. The Spectrum Center Method, *How Does Sensory Integration Relate to My Child* by Alex Freer Balko, http://www.spectrumcentermethod.com.

The Spectrum Center uses sensory integration activities in tandem with the Tomatis Method, because both methods are aiming at the same goal of vestibular stimulation. One is from the perspective of the ear (Tomatis), and one is from the perspective of the body (Ayres).

When the vestibular system, our primary sensory system, is not functioning in children who have developmental issues, their eyes tend to take over to compensate for this lack of needed vestibular input.

This is what I found in Ashley. Ashley always seemed very visual to me. When Ashley was watching television at a most peculiar angle or staring at a minute piece of dirt on the floor, she was really using her sense of vision to receive input that she wasn't receiving through her body.

A lot of children who have self-stimulating behavior, such as watching things spin, are doing the same thing. By watching something spin long enough, one can get dizzy, because the vestibular system has been stimulated. The vestibular system and the eyes are not connecting well, so the eyes, in this case, are trying to give the nervous system the sensation it isn't getting from the vestibular system. In addition, children who have this hyper-vision turn their ears off, since the vestibular system is the auditory system. If those children are focusing intently on something, it just may be that they are tuning out everything else and their attention cannot be obtained. This is also what I saw with Ashley growing up. She was hyper-focused on something she was doing, so she shut down her ears.

The humming that Ashley did was also a form of tuning us out. Humming is an age-old tradition. Monks hum to energize themselves.[16] Gregorian chant is very rich in high frequencies and, although calming, is quite stimulating as well. Gregorian chant also has a very even respiration rate promoting relaxation and orientation. One learns best in a relaxed, alert environment. That is why Gregorian chant is also part of the listening program at the Spectrum Center.

"Music can do all this?" I thought. I was learning so much about this incredible technology. I always thought Gregorian chant seemed sluggish and boring. But it has just the opposite effect! I was learning a whole new aspect to music. And to think this one man, Dr. Tomatis, figured this whole thing out! It was mind-boggling!

The remaining days of the first loop were great for Ashley. She had found her home-away-from-home in the Spectrum Center, and she loved each therapist who worked with her.

16. Paul Madaule, *When Listening Comes Alive*, (Norval, Ontario: Moulin, 1994), 62–63.

"We fight downstairs to see who's going to work with Ashley. We all think she's just adorable!" one of the listening therapists said to me.

They were very kind to us, and Ashley was always so glad to be there. She was becoming one of their favorites. I felt really great about my decision to pursue Tomatis. I liked what I had found at the Spectrum Center.

During this first loop Ashley had started to eat new foods, such as apples, carrots, chicken salad, nuts, peanut butter sandwiches, and even pot roast (all gluten and casein-free). She had never wanted to touch these before starting Tomatis. She liked fruit roll-ups, a most sticky and tacky texture. But tactile sensitivity didn't seem to be an issue anymore. She was also talking more spontaneously.

"Weady, set, go!" she said to us, as we pulled her back in her swing and let go. Her face glowed.

The few words she did have became clearer and more intelligible during the first loop. A duck used to say, "Cack, cack, cack." Now it said, "Quack, quack, quack." Ashley used to say, "More ju." Now she said, "More juice, pwease!" This correlated directly with Dr. Tomatis' belief that if we modify the hearing, the voice changes immediately. The frequencies that Ashley couldn't once hear had now been restored to her hearing, and subsequently to her voice.

By the end of the first loop (15 days after beginning), Ashley had more energy, another belief of Dr. Tomatis that the high frequencies energize and nourish the brain. She now sang the words to songs instead of merely humming them. Her social play was blossoming. She would put her head against the wall with her hand covering her eyes and count to ten.

"Weady not, he I come," Ashley would say, striking up a game of hide-n-seek with us.

Ashley had also begun to sit on the floor with Kacey and hand her puzzle pieces, as they both worked on a puzzle together. This had never happened before! Ashley was playing with Kacey! It warmed my heart to see the two of them now engaging in play.

Ashley had also taken an interest for the first time in baby Sydney. Ashley also started to potty train. She had more awareness of her surroundings and now definitely with her body as well.

It was just incredible! She was interacting with all of us so much more and was really awakening and coming alive! She learned to take turns while playing board games like Bingo and Candy Land.

"Ashwey tun," she'd say, pointing to herself.

"Mommy tun," she'd say, pointing to me.

She was now saying hi and bye spontaneously.

But, she was also experiencing a downside to the listening therapy. Because it was correcting her neurological system, which was basically "out-of-sync," we saw a lot of tantrums that before, we had never seen.

We were told by Rochelle and Alicia that some deterioration in behavior could occur, but with the great results they were seeing in Ashley, they didn't think she would go backward. She didn't seem to be going backward to us. It was more like the terrible twos, which I remembered from Kacey's bout with them, yet had never seen with Ashley. Now they were finally appearing—almost instantly. With respect to language and socialization, those were going full throttle ahead. The terrible twos were scattered about, just enough to keep us on our toes at all times. We just weren't accustomed to seeing Ashley in such an alert, alive state. It kind of took us by surprise. Was it a downside to the listening program, or was nature moving on with Ashley's development?

Come to find out, it was both. It was a good thing. We were told this is often seen as children progress with this therapy, because now they have a clearer sense of who they are and what their bodies can do; they express themselves, now that they can. Since terrible twos are a very natural phase in a toddler's development, it meant Ashley was just catching up with what should have been here all along. The listening was correcting her system, so nature was doing its part, as well. We just tried to weather the storms as best we could.

What really impressed me was that Ashley started to sing more in the car and did something other than sit, suck her thumb and look lethargic during the ride. Whereas Kacey always sang and moved her shoulders to the tunes, Ashley never did. But now, Ashley and Kacey sang together. Every time I looked in the rear view mirror, I analyzed Ashley. She sang, she looked out the window, and she was interested in the sky and the trees now. Mozart was doing something to her!

She was becoming more affectionate and gave us unsolicited hugs. In the mornings she would go to the gate at her bedroom door.

"Dada come!" she would call out, summoning him out of bed.

It was music to *our* ears! Finally, she called Dave to come and get her in the same way that Kacey used to yell, "Daaa" in her crib when she was ten-months-old.

Ashley now needed us.

"Kacey. Hi!" Ashley said, as Kacey unlocked her gate one morning.

She was now recognizing we all had names.

It was just getting better and better. When we read Ashley her favorite dinosaur book before going to bed, she started to participate.

"Wong, wong go, erf wam," Ashley said, reciting her favorite dinosaur story.

"That's right! Long, long ago, the Earth was warmer," I said, repeating it.

"Di-saur big," she said, pointing to Brontosaurus.

"Some dinosaurs ate..." I paused to let her fill in the blank.

"Meat!" she responded with excitement.

"But when the meat eaters came, the plant eaters..." I paused again.

"Wan way," she proceeded to tell me.

"Yep. They ran away!" I said, taking my fingers and walking them across the bed to imitate the dinosaurs fleeing.

When I got to the end of the book, she always knew exactly what to say.

"The end!" and closed the book and put it on her nightstand.

Another remarkable aspect about Ashley's progress was that she started to interact more with her grandparents. A year earlier, Ashley would have screamed and cried if one of them had tried to hold her or play with her, so they just opted not to interfere with her. Now, she was actually going up to them and playing with them. She now had this calm about her when she was around them, that before she never had. I could tell they loved being able to now share moments with Ashley. When they hugged and squeezed her, she didn't mind it anymore. They weren't able to do that for so long! There was now a connection with her!

All of this in 15 days! All of this never seen before! Our eyes and ears were pleasantly surprised at each new thing. And I have to say, I found myself wiping joyful tears away at some of the remarkable things she was doing. How could I ever repay Dr. Tomatis for the changes we were seeing in our little Ashley? How could I ever let him know that he had given us back our daughter? And we still had two loops to go! So far, Tomatis was all I had hoped it would be—and more.

I held up pretty well during the 15 days of the first loop, but I felt worn out from it all. Thankfully, Dave's parents had kept Kacey and Sydney most of the days when I was on the road with Ashley. They provided us with meals and lots of extra babysitting, so Dave and I could take a break and "go out" without three girls vying for our attention.

During the month break from Tomatis, we returned to our normal routine. We had taken those 15 days off from speech and occupational therapy, our special educator and a new pre-school, feeling it was just going to be too much for Ashley. Trying to do all of that, plus Tomatis, plus commuting, was just way too much for this Mommy. I am considered by some to have super powers, but that was going a little bit above even my threshold for routine overload.

But no sooner did we step into our speech and OT office, Shelly and Tina, our new occupational therapist had noticed dramatic changes in Ashley.

"Hi, Tina, hi Shehwy!" Ashley now said to them.

They nearly fell over.

Ashley was the only one they knew who was participating in the Tomatis therapy, so she was their guinea pig. They were starting to see just what effect the listening program had had on her speech and motor planning—in only 15 days!

Ashley had her best session to date after we returned to speech with Shelly. I think Shelly was caught a little bit off guard in her plan of therapy for Ashley that first day back. Ashley soared right passed the work, and Shelly found herself needing to re-group a little bit to find more advanced teaching material.

"What's the boy doing?" Shelly would now ask pointing to a boy with a book open.

"Weading," Ashley would reply appropriately.

This was a big step for Ashley, and it was taking her expressive language closer to age-appropriate and closer to meeting her newly-revised goals. Two weeks earlier, Ashley was still trying to follow directions. Now, we were just amazed at her acquisition of language in (what seemed like), the blink of an eye.

Upon returning to OT, Ashley was now jumping down from 12 inches without assistance and landing on her feet—something she couldn't do previously in OT.

Tina also noticed Ashley's self-help skills were improving. She was now trying to pull off her socks, where before, she couldn't do it and would scream if I asked her to do so. She was starting to pull off her shirt and pants, but still needed assistance. But now she could say, "Help me!"

Diana, Ashley's special educator from the county, was floored when she came to our house for a visit after our first loop. Ashley actually greeted her.

"Hi, Dina."

"How are you today, Ashley?"

"Goom!(good)" Ashley now replied.

It wasn't as clear as some words, but it was an intelligent response to a question, which before we weren't hearing. I thought it was unbelievable!

Ashley was initiating interaction with all of us now. She was enjoying being with us, playing with us, and learning to adjust to her newly-found voice—something that had been a void in her life, and ours, prior to starting Tomatis!

More Wassles, More Tart—Loop Two

Four weeks later, we returned for our second loop of Tomatis. Ashley fell right back into place, as if she had never left. The therapists just couldn't wait to greet Ashley and take her downstairs to play.

At the end of the first loop, I had a critical role by recording a story I read from a children's book. I chose the Frog and Toad stories. The high frequencies in this book are plentiful such as /th/, /sh/, /f/, and /s/. This was my voice tape that the therapists were going to use in the second loop and filter out the low frequencies leaving just the high frequencies. When this is played back, the recording actually sounds like crickets chirping. I had the chance to listen to it in its filtered form—a rather uneasy-sounding recording to you and me. But this was a way to simulate the environment of the womb as they were getting ready in this second loop to re-introduce Ashley to me. They had simulated it in the first loop with Mozart.

I couldn't wait to see Ashley after her first day back and hear from the therapist how she had done. Ashley entered the waiting room as she did many times before, being the first one in line to push the door open. She needed some help with the heavy door. She came running toward me with her arms out wide to give me a big hug. Her smile was illuminating.

The listening therapist kneeled down to talk to me.

"Ashley had a good first day back. She manipulated Play Dough using rolling pins and shape cutters. She tried using scissors with assistance from me. She swung on the platform swing sitting and lying down and demonstrated fair balance. We introduced her to the microphone today, and she did a nice job with microphone work and labeling flashcards. She completed a seven to nine-piece puzzle independently. She played a matching nose game but had a little difficulty matching the correct noses. She brushed her tongue with a sensory brush, but wouldn't let us do it. She initiated singing songs for us with some difficulty with articulation. But she did well today," the therapist said, recapping Ashley's session.

"Bye, Ashley. I'll see you tomorrow," the therapist waved good-bye.

"Bye!" Ashley waved back to her.

During this second loop, Ashley was introduced to my voice tape as well as listened to filtered Mozart. She heard the chirping sounds in her headphones and was now immersed in the sounds of the womb. Her microphone work got progressively more demanding, but she seemed to be keeping up with it. Her vocalization was getting better each day and she was now able to listen to sounds and recreate them intelligently. She was labeling pictures while speaking more clearly into the microphone. She was responding well. I was told she was now interacting with the other children in the listening room and finding it quite enjoyable leading the whole room in song—something the therapists found quite impressive!

We encountered a lot of echolalia during this loop. By that I mean, Ashley would repeat, verbatim, anything someone said. If I asked, "Do you want more juice?" instead of, "yes" or "no" or "more juice," she would answer me with, "Do you want more juice?"

This was becoming quite a problem, and all the therapists, both at the center as well as our own private ones, were encountering the same thing. Apparently, it was just a phase that she was going through by trying out her new voice. She was repeating everything, because this was practice for her. It eventually decreased, but it was an issue for at least a few weeks. But the second loop continued to impress us as her speech became more spontaneous, and she was interacting more with others and initiating play.

During our break after the second loop, new and exciting things were happening with Ashley. The changes were coming nearly overnight. We'd wake up and be surprised by something new she would say or eat.

"More bacon, pwease! More wassles (waffles), pwease!"

Ashley's "f's" hadn't come in, yet and were pronounced as "s." Sometimes it was a stretch to figure out the words she was trying to say, but soon I understood perfectly.

Ashley also decided to give the spoon a try. She was finally getting the motor planning down as well as eating new textures. It was really a big deal to us and a giant step for her.

She was now able to put her shoes on independently. I bought her sneakers with Velcro, so that she was able to put them on herself. It was a way to give her independence from me, as well as a sense of accomplishment of a job done all by herself. It seemed to be a great idea. And it was one less thing I had to do for her.

We were told by Rochelle to listen to Mozart whenever possible. For my anal mind, that meant in the car, at home, everywhere! Now, whenever I put the CD in and Ashley heard the first few uplifting sounds of the music, she perked up.

"Ashley, who's this?" I quizzed her.

"More tart," (Mozart) acknowledging the Mozart music.

We listened to it so often that Ashley became familiar with Mozart and began humming the music. I began to whistle it everywhere, myself. I couldn't get the music out of my head. She must have listened so meticulously, because she could hum with precision, and her pitch was incredible. I considered this form of humming acceptable.

Tina, Ashley's occupational therapist re-evaluated Ashley and found her skills scattered from 20 to 36 months. She was not quite three-years-old. She was now able to open and close scissors and snip a piece of paper without assistance. She couldn't do this before, having neither the strength in her fingers nor the motor planning to do so. She was still having problems with her grip of a pencil or crayon, and a dominant hand had still not emerged.

We were still trying to get her to improve throwing a ball both overhand and underhand. These were skills that she just couldn't grasp. She was soon jumping down 18 inches on her way to a goal of 24 inches that I was told was appropriate for her age. I wasn't concerned so much with the exact height. Eighteen inches or 24, it didn't matter much to me. What was important was that she could land on her feet and not fall to her knees.

Each week of OT, Ashley was improving toward her goals, and that's what was important. She was beginning to stand on the platform swing and not lose her balance. She was beginning to stand on one foot for about three seconds without losing her balance as well. She was climbing all over the furniture at home and seemed fearless. Clearly, her vestibular system was gradually improving, and it was apparent in her overall motor planning and coordination.

She was meeting most of her OT goals and new ones were being written for her. Ashley's major problem was still the oral sensitivity. She was accepting of some new textures, so it was improving, but getting in her mouth to brush her teeth was a battle. Dave and I were always defeated. We tried sensory brushes. We tried electric toothbrushes. We tried Barney brand toothbrushes. We tried toothbrushes that jingled. Our biggest challenge was to get those teeth cleaned. Yet on some occasions, she didn't mind it—if she could control it herself. It was hit or miss with her. I never knew which temperament I'd get each day with regard to teeth brushing. But I decided her kicking and screaming was not worth it. If we needed to skip a night of brushing to just have peace and quiet before bedtime, I chose that route. We muddled through the best we could with certain idiosyncrasies that just didn't seem worth fighting. It was the bigger picture—one getting brighter each day—which was what this journey was all about.

Shelly, our speech therapist, was almost tongue-tied, being pleasantly surprised by each visit Ashley made to see her. She knew that Ashley was capable of speech once the "blockage," (as she called it), was removed. Ashley's speech was blossoming to all of our satisfaction. She was starting to talk in small sentences. I remember one time Kacey came into a speech therapy session with us. She was in a bad mood and started to cry. While holding Shelly's hand on her way to her office, Ashley turned around and looked at Kacey.

"Kacey crying," she told Miss Shelly.

How right she was—and how beautifully stated!

During her sessions with Shelly, she was now working on producing a basic sentence to tell about an action, i.e., "Mommy is sitting," or "the dog is eating." She was starting to understand quantities such as "none," "all," and "the rest." She was working on answering questions with "yes" and nodding her head appropriately. All of this on the way to her long-term goal of age appropriate speech. And she was really getting closer and closer to that goal.

Her daily acquisition of new words and phrases put her quite near her peers. As Ashley's vestibular system was being corrected, and she had found her voice and improved her listening skills, the dam broke. What seemed like a flood of two and a half years of speech, coordination, and balance that was caught up inside of her came spilling out. We smiled proudly and rode the waves with her.

Another Quarter in the Jukebox—Loop 3

A month later, we were back at the Spectrum Center for the third loop. Ashley's progress was just getting better and better. Ashley showed the therapists her newly-found, fine motor skills and balance. They remarked at how her imaginary play had really taken off from a month ago, when they had last seen her. She demonstrated some of her skills while playing with toys in the therapy room.

Later that evening, Dave and I were sitting in the kitchen discussing Ashley. She came up to us and started singing. We always loved to hear her voice. At this point some of her words were still unclear, but we knew the song she was singing. We joined in, too.

What was remarkable about this particular time was that when Ashley finished her song, she would start up another one, and another one, and another one. She was the "human jukebox." She was starting to not only memorize each song on the children's CD that we listened to in the car, but would hum the introductions to them as well!

And she didn't stop! She stood and sang songs for about 20 minutes without our prompting her even once. She barely came up for air between songs. She was full of animation and expression. It was the cutest thing. She had definitely found her voice and was showing off for us—her audience.

I don't know exactly what her listening program had been that first day back of the third loop, but something kicked in, and she started belting out the tunes. My voice tape was always used during every session. Coming off of a break, my voice tape, perhaps, was responsible for this.

Dave and I just looked at each other and cracked up at how wonderful it all was. I had tears in my eyes, because I was laughing so hard—she was delightful and entertaining. The great things we kept seeing from the listening program were just mind-boggling. How could this be happening on only the first day back?

But it was happening, and it was wonderful! I knew the clarity of her words would come later, but the fact that she came up to us and captivated us with her singing and kept it up for so long was priceless. This was why we were committed to this program in the first place—to see results like this.

Part of her microphone work this loop was to repeat words and phrases. Everyday the words would get a little more filtered, so they were difficult for her to understand and repeat back. The phrases would also get a little longer each day. These exercises were to help her with her auditory discrimination. Ashley really had to be a good listener to accomplish these exercises.

Ashley also listened to a text tape of a story. Each day, the tape was de-filtered to add back the lower frequencies, so that finally, she was hearing the entire story in someone's voice. It was not my voice that was used. My voice was the equivalent of emotional stability. Someone else's voice was used so that she would start to listen outside of the womb. This was what Dr. Tomatis called the "sonic birth." Ashley was now leaving the chirping noise of the simulated womb, where she listened through bone conduction, and entering the world of sound the way we all hear it—through air conduction.[17] It was as if she were being re-born. It's an amazing theory! And it seemed to be working like a charm for Ashley!

Ashley was breaking through more and more each day during the third loop. She was playing "Simon Says" with Kacey and the little girls across the street. I joined in on occasion. She was not only following Simon's directions, but she wanted to be Simon.

"Ashwey tun," she said, and moved to the front to think up things to ask us.

"Simon says…toes!" she ordered us.

We knew she meant for us to touch our toes.

With a little more time, we had her completing the whole sentence.

"Simon says…touch yaw toes!"

"Simon says…tun awound!"

I knew this was a giant step toward her rehabilitation. Dr. Wieder's recommendation to us was to get Ashley into some social situations, so she could be a follower—so she could mimic others and learn from them. Now, she wasn't just following, she was ideating. She was creating her own ideas. That was what motor planning was all about. Obviously, her motor planning had been posi-

---

17. Pierre Sollier, The Tomatis Method, "Languages," http://www.Tomatis.com.

tively affected by the Tomatis therapy, enough so to learn this complicated social game for not even being three-years-old.

Just watching her day to day, I saw so much change in her. "Duck, duck, goose" was another one of her favorite games and she picked it up fast. We all sat in a circle on the lawn.

"Duck...duck...duck...*goose*!" she said, laughing and hitting Kacey on the head sparking a "goose" chase.

Ashley's little legs barely got her very far, before Kacey had pretty much tackled her to the grass. Ashley then took her spot in the circle and sat down with her legs "crisscross apple sauce." The game began again. Every time someone was tapped on the head and a chase ensued, Ashley thought she should run too, so she did.

But it was great social interaction, even if she didn't have the rules down just right. It was something I thought she would never, ever, have the capacity to learn and understand. Social skills were one of her weaknesses. But she proved all of us wrong that day. And I was quite happy to be proven wrong! She was turning out to be quite a spunky, happy, perky toddler. I was just so proud of her!

Ashley's spontaneity improved during the eight days of the third loop.

"Daddy, Elmo slippers, put on," she said, as she handed Dave her slippers.

"Uh...oh, Elmo sell (fell)," she said to me one day.

"What should we do?" I asked.

"Pick it up," Ashley astutely responded.

The circles of communication we were opening and closing with her would have made Dr. Wieder very pleased. Now, when I asked her to do something, she followed my instructions.

"Okay, Mommy!"

Talk about tugging at my heart! I didn't think it could get any better than to hear my recently non-verbal, non-social daughter come back and respond in a way that just made me so very lucky to be her Mommy!

Now when Dave's car pulled into the garage, Ashley recognized the sound of the garage door opening.

"Daddy home!" she shouted, and ran to the door to greet him.

And the time I saw Ashley fighting with Kacey over something, I was so tickled to see Ashley push Kacey away.

"Stop it, Kacey!" Ashley said, seeming angry.

Ashley now became more assertive and did not just ignore Kacey anymore and walk away when Kacey teased her. Ashley now stood her ground and expressed herself. Like Tomatis stated, "Finding one's voice is finding oneself."[18]

That's when she started to say, "No!"

When I tried to get her dressed, she screamed, "No!" and took off her clothes. When I asked her if she wanted a particular food, she said, "No!" and put her hands out to push all advances of food away.

Everything was "No!"

I didn't know at first if these reactions were the terrible twos or a reaction to all of the listening stimulation, or just that of a tired little girl who was subjected to so much more than any other two-year-old we knew. But in all of our opinions (Dave's, our therapists and mine), this was the terrible twos! They were in full bloom. She was a month shy of turning three-years-old.

In a quick four months, Ashley had gone from "easy baby" (not caring much about anyone or anything), to talking, singing, and expressing herself as an individual in true toddler fashion. Changes were happening so fast and furious with Ashley that I never knew which personality I'd get each day—a happy Ashley using her new words and communicating her wants and needs, or a cranky toddler whose independence was emerging.

But isn't that the way all normal toddlers are—happy one minute, then throwing themselves on the floor kicking and screaming the next? It was now refreshing to compare her with her peers and the behaviors that sweep over them at that age. Just like any parent of a toddler, we had to keep switching gears and tactics to keep up with her emotions.

But the more I observed Ashley coming alive, joining us as a family, and making her way out of the fog that she had hidden herself in for so long, the more I came to wonder about the initial diagnosis. Was the diagnosis of autism that Dr. Conlon put on Ashley when she was 21-months-old wrong? (We certainly didn't see her as autistic now.) Or was it correct for the time it was diagnosed; but that Tomatis, Mozart and her other supporting therapies were pulling Ashley out of it?

By the end of the third loop, Ashley was asking simple questions.

"Where Mommy go?"

She was answering our questions with detail.

"Uh...oh, spill water," she told me, looking at her foot.

"Where did you spill?" I asked her.

---

18. Pierre Sollier, Tomatis Method, "Autism," http://www.Tomatis.com.

"On my toe."

"Uh…oh, boo boo," she said, pointing to her leg.

"What happened?" I asked with a concerned tone.

"Marker on my leg," she said, recalling she had marked herself up while drawing.

Ashley was becoming even more interested in her bedtime stories and really understanding the plots. Peter Rabbit was becoming her favorite bedtime story, and I was amazed that she could follow the story as well as she could.

"What did Peter do?" I asked.

"Went under gate," she replied.

"Where did he go?" I threw another question at her.

"Misser Gegger garden," she told me.

"Good talking, Ashley!" I said to her.

She could tell us snippets of the story using the pictures as a guide, or answer questions that I posed to her from the story.

On the last day of the third loop, Dave and I met with Rochelle for our end of treatment consult. Ashley was in the listening room. Rochelle just couldn't say enough positive things about how Ashley was progressing, remembering how Ashley was when she first entered the program four months earlier.

"I have to tell you, Ashley is just amazing! There's more two-way language with less prompting. She's using two hands together more. Her vocal work with the microphone is going very well. I was just in to see her in the listening room, and she said, "Hi!" to me. She's alert. She knows her surroundings more. She's saying all the therapists' names spontaneously. It's wonderful to see!" Rochelle said, with enthusiasm.

I was very encouraged by what she was telling us.

"We are just so pleased with the results. We didn't know she would respond so well to the therapy, but clearly this is what she needed. This was the piece of the puzzle that was missing for Ashley to come back to us. But I'm a little nervous. Do you think she'll regress any?" I asked.

"It's possible that you may see a little bit, but her response has been so dramatic, that I'll bet she's just going to keep moving forward," Rochelle said, positively.

I was learning that after three loops of Tomatis therapy, children incur enough changes so the results usually do hold, especially in a child who talks enough to naturally stimulate her ear.

"To summarize what we've done with Ashley, the first 15 days was intensive work on the body. Ashley received more of the lower, vestibular-based frequencies to start the loop—before we began the filtering process—which came about halfway during the first loop. The second loop, she worked on pre-language. We opened up the microphone and just let her say or babble anything, just so she could hear her own voice. There was really no agenda. The third loop she worked on the language. This was the more structured microphone work—the talking, the labeling. We used her own language to stimulate the language center of the brain to get her more connected with her own voice and really worked on the ear-voice relationship." Rochelle explained to us.

"I want to keep this up and build on what we're seeing. Ashley is responding so well, that I'd like her to do another eight-day loop in about three months. She's accomplished so much! We're going to push the language. We tried at the end of this loop to do what's called SREs with Ashley. SREs are 'siblant repeat exercises.' A woman comes on the headphones and tells a little story, and Ashley is asked to repeat the words. Each day the words turn into more syllables and then phrases. Each day the woman's voice gets more filtered with the low frequencies being removed from the words so it sounds muffled. Ashley really didn't want to do these this time, but it's not a big deal. She's young. We expect that the younger children will show resistance to these. She may not be quite ready for these yet. We didn't want to push her. I'd like to try them next loop and see how she does. I'd like to test her prior to the next loop," Rochelle said, sounding encouraged by Ashley's results.

"In the meantime, I'm going to prescribe what's called Samonas. It's a home listening program that works on continuing to stimulate the auditory channel through modulated music, rich in high frequencies. Ashley should do her Samonas twice a day, if possible. This information will tell you all of the minutes for each disc I want Ashley to listen to," Rochelle continued, handing me the sheet.

"You'll need to order these discs and start in two weeks. This will give Ashley's system a chance to calm down from this third loop. If you have any concerns, please call me and we'll discuss it. Do you have any questions?"

"Not about that, but I did want to ask you something. Ashley's still having problems with her stools being runny and very odorous. You had mentioned a doctor that many parents here go to see. Could I have his number? I've been hearing parents talk about him, and I think it may be time for Ashley to be seen by him," I said.

"Oh, that's Dr. Layton. He's very good," Rochelle said, and wrote his number down and handed it to me.

"Well, if there are no other concerns, let's have a follow-up phone consult in four or five weeks."

"Great, thanks Rochelle!" Dave and I said in unison.

"Ashley looks great!" Rochelle said, as we all smiled and walked out of her office.

We made our way back to the waiting room to greet Ashley when she returned from the therapy room. The other parents were also coming back from wherever they had been for the past two hours, and we were talking to one another.

"Is this your first loop?" one parent asked me.

"No, this is actually our last day of the third loop," I said, with a look of satisfaction and relief on my face.

"Did you see a lot of changes?" another parent tuning into our conversation asked me.

"Ashley has made terrific progress from day two of the first loop! We are just thrilled with this therapy. It really worked for her!" I told them.

"This is our first loop. What should we be looking for in terms of changes?" another parent asked.

"Be sure to write down every new thing you see. It may not seem like it's a big deal at the time, but they add up, and you really notice the change," I said to her.

"Ashley went in humming; now she is talking. She is potty training. She is eating a variety of foods; the textures don't bother her so much anymore. Her neurological system seems more corrected from balance to behavior. Take note of it all," I added, reassuring them.

"Good luck!" I said.

As I finished my conversation with that parent, I heard the elevator door open and the children started flying into the waiting room. Ashley came running to us. The listening therapist came over to us and told us what a great day Ashley had.

"She did a really nice job on her audio-vocal work. She was labeling flashcards and singing. She completed a 24-piece puzzle with minimal assistance for focus. She showed good fine motor control stacking blocks up high. She did well," the therapist told us.

"Ashley has come so far. We are really thrilled with her progress," I told her.

"She's a doll! Ashley you take care!" the therapist said, giving her a high-five with her hand.

As we got up to leave the room, the other therapists finished up their conversations and came over to hug Ashley and say good-bye. I knew they were all going to miss her. We took some pictures of Ashley with her new grown-up friends.

Some Really Bad Vibes

Our three loops of the Tomatis therapy were over. Auditory training was so worthwhile and beneficial to Ashley. Dave and I were thrilled with the results.

But at the same time, we were exhausted. We were sad to leave the new friends Ashley had made with all the therapists, and we knew our little girl in pigtails was going to be greatly missed. But we were returning in three months for a fourth loop, so we would see them again soon. But they were three much needed months to rest and get our lives back on track to the normal daily routines.

Each loop of Tomatis therapy meant driving hundreds of miles, having Dave's parents rearrange their schedules to watch the other two children for extended periods of time while Dave, I or both of us were with Ashley. It was a burden on a lot of people. But it was all for the sake of Ashley.

As recommended by Rochelle, Ashley was to be put on a listening maintenance program at home following the conclusion of the third loop. We waited two weeks before starting the Samonas, so Ashley's ears could settle down from the stimulation they had received from the third loop.

The CDs we purchased arrived in the mail along with the headphones. She was to listen to one of the CDs for five minutes twice a day until the fifth day. Then we were to increase the listening by one minute every day until day ten.

On day ten, we were to introduce the second CD for one minute, twice a day. We were to keep this up daily until we were at a maximum of 10 minutes for the first CD and 5 minutes for the second CD, twice a day.

We occupied Ashley's time while she listened. We stacked puzzles in front of her to complete. We had crayons and paper for her to use—endless activities, so as to not let her drift off or become bored and remove the headphones. We put a fanny pack on her with the CD in it for the times she wanted to be mobile while listening.

We incorporated Samonas into our daily routine. Ashley complied with it and even started to look forward to it. She seemed to enjoy it. We saw great improvement in her listening ability and with her language. When the kitchen timer rang after listening was over, she knew just what to do.

"Headphones oss" (off), she said, and went about playing.

Samonas was a continuation of the program Ashley had been receiving at the Spectrum Center. It was prescribed to keep the listening channels of her brain open and to work on distinguishing high and low frequencies. I think it was doing its job.

But in addition to it, we saw something else that we attributed to the listening, since this was the newest component to her therapy that we had recently thrown into the pot stirring it up.

Ashley's behavior deteriorated at times. What used to not bother her, now did. It seemed like the tiniest thing would set her off. Sometimes after swinging Ashley on the platform swing in our basement, I'd leave the swing up. But she demanded that it be taken down.

"Swing down, Mommy! Swing down!" she said, crying to me.

I didn't know why this bothered her so much, but it did, so I took it down. Sometimes if Sydney's baby's swing moved, without Sydney in it, Ashley caught it out of the corner of her eye and went over and stopped it. Sometimes she would just stand for a little while holding onto the swing keeping a safe hand on it, almost in tears. I couldn't figure out why this upset her.

At speech and OT, she usually had no problem leaving me and going in with the therapists. But now, she refused to go with them. She walked a few steps in the direction of their offices, but turned around, screamed and ran back to me as if it were her first day there. She had been going there for more than a year. What was going on?

She was full of anxiety. One evening, Dave left to play cards with some of the guys. Ashley was extremely upset and stood at the garage door and cried for nearly 20 minutes.

"Daddy, Daddy, Daddy!" she continued to shout.

I couldn't console her.

Another time, thinking it would be good for her low tone, I took her to a gymnastics class. I thought bouncing on the trampoline and running through some obstacle courses would be good for her. But she screamed the entire time we were there and demanded that she keep her shoes on while on the mats. The instructor scolded me several times for allowing Ashley to walk on the mats with her shoes. I was kicked out of the gym. I had to carry Ashley, still screaming, in one arm and carry Sydney in her infant car seat in the other. Kacey tagged behind us pouting, wondering why we had to leave so soon. I felt really bad for her. We exited the class with all eyes glaring at me. I so much wanted to say, "What, your child's never had a tantrum before?" Why was this place bothering Ashley so much? I didn't understand.

Ashley now had separation anxiety upon bringing her to pre-school in the mornings. She cried and cried and did not want me to leave. But when I returned to pick her up, the report I got from the teacher was wonderful.

"She seemed to really fit in today, as if she came here full time. She was more at ease, did her work, and she led the class in the song 'Head, Shoulders Knees and Toes.' She was happier than I've ever seen her," her teacher informed me.

"Wow, really?" I asked.

So why was Ashley behaving so oddly at times and having all of these screaming fits? She even smacked the glasses off Tina one day during OT. That was not the Ashley that I knew!

I called Rochelle at the Spectrum Center to inform her we were on day seven of the Samonas, and that Ashley was up to seven minutes with one of the discs. I explained the awful behavior and screaming, flailing tantrums we were seeing—in addition to this great burst of language.

She informed us most children do well on the Samonas and actually need it to stay modulated, but maybe Ashley was the opposite—maybe it was stimulating her too much. She was a little girl, and maybe her system couldn't take it. She advised us to stop the Samonas for a week to see what happens with her behavior.

We stopped as Rochelle advised. Two days later, Ashley was different. She didn't have such a short fuse. She was more relaxed with very little whining and crankiness.

I took Ashley to the Fair at our recreation center. There were many stations set up for the children. We went over to where a lady was churning butter. Ashley milked a (fake) cow. There was face and hand painting. Ashley didn't mind at all getting a flower painted on her hand. She did some arts and crafts and went fishing for a surprise toy. Ashley wandered over to where a woman was playing a guitar and singing children's songs. Ashley started singing and dancing to the music, while parents nudged their children to join her. Everyone was clapping and enjoying Ashley's performance. She was enjoying herself as well, feeling uninhibited and having a blast! Ashley got a real charge out of the event, and her new personality was showing. She was so alive and vibrant!

We re-started Samonas a week after stopping it. Her behavior deteriorated again, but her language was taking off like never before. One day Ashley put her socks on wrong and came to me for help. For one, she was gaining the motor planning to be able to pull her socks on and off. I was extremely excited to see that. It had taken a long time for that skill to emerge. For another, she was telling me what she really wanted.

"Tun it awound, Mommy," she said, asking for assistance.

She was more engaging, talkative, pointing, showing us things of interest, and potty training better each day. But the Samonas was clearly bringing out a little bit of emotional instability in Ashley that we just didn't anticipate at all. At certain times, she would just fly off the handle about the most inconsequential things. But to her, these were real issues.

"Baby Sydney, Baby Sydney! No!" she yelled at me, as I left the room to change Sydney's diaper.

She now wanted to be close to Sydney. She even asked to hold the baby. Ashley would put her arms around Sydney and give her a big hug. Wow—how loving!

Through all of her therapy, Ashley's system was being corrected to that of a normal child. But it never dawned on me the behaviors previously suppressed in her, those seen when a child is coming into toddlerhood, would naturally come out once her system had righted itself. I thought we had escaped them. But we weren't going to get off the hook that easily! Mother Nature was not going to let us miss this wonderful developmental stage!

When Ashley's tantrum got going, Dave and I had to stand back and watch the tornado whiz by. She would remove all her clothes in anger. If I tried to change her wet training pants, she would follow me to the trash can and try to pull the dirty one out of the trash screaming when I didn't let her have it.

"Why do you want dirty pants?" I asked her.

Maybe it was a comfort thing. She never liked change. But, dirty training pants?

Transitions were throwing her off kilter a little bit. She insisted on doing everything herself, and screamed if we did it for her. If this was normal, it was becoming unbearable. I didn't like seeing Ashley this way. And frankly, it was disruptive to our daily life. I really thought Samonas was supposed to be beneficial. But it was bringing out the monster child in her.

We stopped the Samonas for good after speaking with Rochelle again about Ashley's behavior. Dave and I agreed Ashley may be having a negative reaction to the music; the stimulation too much for her little system to handle.

After stopping the Samonas for a second time, Ashley was having really good days again. She was more even-keeled, not throwing tantrums as often, and not being as whiney. But she was still "a bit" (okay, "very much") strong-willed. I think she just wanted to prove she could do things for herself now instead of us always doing them for her, as we had become accustomed. As easy as it was to go into her drawer and find a pair of pajamas for her to wear, she would scream at us for doing so.

"No, put back in drawer," she'd say to us, and then she'd go find a pair on her own.

I had to learn to step back and let her gain her independence. I had to "cut the cord" and realize that Ashley was now becoming a normal little girl, and that I was interfering with her growing up and doing things for herself.

She no longer needed me to be so doting. I always still wanted to do things for her—it was faster that way. But she felt she could do it now. And I had to let her. If she wanted my help, I knew she could now formulate the sentence and ask for it!

CHAPTER 12

▼

DATA SCHMATA!

By now, Ashley was in speech and occupational therapy, special education from the county, and we were doing Greenspan's Floor Time. I had put together a home-based occupational therapy program, and we had completed three loops of Tomatis. Ashley was still on a GFCF diet. I felt I was doing the very best I could and was headed in a pretty good direction with her treatments.

As a result of the recent laboratory testing on her stools, which detected a very high secretory IgA (sIgA) value, I thought it best to update Ashley's pediatrician on her status, as well as get his opinion of her stool results. I hadn't spoken to him in nearly a year regarding Ashley's therapies. It had been that long since Ashley had seen him for a cold or infection. Surprisingly, she had not been sick during that time period. But, he was receiving correspondences from Dr. Conlon, our neurodevelopmental pediatrician, who we saw periodically, so I assumed her pediatrician was staying updated through Dr. Conlon's reports. If Ashley's pediatrician had any concerns about anything we were doing, I never heard it from him—he never called.

During a doctor's appointment for Sydney, I mentioned to him Ashley's high sIgA level, the lack of good bacteria in her system and the overgrowth of yeast. I was seeking his interpretation of the results. I hadn't brought the results with me, but I was trying to determine if any of this could be detrimental to her health. I didn't think it was healthy to have a leaky gut. I wanted to get a referral for a gastroenterologist to delve further into her gut. I had also heard some children did well on Nystatin for their yeast overgrowth, and did Ashley need that?

"I've never heard of the labs you just mentioned. Sounds a bit strange to me," he said, a little wary about trusting results from a lab he had not recommended.

"Why did you use those labs? Who recommended them?"

"We are consulting with a nutritionist. These are very reputable laboratories in the Midwest. They have highly specific testing methods on gut issues. Ashley's got what's called a 'leaky gut.' As I understand it, because of all the antibiotics she received for ear infections over the years, her gut has been depleted of the good bacteria. There is also yeast in her stool. We now have her on probiotics. She's taking lactobacillus and bifidobacteria, but they don't seem to be taking hold. Her stools are very runny and odorous. We've also got her on a GFCF diet. She doesn't get wheat or dairy products."

"There's always going to be a little bit of yeast in the gut. That doesn't seem abnormal to me. But I really need to see the results. Send them to me."

He went back to writing a prescription for Sydney. He diagnosed her with an ear infection.

"Is there another way we can treat Sydney's ear infection? I'm not sure I want to give her antibiotics," I said, very protective now of my third daughter's gut.

Since the time she was a baby, the other physicians in that practice and he had prescribed those antibiotics for Ashley. I wasn't pointing fingers, but he must have sensed where I was going.

"Mrs. Ruben, we treat ear infections with antibiotics. That's medical practice. You can let it go, but I don't advise it. The ear is pretty red," he said, dissuading me from doing so.

I took the prescription from him anyway.

"Do you have any other autistic patients in your practice, besides Ashley?" I asked.

"There is one boy about eight-years-old who we see here," he said.

"Do you know what the family is doing in terms of therapy? Do you know how he's doing?" I questioned him.

"I think he's doing better. I don't know what therapies they are pursuing, but every now and then, I do see the traits (of autism) in him," he told me.

"What are your thoughts about the Measles, Mumps and Rubella (MMR) vaccine? About autism and vaccinations?" I asked.

"There is no data to suggest the MMR causes autism," he said, sounding sure of himself.

"There are plenty of parents who think otherwise—they have seen their children slip away after this vaccine. I know some personally, and I've read stories about others," I told him.

"Again, nothing *I've read* in the medical journals suggests to me that I shouldn't give this vaccine to my patients. I would be more concerned about the need to protect your children from those diseases than about a connection between vaccines and autism. There is no proof of that," he said, writing notes in Sydney's chart.

"I'm just nervous about giving it to Sydney when she's due for it…about the Thimerosal, I mean."

"Thimerosal is no longer in vaccines," he tried to reassure me.

He seemed pretty casual about the use of vaccines. But I wasn't drawn into his laissez-faire attitude. As a mother with one daughter on the spectrum, I didn't want to be going through this all over again with another one. I was concerned—and rightly so! Even if there was no concrete proof in the medical journals of a linkage between the MMR vaccine and autism, the suspicions were still evident. There were scores of children suffering from this disorder, and they had metals in their systems. Their parents were adamant that their children's condition arose from this vaccination. Surely, the pediatrician could have offered something more compassionate than a blanket statement of, "There's no data!"

None of what I said penetrated him. It didn't hit close to home like it did me. He didn't have a large population of autistic children. He had one. Now, with Ashley, he had two. Not enough, I guess, to either become educated about autism or have concerns about how a vaccine could possibly affect our children. He wasn't staring at this disorder all day, every day. I now had genuine fears about vaccines that didn't warrant being brushed aside, because he had no conclusive evidence from a medical journal. My life had dramatically changed due to this disorder. Where it came from, I don't know exactly, but I was trying to possibly avoid it a second time. I wasn't about to play "vaccination roulette" with Sydney.

I learned in the autistic community, parents play so much more of a role than even the child's pediatrician. It was certainly true in my case! He was not "in the know" about a lot of what I had recently researched about autism. I was the one who sought out these specialists and these therapies. I was the conductor of this train. He seemed to have nothing to offer me in terms of direction or map, because he had nothing to draw upon without a populace of autism found in his own practice. I was solo in this. But what I was trying to get across to him was that, although some of the testing I had done on Ashley, and some of the specialists we were seeing were foreign to him, they were not foreign to the community of parents who were out there trying anything and everything to help their children on the spectrum.

With respect to diet and nutrition, he could obviously see from Ashley's prior examinations she was thin, weak and near the bottom of the standard growth chart. Now we knew that sensory integration dysfunction and motor planning played a role in Ashley's limited diet. He never raised these sensory and motor issues with us, and he never, ever, hinted at her being autistic back then when he examined her.

Maybe I didn't pose the right questions to him when she was younger, but maybe he didn't ask them of me, either! Where was his checklist? Not just of her developmental milestones of walking and talking, but where were the questions about if my daughter spun around constantly, or if she could point? Where were the questions about if she fixated on objects or continuously watched a fan spin or flapped her hands or walked on her toes or only ate crunchy foods? He was the doctor! He was the one who went to medical school!—to learn this stuff! Why was I more in the know now than he was?

I brought my anger home and told Dave about the pediatrician's cold reception to all we were doing with Ashley—about his sermon on data.

"Sharon, he's a generalist. He probably has no other patients with autism," Dave said.

That's not true. He told me he has one boy who is about eight, but that he's doing well—whatever that means! I don't know what his parent's have done for him, but it didn't sound like they were seeing all the specialists we are or treating him with similar therapies, or the doctor would have recognized these interventions and our specialists. Or maybe he's just not involved in any aspect of this boy's treatment, similar to how he's not all that involved with us, either," I told Dave.

"I doubt a lot of people out there are doing as much as we are. We've got her involved in everything!" Dave said, believing we were doing all the right things for Ashley.

"Let's look into finding a different pediatrician. Would that make you feel better?" he asked.

"But we've been with him and his practice for so long. You want us to start all over looking for a new doctor? I would have to take the time to pound the pavement looking for someone who may be just as naïve," I said, feeling weight being added to my already sagging shoulders.

"But we need someone who understands us. We speak a different language now, Sharon. This pediatrician has no idea about any of this! If he's not the right one for us to bring Ashley to anymore, let's find someone who's more educated about autism," he said.

I pulled out the phone book and turned to the yellow pages. I went down the list of doctors close to home and found a few.

The next day I called them. My choices were made easier, as only one of them was accepting new patients. I made an appointment.

I dropped the girls off with Dave's parents and went to interview this new doctor.

I stepped into the waiting room. I was immediately disappointed. It was small, not too clean, and rundown. I sat and watched a mother try to control her child sitting next to me. She couldn't. I immediately thought he had some type of behavioral problem. In trying to control his behavior, she mentioned he was just "all boy"—her call, not mine!

I knew I couldn't go around labeling everyone I saw with autism, now that I knew what to look for in its characteristics. But if my sweet Ashley had a problem, why didn't these other children I saw in stores or in the neighborhood or in the doctor's office? Or maybe they did, their parents just didn't know about it. Or maybe they knew and didn't want to talk about it, like I had not wanted to early on. It's not something you just start a conversation off with.

I was led in the doctor's office by a nurse. I sat and waited for the doctor to finish her rounds. I gazed around the room. There was a half-eaten salad in the middle of a messy desk. Her shelves were filled, not with medical books, but with specimen tubes and collection material—a makeshift closet.

I had a gut feeling she probably wasn't what I was looking for in a new doctor. First impressions are everything—and I hadn't even met her yet. But when she walked in, she seemed rather pleasant and was well dressed—I hadn't envisioned her this way from the looks of her office—you know, "cluttered desk, cluttered mind" thing.

I told her I was looking for a new pediatrician—one familiar with autism. She told me she saw a few autistic patients. (That was a few more than our current pediatrician, so maybe I was in the right place.)

She also told me about her son, now 18, who had autism, and who was doing rather well, but it hadn't always been that way.

I felt like she really knew where I was coming from, and I shared with her some of the specialists I had been to see. She didn't know of these particular specialists I had spoken of, nor had she heard of the things we were doing with Ashley's gut or the auditory training. She seemed amazed at the lingo I threw her way when I told her about what we had been doing for Ashley so far. She was certainly impressed and rather interested in hearing more.

However, I felt like I was, again, "teaching the doctor." That's not why I was searching for a new pediatrician. I was seeking guidance. She could no more offer me guidance and insight about treatments than my own pediatrician. And she was a parent who was personally touched by this disorder. She provided nothing novel into Ashley's journey of recovery. She thought I was doing a wonderful job as it was.

After our conversation, I left, walked back to my car and weighed my options. I felt I found another person who could empathize with me, someone with an autistic perspective. But I didn't reap a whole lot from her and couldn't see changing pediatricians—even if she did see some autistic children. I wouldn't be learning any more from her. She obviously wasn't involved in any aspect of her autistic patients' treatments, except maybe in the capacity like ours—a person we kept apprised of Ashley's progress, but who could offer us nothing more on our journey.

So I had found no better deal in her. I couldn't change the layout of her waiting room. I couldn't make it bigger or more comfortable or more kid-friendly like our pediatric office waiting room. What I needed to do was go back to our pediatrician and change his way of thinking toward autism and convince him that what we were doing with Ashley was right—that she was progressing from these therapies. Maybe...I *did* need to "teach the doctor" after all!

And that's when I gave him his first lesson in *Advocating for Your Child 101*. True, he was a pretty decent doctor when it came to my children's colds and runny noses. He often drew text-book pictures of the middle ear on the examination table's paper to further explain an ear infection. And he could write a prescription for antibiotics like a champ! But on the topic of Ashley and autism, he fell short. In my opinion, he didn't make the grade. So I felt he needed to be converted—and educated.

I was back in his office for one of Sydney's well-baby appointments. This time I brought Dave along—cool-headed Dave. I knew I would need him to carry on after I became enraged with the doctor not seeing things my way. He had a tendency to do that.

After the doctor examined Sydney, I talked to him about Ashley.

"I really would like you to recommend a gastroenterologist so we can see what's going on in her gut. I sent you the lab reports. Did you review them? I never heard back from you," I asked.

"I did take a look at them. Specifically, what are her stools like?' he asked.

"They're still runny, they're odorous, and they just aren't normal to me. They are actually noxious!" I said, being very frank.

"The probiotics weren't working, so we stopped them. Ashley's also had terrible tantrums. We didn't know if it was related to the probiotics or not, but we stopped them. I'm just concerned that there may be something we're overlooking—something more serious going on in her gut that could be dangerous to her. Something just isn't right," I said, very worried and near tears.

"How is her speech?" he asked, for the first time in about a year.

"Ashley has really started to come around. She is in speech and occupational therapy twice a week, she receives services from the county twice a week, and we are doing a method called "Floor Time" that teaches her emotional and social development through playing with toys on the floor. We have done three loops of auditory training—the Tomatis Method—and she is on a gluten-free/casein-free diet," I said, summarizing the treatment therapies.

"I'm really sold on Tomatis. I really think this has been extremely beneficial for her."

"What are you doing, again?" he asked.

"It's called the Tomatis Method. Ashley's ears are being re-trained to listen better using high frequency Mozart music. It has helped her to talk and has worked on her motor planning and sensory integration issues. She's singing. She's more affectionate with us. She's playing with Kacey. She's just so different now. I wish you could see her."

"Where are you doing this?" he asked.

"It's at the Spectrum Center in Bethesda. You should recommend this to other parents. Go to Tomatis.com or Spectrumcenter.com and read about it," I advised him.

"What kind of data is there to prove it works?" he asked, sounding a bit doubtful.

Was he not *listening* to me? Did he not believe me? Was he trying to discredit all we had done with Ashley—all of her progress, all of our hard work? Did he think someone couldn't possibly overcome this disorder? That the literature—if he even read any of it—told him autism was a life-long disability, and his rigid thinking couldn't enable him to see past the medical world's grim prognosis of the disorder? Was this concept just too far out there—that this was happening to Ashley—that she was actually getting better? He told me himself (a year and a half earlier) that it was going to be a tough road for me. Did he not think I was up for the challenge?

Data Schmata! Why did I need data? I had proof in Ashley! She was my data! Had he never heard of these types of therapies in anything he read? What was he reading, and who was he talking to that kept him so uninformed about a disorder that is reaching epidemic proportions. These are children. He's a pediatrician! He should know this stuff! But he didn't.

I didn't have data for him. What I had was a whole head full of knowledge about autism, interventions both conventional and non-conventional, and anecdotes from other parents and specialists in the field with which to convince him that what we were doing was right for Ashley—and it seemed to be right for so many others on this journey.

But he was very skeptical about it all—from the labs we used, to the results we saw with Tomatis. I became really annoyed with the fact that my own pediatrician wasn't very receptive to our measures to help our daughter with such a baffling disorder like autism—measures thousands of parents just like me were taking.

Since he didn't have the background in autistic disorders or a slew of patients from which to draw knowledge, he could only spew out, again, what he was taught in school.

"I practice medicine by the book. Medical research is needed to back up any type of theory. If there is conclusive data from the research, we can then take it and apply it to our practice," he said, sounding a bit like my freshman biology teacher.

Hey, I have a Bachelors degree in Biology and a Masters degree in Biotechnology Management! He wasn't telling me something I didn't already know. And he wasn't talking to a dummy! I've spent my entire career in research and clinical trials. If there was one thing I did know about, it was clinical trial data!

But this was Ashley we were talking about! Speaking on behalf of thousands of other parents with a child on the autistic spectrum, I didn't have time to sit and wait for someone to collect data from clinical trials on whether these approaches worked or not, while my daughter was left to withdraw inside of herself even more. I needed these treatments now! I went to the specialists who I found to be some of the best in the autistic community. Obviously, I wouldn't do anything to put Ashley's health in jeopardy—that's why I had a therapy team on board. And that's why I was opening up to him now, so I could have a medical safety net if I needed to bounce things off him regarding testing or treatments.

But I realized at that moment I had come to the wrong person. Just because he was Ashley's pediatrician, I guess I assumed he would be open-minded to any avenues we pursued with Ashley. But given our opposition on nearly everything relating to the topic of autism—and because there isn't a whole lot of hard-core proof out there with a lot of treatment therapies—I was clearly giving him more credit than I should have, thinking he was both interested in our methods of treatment and empathetic toward those afflicted with this disorder.

Maybe these weren't common practices to him, but they were becoming common in the community of children on the autistic spectrum, and I thought he should become familiar with them. If Ashley was in his practice, I thought it was worth his while to get to know a little bit about her disorder, the autistic community we were now involved in, and bring whatever information he could to our situation. But he was unwilling.

Dave took over the conversation. I couldn't take any more of it. After what seemed like pulling teeth, he got the doctor to write out a referral for a gastroenterologist. So, the doctor bent, just a smidgen. I felt we were now being heard, and that he was acquainting himself with some things about Ashley that he needed to know. Maybe by doing so, he could help other children on the spectrum in the future—should he ever have another one in his practice.

We all agreed it was Ashley who mattered most in all of this. But if I was the one leading this journey, I was going to map it out my way. The doctor agreed to be more receptive to some of the methods I was employing, but he was not willing to depart from his way of practicing medicine. He still believed there needed to be hard-core evidence to suggest these therapies worked, before he felt comfortable in recommending them. But I wasn't willing to *not* try something that seemed promising, just because the research wasn't there yet. And I wasn't alone in that thinking.

The parents of children on the spectrum, with whom I had now become acquainted, clearly weren't concerned that medical journals weren't "spilling over" with data. Their children seemed to be doing better from the various treatments they were researching and employing—that's all the proof we need sometimes!

A few weeks later, Dave and I took Ashley to see a gastroenterologist to discuss her leaky gut. My agenda had been to get his opinion of the laboratory results, as well as talk to him about putting Ashley on Nystatin for her yeast over-growth.

The gastroenterologist examined Ashley and found nothing wrong with her, except she was small and thin. After reviewing the laboratory results from our stool analysis and the sIgA results, he suggested we re-try the probiotics—and to be patient, because it could take a while to see results. He didn't recommend Nystatin. He knew our nutritionist, Kelly Dorfman, and her practice with alternative therapies. He thought she practiced in a very reasonable way and didn't

find her to be guiding people into dangerous therapies, even if they were therapies that neither he nor my pediatrician advocated in the absence of clinical data.

He talked to us a little about celiac disease as being associated with autism, but
that tests couldn't be run on Ashley if she was on a gluten-free diet. He too,
counseled us on restricting too many foods from her diet, which could cause failure to thrive. We had a good understanding of the diet. That was not an issue. I
also informed him we were supplementing Ashley's diet with a calcium formula
Kelly prescribed. We weren't about to take Ashley off of her GFCF diet for the
sake of a blood test for celiac disease. We thought the diet was beneficial—we
didn't even entertain that thought.

CHAPTER 13

▼

"GRAND IN" EVERY WAY

We kissed the girls good-bye and left them with their Uncle to baby-sit for the day. Dave and I had reservations at a luncheon to a "Young Children with Special Needs" conference. Temple Grandin, the most famous autistic woman in the world today, was the guest speaker. It was the summer of 2002. I had read one of her books, "*Thinking in Pictures*" and countless other stories about her. Her control and management over her autism was inspiring. Having been told by my specialists that one day Ashley may be a "Temple Grandin," fueled me to learn all I could about what Ashley could become through this famous person—Ashley already had visual gifts.

Temple's book described her growing up with autism, (full of extremely hard times coping with the disorder), being out of touch with everyone, and seeking sensory input from a squeeze machine she designed. She has tremendously gifted visual attributes and has succeeded over the years in her chosen field of animal science, designing livestock handling facilities. She is living proof one could overcome this disorder and become anything.

I didn't know what to expect of Temple. I had never met an adult with autism. I read she thinks in terms of pictures, a video recorder constantly playing in her mind. She struggled with socializing and reading people's emotions and lacked understanding of human relationships. Her livestock handling equipment designs are just incredible. I couldn't wait to hear about her journey. I was so interested to see how it would all play out. How would she relate to her audience?

What would she sound like? Would she have a rapport with us? Would she have unique mannerisms about her that would be obvious to the eye? I wondered about all of these things as we drove to the conference.

Dave and I sat down at a large table in a banquet room. Conference participants started filing in for the luncheon with Temple. As we all sat at our table and started on the salad, I looked up to find the one empty seat at our table being pulled out.

"I'd prefer not to sit at a table for one," a voice said, referring to the empty table in front of the podium.

I was awestruck. It was pretty unbelievable (and such a story unfolding to tell everyone back home) that Temple Grandin had chosen to sit down and eat her lunch at our table before her lecture. I couldn't help but stare, in a polite kind of way. She was dressed rather trade-mark-looking in an embroidered long-sleeved cowboy shirt with a red scarf around her neck. She wore black jeans with a bovine belt buckle.

She immediately started talking to everyone at our table, and we started listening and talking to her. I was very much absorbed with what she was telling us about her early childhood, as much as I could hear over the din of knives and forks striking on the china. And I still politely stared.

Questions were asked of Temple, and she openly shared her responses with us. She talked about her very structured days as a child, yet how she was given downtime each day to just be "autistic," and retreat back into her world without interruption. She had a nanny who taught her the art of turn-taking and sharing—a rather abstract concept to an autistic person. She spoke of her many sensory issues as a child and the famous "squeeze machine" she built and would put herself into to relieve her pressure cravings. She spoke of her intolerances to new clothing which she could not stand—it made her skin crawl. Consequently, she would give her new clothing away. Only very worn-in clothing felt comfortable to her. She found staying in hotels to be most annoying. The sound of elevator bells going off would render her sleepless at night. Yet, the atmosphere of a busy airport was tolerable. Airport sounds were different frequencies that didn't pierce her brain the way hotel noises did.

Her pet peeve was the ring of a cell phone—she was very sensitive to this sound which always disrupted her train of thought instantly—especially in the middle of one of her lectures!

She finished her lunch and pushed her half-eaten rubbery chicken and undercooked rice aside. She reached for the slice of chocolate cake.

"Now, this is the real food of life!" she said, proceeding to devour it.

We all grinned. I felt Temple seemed quite normal.

If this had been an unknown conference participant talking to us, or an unknown CEO of a company, instead of Temple Grandin, I wouldn't have been the wiser that this person had autism. I came already knowing what I did about her, but she surprised me, I have to admit. I was struck by how she was not the picture of autism that I had read so much about in my search for answers for Ashley (i.e., little eye contact, lack of social skills, self-stimulatory behaviors).

In my opinion, she seemed remarkably normal—almost untouched by the disorder. She had a sense of humor and got the others sitting at our table rolling with laughter. But then, I never saw her laugh at her own jokes—perhaps her autism showing through to me for the first time in not being able to elicit emotion. She seemed to have overcome a lot of what I had read she was like as a child. If she was hiding any of her sensory integration issues, intolerances to certain pitches of noise or anxiety-causing situations, she did it with great accuracy—and a few milligrams of antidepressants, she confided to us.

Soon a conference director came over and whispered in Temple's ear saying it was time for her to start her lecture. Temple got up and surveyed the table looking for an extra glass of water. Not finding one at our table, she was not shy in going to the next table to grab one from an empty spot.

She made her way to the podium and attached the microphone to her shirt as the conference director reminded us that Temple had sensory intolerances to the noise of silverware (not to mention hundreds of it) tapping on plates. While imploring us to be sensitive to her issues, Temple interrupted her.

"Just eat your chicken with your fingers! I don't care!"

The room exploded in laughter. We followed her orders and threw our manners aside. She began her slide show.

She gave us a look into how a visual thinker, such as herself, sees the world. She offered up things that she has found over the years to be useful in managing the disorder.

She showed slides that she used as metaphors to tell her story. She stopped at one slide of a cabin lit up in a snowy dark forest.

"This is how the brain looks through MRI (magnetic resonance imaging) when an autistic person feels any type of emotion. There is only one part of the brain that responds to emotion," she explained to us.

She clicked to another slide that showed a lamp store. Every lamp in the store was illuminated and shone brightly.

"And this is how a normal brain reacts to emotion. There are many more areas of the brain in a normal person that responded to emotion."

It was really quite a superb analogy for understanding the differences between these two worlds.

She also showed us pictures of dogs and cats. It was the uniqueness of a dog's nose versus that of a cat's nose that she was able to distinguish the differences between these two animals when she was growing up. She wasn't able to discern the different breeds of dogs, only that their noses were different than the noses of cats.

Obnoxiously interrupted by the ringing of a cell phone, (which went unanswered), Temple immediately responded to the person's insensitivity.

"Step on it!"

We all knew what she meant. Hopefully the owner of the ringing cell phone was quite embarrassed for his or her lack of compassion toward Temple's hypersensitivities—which we had just become aware of—as well as an earlier request to turn them off for this reason.

When she returned to her train of thought (which the ringing phone had disrupted), she shared with us that she didn't learn to talk until she was three and a half, and when she did, she would only stress the vowels in words, not the consonants.

For instance, in the sentence, "The man crossed the street," she could only say, "an oss ee." The high frequency sounds of the consonants ran together for Temple and this unintelligible garble was all she could make out of that sentence. Hearing that, hit close to home. Ashley was exactly like that a few months earlier, before we pursued the Tomatis therapy.

To overcome it, Temple's mentors taught her to stretch out the hard consonant sounds, until she could say them. When combined with the vowel sounds, this created clearer words and sentences. She also had her chin pulled on by her mentors to force her to look them straight in the eyes. She always avoided this interaction. But it worked for her. It pulled her out of her world for the moment and made her focus on them.

She stressed that the talents, not the deficits should be developed in autistic children. In one particular example, she mentioned that too many children today can draw on the computer, but not freehand. This described Ashley too, who now loved the computer and struggled at trying to use a pencil or crayon. Temple explained this was a serious mistake we make with our children; they need to be able to express themselves freehand, which fostered learning to read and write. It did make perfect sense. Temple's drawing talents came out around the third or fourth grade.

She mentioned some children are echolaelic, because they are absorbed in television commercials that play over and over. These advertisements are very predictable and never change—change only leads to frustration. That is why children on the spectrum find comfort in commercials. They aren't able to generalize and know that words have meaning outside of the songs they sing, only that they are contained in that song.

After her lecture, she stopped by the table where her books were being sold. I brought mine for her to sign, as well as carried a picture of Ashley in her dress up clothes wearing a cowboy hat. Ashley's pretend play—that we had just started to see—was captured in a picture that Temple politely signed for her. I was able to maneuver around the meeting attendees who crowded Temple in order for Dave to snap a picture of Temple and me—one for Ashley's scrapbook.

As I thanked Temple for her generosity in signing both my book and Ashley's picture, the crowd around her became smothering. Seeming a bit socially insecure, she did not look up to acknowledge my gratitude—or maybe she just couldn't hear me. Just the same, it was a day I will never forget, and one I will recount with Ashley when she is older. Research never took on more of a meaning than getting to meet, listen to, and learn from one of the foremost authorities on the subject of autism. It was truly grand in every way!

CHAPTER 14

▼

EXCUSE ME,
BUT WHY ARE YOU HERE?

Tomatis—Loop 4

Ashley's progress proceeded full steam ahead. Three months after loop three, we brought her back to the Spectrum Center for a fourth loop. Approaching the elevator, I reached for the button.

"I want to do it," Ashley said.

I picked her up to press the "up" arrow. The door opened. "Press four, Mommy."

She was really blowing my mind.

In similar fashion to the previous loops, Ashley exploded verbally and with respect to motor planning. She was now able to do high fives independently and cross the midline (across the body), string small beads independently and track objects better with her eyes. Three months earlier, at the end of the third loop, she was still having a bit of difficulty with these skills. Now, she wowed the listening therapists.

Her microphone work still consisted of the SREs, the repeating of words with sibilants such as /sh/, /th/, /f/, and /s/ as well as repeating small phrases. Repeating words were easy for Ashley. The phrase such as, "She sells seashells…" was a little trickier for her. It's even hard for me to say at my age!

Ashley spent the first three days of her sibilant exercises at level one. She was having a rough time. When she finally mastered them with 80% accuracy, she

- 162 -

graduated to level two. She worked at this level for a few days as well, the difficulty increasing. During the last couple of days of the loop she advanced to level three. For some children, they move to higher levels each day, but these exercises were difficult for Ashley. As the words got progressively more filtered, Ashley's ear had to work harder to listen. Due to her age, this wasn't out of the ordinary to take a few days to accomplish a single level.

She listened to a text tape in this loop as well, which was de-filtered (adding back the low frequencies) more quickly this time, inviting her ear to move from listening through bone conduction (in the womb) to that of air conduction (outside the womb).

Though she may have not always wanted to do her microphone work on a given day in therapy, it was now commonplace at our house for Ashley to say words and sentences just like her peers. Her own words were easier to say. They didn't come with a muffler.

It was becoming more difficult to fill out her daily progress sheets. I was no longer trying to find those unique changes in her that I reported earlier in the program. The things I had hoped for from the program were now in place.

Our consultation upon finishing up our fourth loop had the therapists raving about Ashley's progress.

"Ashley is one of those children who just really responds well to this therapy," Rochelle told us.

"I wouldn't be in this job (for so long) if I didn't love seeing the results of these children," Alicia said.

I sat in Valerie Dejean's office one day and cried my eyes out as she fed me tissues. She was responsible for Ashley's metamorphosis. As director and owner of the Spectrum Center, she had done all of the programming for Ashley's therapy. Her knowledge of the Tomatis Method—having studied directly under Dr. Tomatis in France, coupled with the incorporation of her sensory integration program—had taken Ashley to new heights in her life, and gave us back our daughter. Valerie knew exactly what Ashley needed in terms of listening therapy and at what pace to give it to her.

I sat and wept and told her how grateful I was to her and her therapeutic program. In seven months' time, Ashley had been put through four loops of auditory training, and had come out swinging. She had emerged a new little girl. I was a believer in this therapy. With the Tomatis Method, we had found our little girl— the one I knew was inside all along—she just needed some help finding her way out.

Our family now seemed whole again. Ashley was playing and relating to her sisters. She was more spontaneous in her speech. Her pretend play was in full bloom. Her joint attention was everything now, (which the doctors had been looking for back then). Neighbors noticed Ashley speaking better, having previously thought she was just shy and didn't *want* to speak—not that she *couldn't*. I told the neighbors about her diagnosis and about Tomatis—their jaws dropped. To them she didn't look like she had any form of autism!

I'll never forget sitting in the waiting room at the Spectrum Center before the day's session during our fourth loop and talking to some of the mothers. They watched Ashley interact with me and listened to her talk.

"Mommy, stand up," she said, initiating a game.

They watched Ashley play with some of the children while she spoke in her newly-found language. One woman gave me a confused look from across the room.

"Excuse me…but…why are you here? Your daughter looks so…normal!"

It was the greatest compliment I could have received. What this mother and the other parents in the waiting room were witnessing in Ashley—what we all were witnessing in Ashley at this point—was a spectacular transformation! To all that observed her, there was no difference in her from that of a normal three-year-old. Noticing a look of disbelief in their eyes—that Ashley was ever anything less than how she presented herself now—sparked me to tell them more about her history.

I told them how Ashley had come into the program seven months earlier humming, grunting and with a few words learned from speech therapy. Now, she belted out songs and spoke spontaneously. I told them about her picky eating habits and her craving for crunchy foods. Now, she tried new foods and didn't so much mind new textures. I told them how she was like a Weeble, wobbling and periodically falling down. Now, she had more balance and coordination and seemed to understand how her body worked. I told them how she used to ignore us and didn't want to be with us. Now she hugged us and loved us.

I think I was hope for all of the parents I sat with in the waiting room—that, they too, might see such results in their children with this therapy. I couldn't guarantee such things, but nearly 80% of the children seen at the Spectrum Center show progress of some nature with this technology.[19]

I held firm to my belief and shared it with the parents that the Tomatis Method was responsible for changing Ashley. Usually not one to impart my

---

19. Valerie Dejean, personal communication, May 2002.

opinions on others, never did I tout anything to anyone more seriously or purposefully in my life than the Tomatis Method and the power of Mozart. But this was important to say! This could be life altering for their children! This could be a ray of light for parents!

"Don't Kill a Fly with A Hand Grenade"

Ashley was now a little more than three-years-old. Her progress seemed surreal. I sometimes couldn't believe Ashley had come this far. It wasn't very long ago that the fog she was in kept us from enjoying our second daughter. But now, she was back with us, and I tried to keep her attention every waking moment.

I always felt the need to quiz her on the language she recently acquired. It just tickled me with delight to hear her voice. I often dreamed about what her voice would sound like if, and when, it came in. Now, I got so much joy hearing it. She had the silkiest, sweetest, most endearing little drawl.

One day we were in the car on our way to a doctor's appointment. It was a bright, sunny day. I turned around to check on Ashley.

"Hi, Ashley."

"Hi, Mommy."

"How are you?"

"Goom (good)."

"What's the weather like?"

She looked out the car window up at the sky.

"It's sunny."

"Is it raining?"

"No, Mom," she said, shaking her head as well.

She had just recently learned to shake her head 'yes' and 'no.' That she was holding this kind of conversation with me was just astonishing. She acknowledged my question, looked out the window to find the answer, and then tuned back into me with an appropriate response and gesture. I could now connect with her.

She was really interacting well and asking so many very purposeful questions.

"What you doing, Mommy?" or "Where'd Kacey go?"

She seemed more in touch with us and with her environment. Ashley was now using language "age-appropriately" and socializing with those around her. She was doing well in pre-school, and the teacher had commented on the significant changes Ashley had made since enrolling almost six months earlier.

She was excelling in all of these areas. Yet the one area still somewhat un-addressed was her "leaky gut." We just couldn't get control over her stools.

The probiotics hadn't worked. The gastroenterologist offered us no new information. Having been on the gluten-free/casein-free diet for about ten months, she still had runny, odorous stools and little "good" bacteria in her gut.

The next arrow in my quiver was to see Dr. Layton, a very reputable doctor who specialized in allergy and integrative medicine for children, most notably those on the autistic spectrum. He discovered that allergies are the underlying cause of a variety of medical problems in adults and children. He's made a career out of successfully treating children with learning, behavioral, and developmental problems due to allergies. He helps concerned parents with issues of "leaky gut" and also performs chelation (metal detoxification) therapy.

It was very fortunate we had come to learn of his name through the Spectrum Center. He saw many of the same children at the Spectrum Center as did most of the specialists to whom we were referred.

Dave, Ashley, and I drove to Dr. Layton's office more than two hours away from our home. I was immediately impressed by him. It was obvious he had done his homework in preparing for Ashley's visit. Dr. Layton had studied very well the history I provided him prior to our visit. The detailed questions he asked were evident that he truly took time to understand the issues with his patients in order to craft a well-educated opinion about the diagnosis of a child.

As he spoke to us from behind his desk, Ashley was playing around with some toys she found in a box in the corner of his office.

"Here Daddy, you blue cup," she said, handing Dave a cup filled with imaginary juice.

"Mommy, you red cup."

She handed me my cup, and I drank all my juice.

"Ashley, what about Dr. Layton? He's thirsty, too," I said.

She walked back to the corner to get another cup.

"Yellow cup," she said, offering him one as well.

"Ashley, can you say hi to Dr. Layton?"

She turned to look at him.

"Hi, Dr. Wayton."

Ashley was exceptionally engaging with him and with us during the evaluation. He looked up from his well-documented notes that I noticed were sporadically highlighted in yellow. He gave us a look that spoke volumes.

"I like what I'm seeing. She's not autistic!" he said, in a matter-of-fact tone.

I was waiting for Ashley to interact with Dave and me so Dr. Layton could see the fruits of our labor during the past two years—he had just noticed.

"She doesn't deserve that label," he said, sounding very sure of himself.

"I think maybe early on, she may have shown signs of PDD with her social communication disorder, but from what I'm witnessing today, the eye contact she's giving me, and the social interaction, she seems like a normal three-year-old," he said, putting a smile on our faces.

Those words he had just spoken were worth the two-hour drive to seek his opinion—the fourth opinion on our journey with this disorder.

"What about the horrible tantrums she's having? Are those the terrible twos just catching up with her?" I asked, curiously.

"She's just exploring her independence and showing her feistiness like any normal toddler. She was unable to do that before," he reassured us.

"But what Ashley *does* still have is a leaky gut, and we need to address that now," he underscored.

He explained that most likely her leaky gut was due to the continuously over-prescribed antibiotics she received for her recurrent ear infections when she was younger—that the good bacteria (such as lactobacillus and bifidobacteria) in her GI tract were destroyed after antibiotic treatment, leaving an imbalance to aid in her digestion.

Clearly, Dr. Layton was suggesting her tantrums were normal and not related to any disorder or probiotic use. He recommended we re-assess her stools for any growth of good (or bad) bacteria, and that we start all over in replacing the good bacteria.

"What about metals? Should we test her for metal toxicity? I've also read a little about secretin. Is this something she needs? Should we be exploring these?" I asked.

"Secretin is a gut hormone secreted by the small intestine. It tells the pancreas to release sodium bicarbonate to break down stomach acid and completes digestion. A child with autism who has a gastrointestinal problem is more likely to benefit from secretin. Approximately 20% of children who receive secretin have excellent results. This may include improved language (more spontaneous), improved eye contact, social skills, behavior and improved chronic diarrhea. The side effects are typically transient hyperactivity. This rarely lasts longer than a week. But just looking at Ashley, she's engaging, speaking and has wonderful eye contact. I don't think she shows signs of metal toxins. Surely I could give her secretin to clear up her gut problem, but that would be like 'killing a fly with a hand grenade.' I don't think she needs that much radical treatment. I don't see her as autistic," he said, being quite honest with us.

"Let's go ahead and get some labs on her. I would like to get another organic acids test and a GI bacteriology and another sIgA. The secretary can give you those kits when you leave. Let's keep the diet intact—keep Ashley on the GFCF diet. I also think you should investigate the Feingold diet which limits artificial flavoring and preservatives. A lot of children are sensitive to these additives. This may be worth exploring as well. After the results of the labs come back, and if she's still lacking in good bacteria, I'll start her on probiotic supplements. I've got a couple in mind that work very well. But let's get through the testing first to see where we are."

We concluded our visit with Dr. Layton and scheduled a follow-up appointment. We left his office with our lab kits in tow agreeing with his diagnosis of Ashley's "leaky gut." Clearly, her gut was an issue. But he surprised us with his opinion of Ashley no longer showing signs of autism. That was truly a gift!

We left with a good feeling about Dr. Layton. That Dave liked him, too, was a relief. I always needed to feel Dave out on the specialists we saw. He sometimes felt they could tell us all sorts of things we needed to do with our daughter, just to get our business—these specialists did not come cheap. The more specialized we got on this journey, the more of a financial burdened it became. Dave was always the cautious one. I was the proactive one—seeking everyone I thought who would be beneficial to us on this journey. But we complemented each other well and agreed on everything we pursued for Ashley.

The next day, I obtained Ashley's stool and urine samples, sent them off to the respective laboratories, and then waited for the results. When they showed up in the mail about two weeks later, they revealed Ashley was still depleted of her good bacteria—none had really grown from the short stint with probiotics months earlier. But what was different about these results was that now she had two very bad bacteria growing. They weren't there earlier when she was first tested.

"How did *they* get there?" I wondered.

Before I had a chance to speak with Dr. Layton, I delved into website after website trying to figure out what these bad bacteria were and how they got into my daughter's stool. The information I found sounded dreadful.

In a phone consult with Dr. Layton, he prescribed a new regimen of probiotics for Ashley. We were to give her capsules containing the bacteria she was lacking in addition to cranberry extract to try and kill the bad bacteria and cow's colostrum to boost her immune system.

Within a few months, her stools were more formed, but still a bit odorous. It led me to believe that we needed a higher dose of the probiotic. Dr. Layton recommended increasing the good bacteria two-fold to put more into her system and to try to combat the odor. We remained on this regimen and were to test her stool again in six months.

CHAPTER 15

▼

FROM JAMMIES TO JUMPER

Ashley graduated from nursery school in the summer of 2002. I was really proud
of her as I watched her sing along with her classmates during the ceremony. She
really seemed to enjoy singing, and her teacher remarked at how she knew all the
words to the songs, more so than any of the other students. Singing was now her
strength.

After a few flops in daycare settings, I felt I finally found a private school that
was just right for her. There were only 10 children in the classroom, which made
it a lot easier for her to receive the attention she needed and to make the auditory
processing a bit easier. The classroom was quieter and less threatening. I was
comfortable with the teacher and her style of teaching. I hadn't shared Ashley's
diagnosis with her. Ashley seemed fine now. I told the teacher what situations
Ashley learned best in, and she was very receptive to incorporating my suggestions into her classroom. She gave me a lot of feedback every time I picked Ashley
up from school. The teacher started to learn exactly what I needed from her and
from the classroom environment in order to have Ashley perform at her best. I
thought that this school was working out well for Ashley. I then found out the
teacher wasn't returning for the new school year. I needed to re-think Ashley's
school options.

I kicked around the idea of putting her in the Montessori school that her sister, Kacey, attended. I really had dreams of them being at the same school, holding hands, and running around on the playground together. My hopes and

dreams of this ever occurring had been snuffed out by the shocking diagnosis we had received two years earlier. But having seen the results that speech, OT, Floor Time, special education, nutritional intervention, and four loops of Tomatis had had on Ashley, I felt she would fair just as well as the other children her age there—normal as any other.

I chose Montessori, because the classrooms are geared toward the size, pace, and interests of the students. Classrooms are designed to give students the freedom to move about. They are equipped with material arranged on low shelves easily accessible to students. For the younger children, the practical life exercises ranged from spooning beans from one bowl to another (gaining fine motor coordination skills), to polishing silver pieces (gaining hand strength needed to grip a pencil for writing). The sensorial exercises provided stimulation of all the senses from tactile exercises (running fingers over sandpaper numbers and letters), to smelling different aromas using a blindfold, to hearing different amounts of sand when shaken in canisters.

The Montessori material and exercises carry many purposes from working on coordination, to keeping an attention span during a task, to paying attention to detail, to following a regular sequence of actions. They ultimately provide good working habits as the child finishes a task and puts it back on the shelf before beginning another activity.

I knew this environment would be great for Ashley; from the standpoint of the Montessori philosophy—enabling the child to learn in a natural setting, at her own pace, with material of her own choosing, creating a more responsible and independent individual. A lot of what an adult considers ordinary, such as washing dishes, polishing shoes, and folding towels are exciting tasks to children and allows them to imitate adults. Imitating is a strong and necessary urge in a child's early years. As much as the Montessori material teaches retaining attention and maintaining coordination, these jobs are really the precursors to the meat of academics, "reading," "writing," and "arithmetic."

But still, I was scared. Was it the right time to introduce Ashley into this type of setting? She had been accustomed to a pre-school with only nine other children in the class. The class was quiet, and there wasn't a lot to distract her attention. She was doing the same work as the others, and was starting to potty train with the other little girls who all congregated in the bathroom.

Montessori was going to be different in so many ways. Her classroom was going to have children ranging in age from two and a half to six-years-old. The jobs were primarily independent. A child usually works by herself on a particular task, completes it, has it checked by the teacher, cleans up, returns the project to the shelf, and gets another task to perform. The social interaction can be minimal. What Ashley needed most was social interaction. Her language was just now coming out beautifully. I didn't want to stifle that.

Going to the potty meant putting on a necklace and leaving the classroom to go to the bathroom. She was going to need her self-help skills more than ever here. Was Ashley ready for such independence, or was I pushing it too soon?

It concerned me a lot that what I was doing by putting her in this type of classroom could backfire. Would Ashley's behavior (that she sometimes exhibited), kick her out on day one, or would the teacher have the courtesy to give me a warning letter first? Would she throw all of the beans—which she was supposed to be spooning from one bowl to another—into the air just to see what a bean shower felt like? Would she throw the child-size porcelain tea set on the ground after she had had enough of trying to pour water into a teacup without spilling a drop? Would concentration turn into frustration? Would I somehow end up in next year's Parent Handbook as an example of what *not* to have your child do in class? All the possibilities swarmed around in my head at a ghastly speed.

The respect even the very young children have for the Montessori philosophy and the material is quite a sight to behold. When one walks through the halls during class time, the atmosphere is calm and serene and discipline fills the air. The students, clad in matching uniforms are hard working and know their place in the classroom. There is no room for a child who doesn't respect the teacher, the material, or curriculum.

On the other hand, I felt Ashley was now speaking well and comprehending enough to get by in the classroom, as much as any other three-year-old there. The benefit that she'd be getting working with the Montessori material and learning the work habits and getting self-esteem from performing the jobs, in my mind, out-weighed the doubts I had about her readiness and maturity level.

It's probably wrong to use maturity and three-years-old in the same sentence, but in Montessori, if you don't possess it coming in, you surely acquire it and take it with you on the way out. And you bring it with you the next day. The Montessori setting almost cries out for discipline once you step foot in the door. It looks totally different, it feels totally different. It *is* totally different. The Montessori classroom is filled with expensive material that is self correcting. By this I mean a child is able to learn through visualizing that she has made a mistake and needs to correct it—the material only works in one way. Stacking blocks to form a tower only works when the size decreases on the ascent. A child immediately knows she needs to correct the positioning of the blocks when she puts a larger block on a smaller one and the entire tower collapses. There's a need for the child to be able to understand about taking care of the material and not abusing it. A public classroom has a very different set up from that of Montessori, and there's usually very little in that type of classroom that one can break or misuse.

So was Ashley's maturity level ready for Montessori? And was Montessori ready for Ashley? To stave off any concerns in my mind of Ashley's readiness for such an independent learning program, I thought about keeping Kacey and Ashley together in the same classroom. I could feel a little more comfortable with Kacey being there, knowing what Ashley's issues were. She could look out for Ashley and teach her about the classroom. Kacey was now going to be one of the oldest students in the class, and the older ones have the privilege of teaching the younger ones—this was also the philosophy of Maria Montessori, founder of this teaching method.

I informed the director of the Montessori school about Ashley's diagnosis and the therapies we were pursuing with her. I explained to him about Ashley, not only to rationalize my desire to want my daughters in the same classroom, but to also educate him about autism. I was pretty sure Ashley was not going to be the only one ever to be educated in this school who was on the autistic spectrum, or who came with learning disabilities. Ashley was the first one brought to the director's attention. But there could be, (probably would be, maybe already were) other students in the school who exhibited some autistic tendencies—perhaps so mild they eluded everyone, but nonetheless, fell on the spectrum.

By bringing autism to the school and to his attention, the director was now my ally. Wanting every child to succeed, he allowed not only Kacey and Ashley to be together in the same classroom, but granted permission for Ashley's county educator to join her in the classroom once a week to teach her strategies to cope in this new environment. Ashley was showing so much progress, but she still had some transition problems. We revised her IEP, the Individualized Education Program, during the summer for the following school year to work on easing the difficulty she had with moving from one task to another and on tempering her behaviors when she got frustrated.

Summer came to an end. The morning I thought I would never see two years earlier, arrived complete with sunshine and two girls leaping into our bed as they did every morning.

"Where's my weemote, Daddy?" Ashley said, searching the wrinkled sheets.

I watched her from one eye underneath the pillow where my head was buried.

"Good morning Ashley," Dave said, groggily.

"Morning, Daddy!"

She found the remote and turned on the television.

"Twenty six," she said, turning it to the PBS channel.

"Wook, Daddy! Elmo's on."

She bounced on the bed with delight when she found Sesame Street.

"La la la la, la la la la, Elmo's World! Elmo wuvs his goldfiss, his cwayon, too. Dat Elmo's World!" she sang.

I opened both eyes and sat up.

"Morning, Ashley."

"Morning, Mommy."

"Ashley, do you know where you're going today?"

"Schoolly!" Kacey said, enthusiastically jumping on the bed with Ashley.

I could always count on Kacey to beat Ashley to any answer to my questions.

"Let her tell me herself, Kacey," I insisted.

"Ashley, where are you going today?" I repeated.

She still didn't answer me, preferring to watch Elmo.

"Ashley, what's your teacher's name?"

"Mrs. Rojas," she correctly replied, as she pressed the up arrow to increase the volume on the television.

"That's right! Are you going to see her today?"

"Noooo!" she whined, as if I were bothering her.

That wasn't quite the answer I was looking for, but it was early. Maybe she was still sleepy.

We went downstairs for breakfast like any other day—except, it wasn't just another day. Summer was over. Instead of lounging around a little longer in jammies, it was time to get those studious-looking uniforms on the girls. Kacey was very excited and nearly hurdled into hers. She couldn't wait to see her schoolmates. Ashley, on the other hand, wanted no part of this event.

It was a new school year, a new school, a new teacher, and a chance to be with Kacey in class. It seemed like a good time to turn over a new leaf with Ashley's dressing behavior. As much as I prepped Ashley the day before by getting her into her uniform (hoping it would spark interest on school day), it didn't. Ashley fought us all the way and even went so far as to march back upstairs, with leaking eyes, and picked out her favorite summer shorts outfit as a replacement to the required red and blue plaid jumper.

"Green shirt and shorts," she said, stomping down the stairs sniffling and waving the clothes at us.

How was I going to explain that the Montessori uniform was not green with garden tools on it? The best we could do was have Dave grip her with all his strength while I maneuvered the white shirt and plaid jumper on her. Once the uniform was on, it wasn't coming off, either! There were too many technical fasteners to get through; from zipper to hook and eye to buttons. She was in there for the duration. Thank goodness! Wow, that killed a good 20 minutes I hadn't budgeted into the morning!

I had the grand plan of videotaping Ashley's first day arriving at school. I pictured myself walking backward after getting the girls out of the car, talking into the camera, and commentating all the way through into the classroom. I wanted documentation of this momentous occasion. After all, my dream was coming true. Ashley and Kacey were now at the same school and, in my opinion, Ashley had triumphed over her disorder of autism. It was monumental to us.

We put both Kacey and Ashley in Dave's car with a little whining from Ashley, as she clung onto her jammies. I put Sydney in my car so I could take her to Dave's parents. Dave turned one way to go to the school, and I turned the other. Two miles down the road, I called Dave on the cell phone.

"Did you get the lunches?" I asked.

"Uh…oh, I'll go back!" he said.

"No, I'm right here, I'll go," I said, making a quick U-turn at the next light.

I pulled into the driveway, ran inside, grabbed the lunch boxes, got back in the car, and headed to his parent's house. I dropped Sydney off with a quick kiss good-bye, got back in the car and headed to school to meet up with Dave and the girls.

As misfortune tended to follow me, I met up with a traffic jam that was the aftermath of an accident on the highway. I called Dave who was sitting in the parking lot waiting for me. With 15 minutes left before the bell was to ring to line the children up, I knew I wasn't going to arrive at school in time to capture their first day on video. Dave took the girls onto the playground and watched them play, giving me play-by-play details over the phone. I screamed at every car in front of me for keeping me from where I should be—on the playground watching Ashley's first day of school.

"Do you people know how much this means to me? Do you know what she's been through these past years? I'm not going to make it! I'm not going to make it!" I screamed, threading the car through a tiny gap left by a woman putting her makeup on as she drove.

I looked at the clock in the dashboard. Five minutes to go. I inched my way closer to the school.

"Dave, stay where you are. Don't leave, I'm right here, close to the school!" I said, rounding the corner with the school in sight.

"Hurry, they're going to line up soon," he said.

I abruptly parked, shot out of the car with the camera and lunch boxes swinging in the air and ran across the street toward the school. I slammed the gate to the fence behind me and sat down next to Dave.

"Where is she?" I asked, winded from the sprint.

He pointed to the slide where she seemed to be having a great time. I removed the camera and started videotaping. The bell rang and the children swarmed from the playground equipment as if someone were handing out ice cream. They all ran to line up—all of them—except Ashley.

She was quite content where she was and didn't want to leave. Kacey went over to her and pulled on her arm to take her to Ms. Rojas' line. But it only made matters worse. Kacey looked at us begging for help and gesturing for us to come get Ashley. Ashley wouldn't budge.

Dave and I knew starting out on the playground might be a bit tricky with her transition difficulties. Once she got going on something, she had a hard time switching gears as easily as some of the other children.

We witnessed this during Kacey's spring program at the end of the previous school year. Dave went to the playground to be with Ashley while one of the classes performed "on stage" under a large tree. After playing a bit, Dave tried to get Ashley to leave the play equipment and come over and sit down, but she screamed in protest. Every parent sitting in their lawn chair looked at Dave and Ashley. The ones sitting near me looked at me knowing those two came with me. I sunk a little lower in my chair. Ashley's tirade and behavioral antics cut right into a sixth grader reciting the preamble of the Constitution of the United States—a dedication to the events of September 11th.

In order to move things along on this first day of school, Dave picked up Ashley and took her to the appropriate class line. Some children were well behaved and knew the routine from last year. Others were new and didn't quite know what to do. Some, like Ashley, were crying for their Mommies and Daddies. With lunch box in tow, Dave carried a sniffling Ashley into the classroom. Ashley put her lunch box on the shelf as Dave bent down still holding her. He tried to put her down but she preferred to stay tightly clasped in his arms.

"Put her down and let her go to circle time," I begged him.

He was a bit hesitant to let her go, not wanting her to revert into a full-fledged tantrum. But I wanted her to know that she was now in "big girl" school and she was to make her own way and sit down with the others—that Daddy wasn't going to hold her all morning. Sometimes, Mommy gives tough love.

Dave put Ashley down, and she timidly moved toward the others in circle time. I grabbed Dave by the shirt and pulled him out of the classroom. Noticing we had left, Ashley ran out of the classroom and down the hall screaming for us. She was retrieved by Mrs. Rojas' assistant who brought her back to the room and closed the door. The other parents in the hall looked at us.

"She's mine!" I confessed.

We peered into the window of the classroom and saw her sitting in the assistant's lap. Circle time had begun and Mrs. Rojas was saying the days of the week.

"Ashley, you know those," I said to myself, hoping she would join in. She was calming down, but didn't want to participate. After about 10 minutes, she had moved out of the assistant's lap and into a spot in the circle next to Kacey. Ashley was listening to Mrs. Rojas talk. But as some of the others were sitting there nicely paying attention, Ashley, every so often would roll on her back, suspend her feet in the air, and expose her underwear. Not a good way to start the year off. I stood and watched for a while, ducking every time I thought she spied me lurking.

Dave had since said good-bye to me and left the school. He was on his way to work. Ashley's new special educator from the early intervention program, Miss Brenda, had arrived. After I greeted her and spoke with her briefly in the hall, Brenda walked into the classroom to be with Ashley. (She had met Ashley a few weeks earlier at a speech therapy session to get to know her and for Ashley to feel comfortable with her once school started.)

Now that Brenda was there, I felt more at ease and decided to just let whatever happens, happen. I'd surely hear about Ashley's day when I picked her up in three hours. I left to pick up Sydney.

I arrived back at school a little early to peer in on what Ashley was doing. The students were eating lunch. Ashley walked around the room eating while the other children politely sat in their seats eating sandwiches and sipping drinks. Ashley scanned the room looking at all of the different Montessori material on the shelves. She wasn't touching any of it, thank goodness, but seemed curious about all of it. Every so often, Mrs. Rojas brought Ashley back to her seat and reinforced the need for her to sit at the table and eat with everyone else. Eventually, something else would catch her eye, and she'd be back up wandering. I went into the classroom when it looked like everyone had finished eating and were starting to clean up.

"Mommy!" Ashley said with a big smile on her face, running over to me.

"Hey sweetie, how was your day?" I asked, giving her a big hug.

Ashley was about to leave the room without cleaning up her table, but I directed her back to her lunch box. I helped her clean up while holding Sydney in my arms. Some of the other children were sweeping the floors and brooming off their tables. Kacey came over to help us clean up Ashley's spot. I captured Mrs. Rojas's attention and asked her how Ashley's day had been.

"Good," she said, in her Spanish accent.

"She moves around a lot for circle time. She does not have that attention span yet, but she's young, it's okay," she reassured me, patting me on the shoulder.

Ashley behaved pretty appropriately for a three-year-old. There were other children I saw in the classroom that seemed to behave the same as Ashley. I thought she did well for the first day, after she calmed down that morning. From what I observed, she seemed to fit in just as much as the next little girl or little boy in there who had no diagnosis (to my knowledge). I couldn't expect any more than that from her on the first day.

The fact I wasn't presented with an itemized list of all the material I envisioned her breaking, throwing, or eating, meant she made it through to my satisfaction that first day. We can only improve upon it, I thought as we all left the building and headed for home.

For days to follow, Ashley seemed to grow more and more accustomed to the routine of Montessori. It was still a struggle to get her dressed in the morning, and I really don't know why. But once she was out the door on her way to "schooly," (as she referred to it now), she was fine. She blended in well, she was starting to socialize with the other children and even found a few girls her age to pal around with. That's what I was waiting for—a pal. It's just what she needed. And Kacey was still there as security for her.

I had given Mrs. Rojas information on sensory integration, the GFCF diet, and Ashley's auditory training program. I wanted Mrs. Rojas to understand that Ashley may exhibit certain behaviors due to sensory integration issues, like spinning around. Ashley needed the movement—the vestibular input. I didn't want Mrs. Rojas to discourage Ashley from getting that input. But Mrs. Rojas responded by telling me some of the children in her class also acted that way, suggesting to me that it was normal child behavior. She didn't see it as a behavior stemming from a disorder and couldn't thoroughly comprehend Ashley's diagnosis. To Mrs. Rojas, Ashley looked similar to other students her age.

I also told Mrs. Rojas it may take Ashley a while to process something being said to her due to auditory processing difficulties. (These were still being addressed by the Tomatis therapy.)

For example, it was necessary to speak literally to Ashley. This was evident in Ashley looking up at the ceiling when the teacher's assistant told her to put her smock up. It was an "Amelia Bedelia" moment.

Mrs. Rojas was aware of Ashley's special food requirements and kept an eye out during snack or lunch time that Ashley only ate the foods I packed for her. Ashley was really good about that, anyway.

But I just felt it necessary to have Mrs. Rojas understand a little bit about Ashley's history, why she had been labeled on the autistic spectrum, and what we were doing to facilitate her progress. I also informed her about Ashley's low muscle tone which interfered with motor planning and fine and gross motor activities, and that we were addressing these issues with OT and Tomatis. Ashley was still a little timid in holding a pencil or crayon correctly. She still did not have the finger control needed to use it properly. But that's what Montessori equipment did best—worked on the precursors for reading and writing. I knew it would only get better in time.

Since I brought some of Ashley's issues to the attention of Mrs. Rojas, she remarked at how impressed she was with Ashley's manipulation of scissors and cutting ability for someone her age.

"The other children cannot do that so well," she told me.

The scissor work Ashley did at home and at OT was obviously paying off. Months earlier, Ashley was unable to hold a pair of scissors, much less cut or snip paper. Her fingers were weak, and she lacked the motor control. But it seemed we were addressing the right things in therapy. They were certainly getting noticed in class.

After watching Ashley during the first few months of school, Mrs. Rojas admitted she did not see what we were talking about with Ashley's medical history and her placement on the spectrum. She just thought Ashley was a typical three-year-old—a rather bright three-year-old. My concerns seemed almost trivial as she reassured me that a lot of the younger children had either behavior issues or didn't concentrate on things well—that they were still young and would eventually mature. It was difficult to explain to her just how Ashley used to be and how much progress she had made since the onset of her diagnosis. Ashley didn't appear like that now. Mrs. Rojas only had this normal Ashley to go by now.

Everyday when I picked the girls up from school, I would briefly discuss Ashley's day with Mrs. Rojas.

"She's really paying attention now in circle time, whereas some of the other children are looking away from me and not participating. She answers me when I ask her a question, and she enjoys the music and singing," Mrs. Rojas said to me.

"Is she working on her jobs?" I asked.

"Oh, yes. She's working with the material. She doesn't always clean up, but she's learning."

On the days of Brenda's visits I would also get a call from her telling me how well Ashley was doing—that she was responding to all of the strategies she was using with Ashley to get her to be more social and attentive with fewer transition problems.

I liked what I heard from both of them. Ashley understood the jobs that she worked on. From washing a rock to spooning beans to mixing bubbles with a wisk, she was meeting the challenges of these practical life activities, as well as slowly learning the routine of cleaning up after herself.

Mrs. Rojas was actually impressed with all that Ashley knew coming into the class. For being three, she knew her numbers up to 50, all her colors, all her shapes, all her days of the week, all her seasons and all her weather conditions and so much more.

"We do a lot of playing school at home," I told her.

"Oh, yes, she's very smart. Kacey probably helps her a lot, too, yes?" Mrs. Rojas asked.

"We work really hard with Ashley, and Kacey's a great teacher for her," I replied.

There was no doubt in my mind about Ashley's cognition. Early on, after receiving the diagnosis and being frightened about what was happening to my little girl, I wondered what the future held for her and how she would make out educationally with such a diagnosis. But as the therapies proved to be making their mark on Ashley, and she was coming back to us, I could see for myself Ashley was super bright—a sponge absorbing everything.

I knew Ashley had the capabilities to cope in the classroom when it came to doing the jobs. It was the behavioral side to things I worried about most. But with Mrs. Rojas' attention to Ashley's needs and Brenda's strategies to keep Ashley focused, my fears of putting her in a school—possibly above her capabilities—were put to rest. I was grateful to hear how they thought Ashley fit in well in the classroom surrounding and was acquiring the skills and learning like the rest of the students. It was more reassurance that we were on the right track with Ashley and her therapies, enough so that we felt good about our decision to put her in Montessori. Ashley belonged there. Ashley was learning there. Ashley was one of them there. No other parent would have ever suspected that Ashley wore a label of a different kind in her jumper!

CHAPTER 16

▼

A LABEL IN QUESTION

During one of our speech sessions, Shelly re-tested Ashley for receptive vocabulary and found her above age level.

"Don't take this the wrong way, but she seems very *normal* to me, Sharon," Shelly said, as we discussed Ashley's results.

"Shelly, I can't figure this out. She's been diagnosed with autism, yet her teacher has seen such an improvement in her and thinks she's just as normal as the next child in her class. I'm confused!"

"Hey, Mommy, get the ball," Ashley said, interjecting our conversation.

I picked up the ball on Shelly's desk.

"Hold your arms out," I said, throwing the ball to her.

She threw it back.

Shelly was watching me have just a normal, natural interaction with Ashley. We both remarked how not but a year and a half ago, she was non-verbal.

On this day, after being tested, she was above average. As much as I didn't understand how Ashley's language and social communication didn't evolve correctly—resulting in her being placed on the autistic spectrum—I was equally puzzled wondering how she leaped into language almost a year above her age.

"She's quite amazing. We always knew that Ashley was special. She just needed a push. I don't know what was blocking her at the beginning. I was convinced it was an ear problem due to the many ear infections she suffered. But an auditory processing problem makes sense to me," said Shelly.

"Look at her now. She's normal. She's normal!" I said, watching her play.

We smiled and shook our heads. We talked about Ashley and her achievements—the interaction, the eye contact, the ball she tossed to me. They were all glaring indications of the progress Ashley had made since this journey had begun.

"If Tina could only see her now!" I said, glowing.

Tina, the occupational therapist, had since left the practice and was no longer around to see Ashley throw a ball underhand. This was a skill Tina always tested Ashley on and one keeping Ashley from moving up to an age-appropriate level. Ashley couldn't master it.

Tina had only left a week earlier, but that was the thing about Ashley; she would make progress so fast, even within a given week. She was now mastering things she couldn't do during the previous week upon testing. It was hard to keep up with her, because I constantly had to change my tactics with Ashley. I had to keep challenging her with new things. The week before, the tasks were too difficult for her. The following week, they were too easy.

"We shouldn't treat her any differently than Kacey. Ashley understands everything we put before her," Shelly advised me.

I nodded in total agreement.

Shelly still agreed that there were times when Ashley had her moments, be them sensory integration issues, transition problems, or call them normal terrible twos or threes. Whatever they were, we hadn't seen them in a while, since we stopped the Samonas months earlier. I had also reintroduced the Wilbarger protocol. It always seemed to calm her and organize her central nervous system. But being three, we knew we were to still expect a lot of defiance and her wanting things to go her way—she hardly disappointed in that area.

But presently, it was great to hear from Shelly that Ashley was a changed person from the lost little 19-month-old that came to her a year and a half earlier. Shelly assured me Ashley was going to make it out there in the world just fine, and she was going to shock a lot of people with her brightness. She certainly shocked us at every turn.

Shelly made the decision to retire from her profession. I was sad to see her go. But for the duration we had her on our team, she was truly dedicated to helping Ashley overcome her obstacles. Shelly wrote me shortly after she left. She had always looked forward to her sessions with Ashley, no matter how little she could extract from Ashley on a particular day. She had patience the likes of no other, and I knew she would never forget the days, months and years that Ashley grew on her—physically and developmentally.

Dear Sharon,

Thank you so much for the beautiful flowers. Ashley did a wonderful job making the presentation to me. I'm trying to settle into my new life. It is difficult for me to think of Tuesdays and Thursdays without Ashley. Since October of 2000, our first evaluation, Ashley has progressed from a goal program designed to elicit five different sounds to recently Ashley telling me, "I don't want to do anymore, Miss Shelly!" I'll never forget those first words "in" and "out," as she attempted to throw balls in and out of the ball pit. I don't think I know of any other child whose first words were prepositions. When she said the word "kangaroo" out of the blue, I know that was a day both of us will just never forget.

At the time that I thought we were sailing along and filling in the missing pieces from the ear infections, Ashley's diagnosis of autism came. I was stunned, as you know. I started reading, and you started reading everything. You really educated me with Tomatis, and it seemed to have been the missing link, as you say, for her. As Ashley was progressing and her language took off, I found myself not being able to write fast enough on my progress notes to capture all the wonderful things she was saying in our sessions. Ashley didn't like being tested that much as you recall, so I had to be creative in my attempts to gather the data on her skills. But toward the end of my time with her, she started to cooperate. I was amazed at how she scored at a four-year-old level being only three-years-old.

Unbelievably, we had 20 months of speech together. No other child pushed me to find new ways and material to continue established themes and build upon her language more than Ashley did. Her goals kept changing, as she was mastering them at a very fast pace.

Sharon, it is important that any new therapist and teachers in her life know about all the pieces in Ashley's unique puzzle. Be very proud of yourself and understand that your timeliness with her symptoms, your dedication in bringing her all the best therapies, and seeing all the best specialists, has made all the difference, I truly believe, in her extremely, rapid progress—not to mention her determination and strong will, as well. She was definitely slow to take off, but I'm sure you can't even keep up with her, now. And I know you're just tickled with each surprise she brings you. She is a remarkable little girl whom I am going to miss. She added so much to my life, and I'm so happy that I was part of your journey.

All the best,
Miss Shelly

Tomatis—Loop 5

We continued with Tomatis for a fifth loop. Bringing Ashley to higher levels of listening was only the right thing to do with her—I didn't want to stop a good thing. She still had some right-ear, left-ear discrimination problems so there were still kinks that needed worked out with her listening.

The listening therapists were delighted to see Ashley back. I was quick to point out that Ashley had made tremendous progress in just the few months we had been away. Ashley's program still consisted of the active microphone work. It had been three months since we had last been there, so the therapists started back at level one for her SRE exercises—the words and phrases she had difficulty mastering in loop four.

During this fifth loop, she didn't have so many problems with her word exercises. The words were still muffled and quite challenging. But Ashley stuck with it, and her hard work paid off. She went from level one the first day, to level six by the end of the loop! She had only gotten to level three during loop four, and it had taken her eight days to get there. Her ears were definitely working now! All in all, the fifth loop built upon her acquisition of language and continued bringing her to a point of right-ear dominance.

I had a follow-up phone consult with Rochelle from the Spectrum Center.

"How's Miss Ashley doing?" Rochelle asked eagerly.

"She's doing really well," I said, excitedly.

"She's in school now with her sister. We put her in Montessori, and she's doing great there," I happily shared.

"Excellent!" Rochelle said.

"She's totally mainstreamed in?" Rochelle asked.

"She has a special educator from the county's early intervention program who attends class with her once a week, but for the most part she's functioning on her own. It was a rough adjustment for her early on, but she came around, and she seems to enjoy it now."

"She's probably going to love it," Rochelle said.

"So far, yes, she seems to. She's doing her jobs like she's supposed to. She still has a bit of trouble maintaining attention during circle time, but the teacher tells me that it is perfectly normal. Other children her age exhibit the same behavior—that it wasn't anything to worry about—she'd outgrow it. Her teacher also reminded me that Kacey was that way at first, too."

"You know what, Sharon? If that's the only thing we're dealing with, that's great!" Rochelle said.

"Yes, that's the only real issue I see now. I was worried about tantrums and sensory overload—Ashley not being able to cope—those types of things. I don't see any of that, and I watch her there a lot. I feel really optimistic—her being at that school," I said.

"I'm sure the teacher just loves Ashley. How could you not?" Rochelle added.

"I'm still brushing her every now and then when she does get a little crazy on me," I told Rochelle.

"And her language continues to increase?" Rochelle asked.

"It's amazing. I write down a lot of what she says so I can keep track of the progress, and here are just a few examples, if I can share them with you."

"Sure, let me hear," Rochelle said.

"Well, she and Kacey were playing, and they started fighting over something and Ashley said, 'Go to time-out now Kacey! Now!' Isn't that great? She makes sentences like any other three-year-old in my opinion. Here's another. 'Daddy, I making puppet show—Fwee Widdle Pigs.'"

"That's wonderful! She's using the language. She's pretend playing. She's addressing Dave. What more could she put into a sentence? It's beautiful." Rochelle said, excitedly.

"I also walked in the house after shopping one day and was greeted by Ashley with, 'Mommy, you're back!' It's normal. It's appropriate. It's just really good stuff. There was a time when Ashley didn't care if I was coming or going. Now she's excited to see me! It's all really coming together for her," I said, beaming enthusiastically through the telephone line.

"That's just great!" Rochelle responded.

"There is one thing I wanted to run by you, Rochelle, and that is, on cloudy, dreary days, she seems to tantrum more and is more out of sorts. I feel like she really needs a lot of sensory input then. Any thoughts on that?" I asked.

"It could just be that to get an optimal level of functioning, she needs the intense input of a bright sunny day. You know, it's not something I hear a lot about." Rochelle said.

"Well, she's unique," I said, chuckling.

"She *is* unique—in a very good way, she's unique," she said to me. Does play continue to be more imaginative?"

"Yes, she's really doing well with her Floor Time. Now, she's assigning roles when we play, so that's coming right along," I said.

"We have also been to see Dr. Layton about her leaky gut issues, and we are following through with prescribed probiotics. So, we are addressing that problem. He also mentioned that when he saw Ashley, he did not see any signs of autism. She had a great visit with him. She was engaging, showed good eye contact, gave him toys on his desk, and interacted with us a lot. He was really impressed with her," I said.

"You know, Sharon, I think it will probably be hard to find a professional at this point who would put that diagnosis on her," Rochelle hinted.

Wonderful! Another professional questioning the appropriateness of her label—I liked hearing that from Rochelle.

"So, the next step for Ashley will be to test her, which I think will be amazing to really see," Rochelle said.

"We will be back next month for testing, so you'll get to see Ashley then," I said.

"Sharon, Ashley's doing wonderfully! And Montessori is a sensory approach. If it's one thing that Ashley has shown everyone, it is that she is a strong responder to a sensory approach. Ashley is that ray of hope. Most of these children progress with Tomatis, but it's at what pace that differentiates their progress. Ashley is a fast moving child—amazingly fast moving. You guys have done an excellent job with her. You and Dave have put a lot of work into it, too—tons of work!"

"Well, she's still a work-in-progress, as you know, Rochelle."

"And she will be for the next couple of years. But I think down the road, you are going to look back and say, 'Wow!'"

"I hope so. Thanks Rochelle, I'll see you soon."

"Take care and give that cutie a big hug for me." We both said good-bye.

Coincidentally, that very same day, I received a letter from Dr. Layton that he had sent to my pediatrician. I was in a terrific mood after speaking with Rochelle; her telling me she thought Ashley no longer carried the characteristics of the label. Dr. Layton's letter filled me with more confidence that Ashley had arrived.

To Whom It May Concern:

Previously, Ashley had been diagnosed with Pervasive Developmental Disorder (PDD-NOS). The developmental history includes Ashley not turning around when her name was called, over focusing on videos, no words and decreased eye contact. Regarding speech, there had been slow progression. However, since starting a diet consisting of casein-free (no milk, cheese, yogurt, ice cream) and gluten-free (no wheat, oat, barley and rye), Ashley's language has significantly improved. An auditory training program has also been beneficial. When seen by me at three-years-old, her receptive language had been measured at four years, two months, and expressive language is age-appropriate. Additional issues include loose, foul-smelling bowel movements. A previous stool analysis showed no good bacteria (zero lactobacilli and bifidobacterium) and a very elevated secretory IgA of 1495. Food testing was positive for egg whites, soybean, garlic, and orange. At this visit, after taking a history for over an hour, it was my opinion that Ashley was not autistic. It was certainly a concern before medical interventions (the past two years) that she was on the autistic spectrum. In fact, the diagnosis of PDD-NOS had already been rendered. It is obvious that she no longer has PDD or autism, as she was engaging with both her parents and me during the visit. I believe now she has an expressive speech delay that is improving. I thought it was necessary to recommend certain tests and intervention to be sure that Ashley turned out to be a normal child. I am pleased with the progress Ashley made even before seeing me. By addressing "leaky gut" issues, probably affected by the frequency of antibiotics her first 15 months of life, I should be successful in helping Ashley reach her full potential. Although many of the interventions already undertaken including casein/gluten-free diet as well as supplements I recommended are often downgraded by many pediatricians and developmental specialists, it is quite obvious that Ashley and a significant number of children with developmental delay issues do improve. For this particular patient, dietary intervention, supplements and numerous other early intervention therapies provided substantial medical benefits.

Sincerely,
Richard E. Layton, M.D.

I immediately got on the phone and called my parents. I had to share the news of this letter with someone. Dave was not reachable at that moment.

My father answered, and I read the letter to him. I accented the part about the doctor not thinking Ashley was autistic any longer.

"Sharon, that's wonderful! You know, I am *so* proud of you and how you have handled this whole situation. Ashley looks great! I am just amazed at the amount of work you guys have done with her. These have really been tough times on you and Dave, and every time your Mother and I see Ashley, she looks better and better."

"Well, she's the product of a lot of intervention. I couldn't just sit back and do nothing. She's my daughter. I had to find out what was wrong and how best to go about correcting it."

"Yes, but you immersed yourself in this like I don't think another could do. I'm just awestruck at the things you are doing for Ashley—the things you read about, the doctors she sees—how you even found them! You've done just a fabulous job with her. It just makes me so proud to see you all grown up and with a family of your own. When faced with a life challenge like this, you are such a fighter," he said, nearly making me cry.

It was always good to hear from my father that he thought I was doing a great job—on anything—but particularly with Ashley. The little girl he raised in ponytails was now grown up with three girls of her own in ponytails, and fighting the battle of her life—and seemed to be winning.

His pride toward me meant a lot. The support from all of my family meant so much. And it also kept me going. Why was I the chosen one in all of this? I guess we'll never know. But I hope that I was an inspiration for them all. That the youngest daughter and the baby sister had grown up to make a special impact on not just a child, but on others around her, including the community afflicted with PPD and autism. It was my mission to cure Ashley. Now it was my mission to help others through this nightmare.

The following week I had a scheduled phone consult with Dr. Layton.

"Hi, Sharon. How's that cute, little lady of yours?" he asked.

"She is doing great! I wish we were up there so you could see her today. She's in Montessori school now. Her language is through the roof, and she has taken a big leap in her social skills. I've given her teacher a lot of information about her background. They are all informed about her history at school. But frankly, her teacher can't see any of it—how she used to be—which is a good thing," I said to him.

"Well, yeah, it was tough for me to see it, when she was here, too. My opinion of her was mainly that of the leaky gut. Now as for the supplements, she's on the probiotics?"

"Yes. She's on the probiotics, the cranberry extract, and the colostrum. Her stools are a little bit firmer, but they are still odorous. I wanted to know if we should increase the probiotic dosage."

"What about the artificial flavorings and preservatives? Have you stopped those?"

"Well, you know, we didn't put her on the Feingold diet, because she's already so limited. She doesn't really get any artificial flavors or colorings, anyway. I'd like to start putting some things back into her diet, and I wanted to talk to you about that."

"Her language is fine?" he asked.

"I think her language is going great. There's back and forth communication. She's engaging. She's pointing at things of interest. Yes, I don't even think that's our concern anymore," I said, happily.

"Any social concerns?" he asked.

"I don't think so. Right now she looks and acts like a typical three-year-old. She's playing in groups more. In circle time she's interacting and even hugging and laughing with the children."

"What about reciting videos? I know you had a concern about this when I first saw you."

"She still does it a little bit here and there. But I think she does it, because she has a good memory, and she's acting things out that she sees on the videos," I said.

"But if that's isolated like that, the fact that her language is spontaneous is the important thing," he said. "And the gluten free/casein-free diet has helped her, right?"

"I think it was one of many things we tried that really gave her eye contact and started her babbling. We've been doing Tomatis also, as you know. I think that has had a tremendous impact on her acquisition of language and her overall body awareness. She's not as defensive as she used to be to food textures or has those tactile issues any longer," I said.

"And the other forbidden things such as orange, garlic, soy, those came from testing her, right?" he asked.

"Yes, they came up positive—to avoid them—but frankly, I don't know what they were doing to her," I said.

"Well, let's find out. Let's do some food challenges with her. Start on a Saturday, because if there's a problem, she has a day to recover. Do these weekly. Now, of the orange, egg, soy, and garlic, what's most important?" he asked.

"I'd like to start with egg. That gives me a few more options with her diet. I'd like soy to be next, then orange, then garlic."

"Make these foods abundant in what you're putting back. Don't just give her something that contains a little bit of soy, or a little bit of egg. Give her a heaping dose of tofu, if she'll eat it, or try soy milk, or soy hot dogs, or straight oranges, or orange juice. That way, if she can tolerate a lot of it, there's not going to be a problem introducing foods that contain just a little bit of it."

"So we're still going to keep her on the GFCF diet? What's your feeling on this? Is this going to go on for years?" I asked.

"No. Let's get these foods in, and if she maintains with how she's doing, the next thing I'd say is to go for the gluten. It really opens up a whole world of options for her. The casein is much easier to track. The gluten is really tough. Get through with these, and we'll see where we are. Did Kelly ever have Ashley on digestive enzymes?"

"No, we talked about enzymes, and she told me to go online and read about a few of them, which I did, but I never followed through with giving them to Ashley."

"If we were more worried about autism, I'd be going for one of the more potent ones, but I don't think she needs the ones that are geared toward that population," he said. "I'll recommend one that the Apothecary carries, but I'd wait. You can start the digestive enzyme in two to three weeks.

"Do the egg test Saturday, then increase the probiotic four days later. If you increase the probiotic now with the egg challenge, she may have a die-off effect with the bacteria, and it might influence the egg test. So, increase the probiotic in four days, and then add the digestive enzyme in two to three weeks, but three days after a food challenge," he said.

"What am I looking for in a reaction?" I asked.

"Well, you'll know in 24 hours if there's a problem. She may act bizarre, become hyperactive, and may have an upset stomach," he said.

"Well, when she has a tantrum, how do I know it's just a three-year-old tantrum versus a reaction to the food?" I asked.

"Well, you don't. You know the way she is. This would be over and above. See, that's the problem with a three-year-old. The terrible twos can really be the terrible threes, and you never know what you're going to get. But if she's becoming more strong-willed, more 'why this, why that,' if she's defending her own turf, that's normal three year old stuff. It is tough going through it, but for you it is good, because she's now more in line with what your older daughter is like. As for calcium, since she isn't receiving any, now that you stopped the universal formula, let's add that back to her diet, probably on a Wednesday, not on the same day as anything else. There's a good supplement I'll recommend," he said.

"So over the next four to six weeks, try the four new foods, bump up her probiotic, and add calcium back into her diet. Once you get through all of this, and if she's doing the same or better, we may re-introduce gluten in six to eight weeks," he said, repeating his instructions.

"So when do you want me to check back with you?" I asked.

"Well, if you get through all of this, let's just talk in about three months. I love seeing all of you, but you really don't need to make the long trip up here. We'll just talk then. But please call me for anything, especially if there's a problem. Sounds like she's doing great!" he said.

"Thanks as always, Dr. Layton."

"Bye, now!"

I thought Dr. Layton was a wonderful doctor, and I'm glad we sought him out for his advice and guidance. He had reiterated to me that he didn't think Ashley's condition was autism any longer, because of the fact that her speech was now age appropriate, and she was social and spontaneous. To him, someone who is autistic lacks spontaneity. Ashley hit him as being a pretty spontaneous child the first time he saw her. He agreed that she may have exhibited some autistic characteristics early on, and may have had developmental delays coinciding with autism, but that now, she didn't show any of the defining characteristics or self-stimulating behaviors usually seen in the autistic population.

Having seen children for more than 30 years, he told me he could pretty much walk into a room and size up a child—things would just click with respect to thinking someone was autistic or not. He told me he knows some children are autistic even before he sees them—he can hear them. These children have a sound about them that is unique—an "Eeeeeeee" sound to them.

When he looked at Ashley the first time, he was confused—he didn't see or hear anything suggesting autism—nothing clicked for him.

Granted we had been through more than a year and a half of treatments by then. She appeared totally different from the history I originally sent him. He also mentioned that when a child is labeled autistic by another doctor and his opinion is that the child is not autistic, within a year, someone else (the diagnosing doctor) agrees with him. It's all clinical pediatrics with him. It's nothing he's read in the literature. It's his experience. It's listening to the history of the child, knowing what's normal and what's abnormal.

Dr. Layton thought Dr. Conlon might change his opinion of Ashley once he saw her again. Well, we would wait with baited breath with that one. That follow-up office visit with Dr. Conlon was in a few months.

Per Dr. Layton's recommendations, I re-challenged Ashley's diet with the egg, and didn't notice anything different in her behavior outside of the terrible twos (and now threes) that we were accustomed to seeing. The "defending her turf" was always in full bloom—we considered that totally normal. We added egg back into her diet. That was a plus. She could now have eggs or French toast (GFCF bread), and cooking her special foods had just become *a lot* easier now that I didn't have to use an egg replacer. I could never get the right proportion of that egg replacer-to-water thing down just right, anyway. So, this was a giant bonus for me.

Upon re-challenging with the other foods, we didn't see anything drastic in her mannerisms, either. We saw some separation anxiety that we hadn't seen in a while, but I didn't think it was due to these foods. The separation anxiety was short lived and only in isolated incidents. So, I put these foods back into her diet and opened up a world of food possibilities for her.

Tomatis—Loop 6

In my biased opinion, Ashley had recovered. It was also becoming the opinion of most of our specialists, as well. We had returned to the Spectrum Center during our break after the fifth loop to have Ashley tested. It had been nearly a year since Ashley had started Tomatis. The therapists performed tests to see how well she could discern words that were said in a background of noise, such as in a crowded restaurant. Ashley did pretty well, but she still had some right-ear, left-ear discrimination issues. I decided to continue with a sixth loop to address these kinks that still needed to be worked out. Plus, it was always a language and motor skills boost for Ashley.

During the Christmas holiday of 2002, Ashley went back for her sixth loop session. Our first day back at Tomatis (in three months) found Ashley right at home. Her program remained similar to previous loops. She showed good balance on the swing, connected dot-to-dot for eye tracking, was working on drawing with a mature grasp, and using appropriate language and peer interaction.

Her language was above average in both receptive and expressive as tested by our private speech therapist. Ashley was holding conversations with us. Now she was saying things like, "Look, Mommy a bird flying in the sky" or "Bye Kacey, have fun at Grandma's!" or "I need a drink, I'm firsty!" This three and a half year old was now saying all of these wonderful sentences that were meaningful and so appropriate. She was more self-sufficient with her skills like dressing and undressing. She was now playing with Kacey and Sydney, like three sisters would play on any given day. It was just bliss to Dave and me. I sometimes just gazed at the three of them playing and laughing—Ashley was so happy! I smiled with delight at how far she had come—how she found her way back. Our family was whole again!

Dave and Ashley loved to play pretend. It was now a concept she grasped.

"Daddy, you be the wolf. I be the pig," she said, striking up a dramatization of the Three Little Pigs, complete with puppets I had made.

"Not by the hair of my chinny chin chin!" Ashley said, running through the house when Daddy wolf came out of the pantry chasing her.

Then, there was the Spanish that started to pour out of her. Kacey and Ashley were learning Spanish in school. Ashley picked up on it immediately. She knew the Spanish numbers up to 20, all of the colors of the rainbow, and body parts from "cabeza" to "dedos"—head to toe. It blew the therapists at the Spectrum Center away when Ashley recited Spanish to them. It wasn't that long ago we were trying to get her to learn English! Now my three-year-old surpassed me in my knowledge of the Spanish language. That was just fine with me!

It isn't unusual to be able to pick up a foreign language while undergoing the Tomatis therapy. Each language uses different frequencies. French is spoken in the frequencies between 1000–2000 hertz. The British use frequencies from 2000–12,000 hertz. The French find it difficult to speak the English language, and the British have difficulty speaking French—they are each deaf to the other's frequencies. Dr. Tomatis discovered that by training the ear to hear foreign frequencies, the ear could pick up learning these frequencies and thus, one could be taught a foreign language easier.[20] Some people pursue the Tomatis Method just for this reason.

Ashley's ears were now becoming so attuned to language and music that she could differentiate sounds like never before. Her ears were almost bionic to me. She was hearing noises from far away that only two years earlier had never processed for her. Listening to Mozart, she could now discern each instrument when it played. It was quite amazing!

"Mommy, that's a French horn. Mommy, that's a flute!" she would say at the appropriate time when she heard the instrument.

I don't know too many toddlers who have such an ear for music like that.

---

20. Pierre Sollier, Dr. Tomatis, "How We Listen," Listening and Learning, http://www.Tomatis.com.

Strangely enough, the sixth loop enabled Ashley to completely potty train, and to correctly hold a pencil, promoting a right-hand dominance—she had been mixed dominance up until then. These were the amazing things about the Tomatis Method and the Spectrum Center's program—the therapy worked on the whole body. In Ashley, it promoted not just her speech and language, but it liberated her from the repetitive characteristics of autism, like hand flapping and toe walking. Her sensory integration issues faded, and she was no longer offended by a lot of gooey textures. She was trying and eating new foods. Her balance and coordination had improved dramatically. She was riding a scooter with accuracy, playing hopscotch like a champ, and getting stronger in her arms and legs.

But then we tripped up. Ashley's behavior headed south after the sixth loop. I wondered why? She was doing so well! What could have provoked this? We weren't doing Samonas any longer. It couldn't have been that! Why was Ashley so out of sorts? I couldn't understand or rationalize it. I had re-challenged her with new foods. She seemed to tolerate them just fine. It wasn't the soy. It wasn't the egg. Why was she so emotionally unstable at times?

Then I found out what was wrong. I learned from Valerie Dejean during a follow-up call a few months later, that my voice tape had not been used during the sixth loop. Without the support from my voice tape, Ashley felt a disconnection, and frankly, needed me! She wasn't ready to have the "cord cut" just yet. How strong the bond between a mother and a daughter!

During a mini-loop a few months later, my voice tape was inserted back into her program, and she was completely fine. And, what about her social communication issues that placed her on the autistic spectrum two years earlier? Well, they no longer existed in my opinion. She was playing and socializing with everyone! She was leading. She was following. She was talking. She was laughing. She was even telling jokes! She was spontaneous and original in her thought, as well as symbolic in her play—characteristics absent in autism. The diverse therapeutic capabilities of the Tomatis Method had well been proven in this little three and a half-year-old—knocking autism on its ear!

If there was any hint of autism still in Ashley, you'd have to find it with an electron microscope!

CHAPTER 17

▼

CLOSING (AND LOCKING) THE DOOR ON AUTISM: THE END OF THE JOURNEY

In my two and a half years on this journey, I never found out why autism had come to call on Ashley. I'll never find out. I cried. I blamed myself. I blamed others. I hid from my friends. While my friends were going to "Mommy and Me" classes with their children, I was going to "Mommy, Me and Therapy" classes. It didn't seem fair. Sometimes I hid from the new life I now had to lead—it was sometimes an unbearable battle to fight.

But I pulled myself together with a lot of support from Dave and our families and considered it the challenge that I must have been chosen for. And through all the progress—that I honestly didn't expect to see so soon, but was hoping for—I never hesitated to query all of our specialists time and time again about their opinions of Ashley and the diagnosis of autism. I just didn't see it anymore!

Their opinions of "I don't see it, either" or "You'd be hard-pressed to find someone to put that label on her now," or "She doesn't deserve that label," as good as those felt to my heart, were not the "be-all-end-all" opinions. There was one last hurdle to overcome, one last judgment to be made—that of Dr. Conlon's—the neurodevelopmental pediatrician who had diagnosed Ashley on the autistic spectrum years earlier. Dr. Conlon's opinion of her current, transformed appearance was the most important to obtain and would be a true barometer of how much she had progressed on this journey. I always feared the times I walked into Children's Hospital. It seemed nothing good ever came of our visits—a diagnosis on the spectrum, an EEG I couldn't bear to watch, laboratory tests gone awry. It was just always bad news. Always!

But this time, I was hoping it would be different. We were going to meet Dr. Conlon in a different satellite office, in a different city, with a noticeably different daughter. I was conspicuously different as well. I was happier. I had more poise. I was as strong as an ox with self-confidence, as well as with conviction about Ashley's developmental abilities—not her developmental disabilities. I was smarter than I was two years earlier having taken a crash course the hard way in autism and therapeutic interventions! I was now more likely to stand up and get in one's face to voice my concerns or question one's medical opinion with my newly-acquired education rather than sit back, accept a drab diagnosis and turn meek and reserved. I was a picture of "Don't come and do battle with me, unless you want to be defeated!" I was woman, hear me roar!

So with a change of venue and changes in all of us, we were hoping for a different outcome from this visit with Dr. Conlon—one of *no* autism. I was going into Dr. Conlon's office and parade Ashley in front of him and to make sure he saw what we were seeing now every day—a verbal, social, vivacious, spunky little girl with no doubts in my mind that she *did not* have an autistic disorder any longer. I was confident and convinced of it!

We arrived at Dr. Conlon's office for the follow-up consultation. It had been about eight months, since we had last seen him. Ashley looked completely different. She had grown taller, had gained weight, and had become more socially and behaviorally mature.

While I talked to Dr. Conlon, Dave played with Ashley and Sydney. Dr. Conlon could tell immediately that Ashley was not the same girl he had diagnosed with autism more than two years earlier.

"I remember early on it was hard to capture her attention, and she would be fascinated with my black box, not to mention her lack of speech. These were concerns that I had back then—that she didn't share attention with us and couldn't communicate or socialize," Dr. Conlon said, noticing the dramatic changes in Ashley right away.

"I just don't see autism anymore. Her therapists don't see it. Her special educator doesn't see it. She's been through six loops of Tomatis. They think she's a miracle! It's just not there anymore in my opinion!" I said, trying to build to my plea to take her off the autistic spectrum.

"You have been great advocates for Ashley. She's had a tremendous amount of intervention. And that's the purpose of intervention, to see if we can make a difference in the outcome. I would like her to be re-tested by your speech therapist for semantics and pragmatics and observation of how she uses language. Does she initiate? Does she turn-take? Does she maintain what we expect for a near four-year-old in terms of topic play?" he said.

"She does all of those things for us and for her therapists. At school, she plays with other children on the playground. She interacts in the classroom and participates when called upon by her teacher. I think she is right there with her peers. I think she's just as normal as the other children sitting in that classroom!" I told him.

"I'm just looking at her playing right now and interacting with Dave and her sister. She looks great, I agree. My feeling is that, she probably isn't in this category where we were a while ago."

Now he was starting to say some things I really wanted to hear!

"She has made remarkable leaps, but that's one of my concerns and hesitations. Not that one can't grow out of it through interventions, but usually what we're seeing is an individual who is quite high functioning, but is still having some mild pieces to the disorder. But it may be that Ashley is one of those few where there really is no longer a diagnosis. There's been data published that when some children around two-years-old were diagnosed on the autistic spectrum and then received early intervention, they were subsequently taken off of the spectrum at four-years-old due to their improvements and eradication of their autistic symptoms."[21]

It was all I needed to hear! It *was* possible to recover from this!

"But I just want to feel comfortable in closing the door on this. As I said, I think social communication and pragmatic language can still be an issue in these children and not be part of an autistic spectrum diagnosis. If there are difficulties with these in Ashley, we would want to still work on them but they, more than likely, would present off of the spectrum," he said, trying to cover all the bases and making sure I had a complete understanding of the issues at hand.

"Even from the beginning, if you remember, her capabilities, especially visual, were very high. If we were to pick children early on to really come so far, I think Ashley would have been one of them. She really showed us early on, that despite her social and language deficits, she possessed a very high ability for learning. So,

---

21. Stone, Wendy L., Lee, Evon B., Ashford, L., Brissie, J. 1999. 40 (No. 2): pp. 219–226.

to be sure about all of this and for me to feel comfortable in making such a decision, I want to review the latest testing from your therapists. Send me all of those reports, and I'll review them and address it in the follow-up letter to your pediatrician. You've really done a great job with her," he said, wrapping up our consult.

"That sounds great, thank you. I'll get you all of the reports and send them promptly," I replied, shaking his hand and leaving his office.

Finally, a happy consult! It had gone just as we had hoped. We would just have to wait for his final report to confirm what our hard work and interventions were blatantly telling us—that we thought Ashley no longer belonged on the autistic spectrum—that everyone she came in contact with thought she no longer presented on the spectrum.

At our next speech therapy visit, I informed our new speech therapist that Dr. Conlon wanted Ashley re-tested as well as wanted a sample of her socialization skills. Since Ashley was in private therapy and not in a group where she could interact with other children, I videotaped her at home with her sisters to give to the speech therapist for her review. She wrote up her findings.

Brenda, Ashley's special educator, was at the house for a visit the day I videotaped the girls playing. She collected her own data on Ashley for an evaluation to determine the need for further early intervention services from the county. Brenda hinted to me that Ashley's progress and attainment of all of her goals, (now being age appropriate), would probably not warrant further early intervention services from the county.

With the videotape, the re-test for pragmatics and semantics, and the write-up from the county, the final pieces of data that Dr. Conlon needed were being prepared.

The speech therapist shared Ashley's scores upon re-testing her. Ashley was three years and ten months old at the time. The comparison of Ashley's scores from that day—with her baseline score when she was one year and seven months collected by Shelly—was not only astonishing, it was a bull's eye for me! It was the data I needed to strengthen my argument that Ashley warranted being removed from the autistic spectrum.

	Standard Score	% Rank	Age Equivalent
October 2000 (1 yr, 7 mo.)			
Auditory Comprehension	68	2nd	0–8 months
Expressive Communication	63	1st	0–5 months
Total Language Score	66	1st	0–7 months
January 2003 (3 yrs, 10 mo.) Auditory Comprehension	108	70th	4 yrs, 2 months
Expressive Communication	102	55th	3 yrs, 9 months
Total Language Score	106	66th	3 yrs, 10 months

Once having the language of an infant when she was 19 months, Ashley had almost done the impossible. She had made up nearly four years of language in a little over two years! Averaging it all out, she scored at a three year, ten-month level—ironically that is how old she actually was!

Ashley was asking questions, she was using pronouns, and she was able to use language to interact with adults and children. When posed with a question, she could answer appropriately. She was playing appropriately with toys and role playing. She was showing age appropriate turn-taking. Her speech was 100% intelligible, except for an articulation problem called a liquid glide. Ashley rolled her l's and pronounced them as w's like in "Ashwey." But the speech therapist told me this was normal for her age and, other than that, saw no reason to continue with her therapy—Ashley had met her goals and then some. Ashley was released from speech therapy at that point having had two years and three months of this intervention—more than half of her young life!

Subsequently, Ashley no longer needed occupational therapy services and was released. Upon observation and review of Ashley's milestones, the special educator from the county, Brenda, found no reason to render further early intervention services. Ashley was released from the county's Child Find program, appropriately enough, on her fourth birthday!

I re-tested Ashley's stool sample and found her good bacteria was finally grow-ing—her gut was healing. I took her off the gluten-free/casein-free diet that she had been on for more than 18 months—a little less than half of her young life!

With all this data and discharge summaries from the speech therapist, the spe-cial educator from the county, and classroom and performance notes from Ash-ley's Montessori teacher, I sent the entire package to Dr. Conlon for his review. It was now a matter of his assessment from all of the information, (along with his own interpretation of what he observed in Ashley during our last consult), to convince himself that removing Ashley from the autistic spectrum was the appro-priate action to take.

Just a little bit longer to wait for his verdict, but Dave and I were certain that he was impressed with what he now saw in Ashley—a transformation, rarely seen in his practice. There was no hiding the truth. Data can't fib!

I've Got Mail

The afternoon I went to the mailbox and saw a letter from Children's Hospital, my heart fluttered. I had waited for the letter for months. I was ever so optimistic that this letter was going to be the bow that tied this whole journey up into a nice, neat package—unlike the day of Ashley's autism diagnosis two and a half years earlier that unraveled my world, leaving it tattered and me in need of an emotional seamstress.

My hands were shaking as if it were bitter cold outside, but it was a sunny day in June. I carefully opened the letter. This was hopefully going to be the most remarkable piece of memorabilia I would add to Ashley's scrapbook. I carefully proceeded to preserve its condition. I unfolded the letter, took a deep breath, and read it while walking up the driveway. It was addressed to Ashley's general pedia-trician.

I had the opportunity and pleasure to see Ashley back for a neurodevelop-mental pediatric follow-up. It gives me great pleasure to send this letter updating Ashley's tremendous progress with her communication skills. As you know, Ashley has a history of pervasive developmental disorder, not otherwise specified (PDD-NOS). This was made when she was just less than two-years-old. Her parents have pursued traditional interventions including speech and occupational therapy, as well as special education intervention and complementary and alternative interventions such as dietary, probiotics and other supplements. Ashley also received an auditory listening program, i.e., Tomatis. The family feels convinced that this latter intervention has made a difference in Ashley's progress. Her parents have been excellent advocates and have sought a multi-modal intervention program that has been successful.

It is truly exciting to see the progress that Ashley has made, and her communication skills are quite like other children her chronological age. She has developed good social communication, and her pretend play has evolved. It appears that Ashley is an integral part of her Montessori classroom, and her teacher feels that she interacts well with her peers. A small percentage of children, who are initially felt to be on the autism spectrum—at the high end of the spectrum—may not meet criteria as they grow older. It is clear from the evaluation today, in conjunction with a review of recent evaluations from her private therapists, that Ashley no longer meets criteria for an autism spectrum disorder. It is with delight and pleasure that I complete this letter and look forward to hearing from Ashley's family about her ongoing successes.

Most sincerely,
Chuck J. Conlon, M.D., F.A.A.P.
Chief, Neurodevelopmental Pediatrician

It was official! We did it! Ashley was off of the autistic spectrum!

She was no longer considered as having any form of autism! Our hard work had paid off! All of the doctor's visits, all of the speech and occupational therapy sessions, all of the special education services, all of the laboratory testing, all of the vitamin supplements, all of the GFCF diet foods, all of the Floor Time, all of the swinging, all of the brushing, all of the Tomatis, all of the research and reading—our journey was finally complete! We had arrived at a most perfect destination.

I ran inside to find Ashley. She was right where she was when this whole journey began—in front of the television watching a Barney video. It was still her favorite. But unlike two years ago, now she had no problem leaving the world of Barney, the songs, and vivid colors for a few moments and focus on something else—me. As I bent down and hugged her, one last tear fell from my eye.

"I love you, Ashley!" I said, squeezing her tightly with the letter dangling in my fingers.

"Gimme a smooch!" she said, grabbing my face and planting a kiss on me.

She hugged me and looked straight into my eyes.

"I love you, too, Mommy!"

In a most ironic, but appropriate moment, the "I love you" song started to play as the Barney video had come to an end. The timing was impeccable.

"Hey, Mommy, whadtha duck put in soup?" she asked me, still tuned into my face.

I put both hands on her soft silky cheeks.

"Uhm, I don't know, sweetie! Whadtha duck put in his soup?"

"Quackers! Quack, quack!" she said, breaking into a gut-splitting laugh.

"Hey, that's pretty good, Ashley. Got any more?" I asked, finding pure delight with her joke.

"Yeah. Where'd the sheep get a haircut?" she asked, still giggling from her first joke.

"Hmm?" I said, crossing my arms with the most perplexed look on my face.

"Where *did* the sheep get a haircut, Ashley?"

"At the baa baa shop!" she said, cracking up again.

"Wow, Ashley, those were great jokes! Gimme a high five!"

She slapped my hand, and I headed to the kitchen. Ashley went back to catch the last few tunes of her video.

"Ashley, you're amazing!" I shouted back, smiling from ear to ear.

"You're just *so, so* amazing!" I said, under my breath, shaking my head in disbelief of the conversation we had just had.

For more than two years, I had left Ashley in so many capable hands—even Mozart's! They molded and sculpted her. Their masterpiece was now complete.

She was unveiled!

Still in pigtails, she was a work of beauty!

AFTERWORD

▼

When parents are faced with the news that their child has been diagnosed on the autistic spectrum, their world comes crashing down. It is hard to make sense of it all—then once we do, we must pick up the pieces of our shattered dreams. We all have dreams for our children. Aside from the professional titles of doctor or lawyer we conjure up in our minds wanting them to become, we all want the same dream—to have them grow up healthy, happy and have more than we had.

Devastating news of any kind (regarding our child's health) immediately crushes those dreams—our child's future of being successful, living life, enjoying life—snuffed out ever before it really gets a chance to be ignited. Coping with such news makes you go cold, it makes you withdrawn, it puts you in denial and worse, can throw a family and a marriage into a tailspin. The medical bills, the constant attention to the child's special needs, the lack of sleep, and the stress and strain of every day trying not to lose hope, can do you in.

But given the cards you've been dealt, you have to make a winning hand out of it, somehow. Folding is not an option. Explore every possible opportunity for your child. Get professional second and third opinions. Leave no stone unturned. Read. Become absorbed in what your child is going through from an internal perspective. It can be exasperating coping with the adverse effects of this diagnosis that our children show outwardly. Imagine how your child must feel on the inside—the frustration, the fear, and the need to hide from us. Our children are trying to make sense out of a senseless world. Their bodies are disorganized and react to things the only way they know how. They try to communicate through various behavioral avenues, but we don't have a decoder—we fail in our attempts to really understand what is wrong. This feeling leaves you drained, discouraged beyond belief, and completely helpless toward the child you love so dearly.

That is why I feel early intervention and a variety of modalities can be instrumental in relocating the child within. I never knew half of the therapies we used were even in existence until faced with needing them. I never knew what the state and county could do in terms of early intervention services until I was steered in that direction. I never knew there were so many parents out there in the same boat, and that support for one another was essential for the sake of keeping sane and keeping informed. I never knew I could be so devoted in finding Ashley a way out, and never knew the cost it would take. But the cost became secondary. I would have sold everything I owned in order to provide her with the best possible treatments.

But one of the least expensive things that proved to be an essential part of this journey was my perseverance in constantly seeking information and gathering knowledge. I wanted to know about all possible treatment options—so I could employ them all.

I studied our therapist's techniques during their sessions and re-created them for Ashley at home. I made educational and therapeutic material to build her skills and ease her behavior. I taped pictures from one end of our house to another to quiz her. I purchased occupational therapy equipment and made a therapy room in our basement. I bought a store full of pretend play toys and spent more than two years of Floor Time with her. I read books on a myriad of subjects from recovery stories, to learning how to play with Ashley to engage her, to cooking for a child with special needs. I went to conferences and seminars, scoured the Internet for information, and networked with other parents to find specialists to add to our team. It was endless. I was tired and burned out. But I had to get up everyday and begin anew.

But in the end, the hard work paid off. Ashley came back to us and joined us in our family—right where she belonged all along. She was de-railed for a few years, but we got her back on track. Now, when I see her smile, I light up.

Catching Ashley's symptoms early on and having her diagnosed at such a young age was probably what gave us the edge. This is what I've heard from not only our specialists, but from other parents whose children were identified with the disorder at six, seven, even at eight-years-old—they had lost so much time and were now losing hope fast.

Denial can be an overwhelming force that can impede your common sense and stall you from getting the proper diagnosis and treatment for your child. Getting past the denial factor was harder for me than the actual journey. I felt out of control, scared, and beleaguered at the turn my life had just taken. But traveling down the road to recovery put me back in control. Educating myself taught me that I had options—lots of them. The prognosis of a life-time disability, which is scattered throughout the literature on autism, only made me want to defy the odds that much more to fight and beat this disorder.

On many days I wanted to give up, either due to sheer exhaustion, or because getting through to Ashley proved fruitless. But I persevered. I pushed her, and I pushed her, and I pushed myself, too. I wasn't about to give up. When I started to see progress with Ashley, I set the bar even higher and pushed her even harder. Treating a child this young is very difficult. I didn't know if she didn't understand me at times, because she wasn't old enough to grasp the concepts yet, or if the diagnosis was getting in the way. It was hard to tell sometimes. But Ashley shocked me at every turn. I have to give credit to this little girl who never gave up the fight.

I don't consider Ashley's recovery a miracle. This disorder *can* be battled and won. What's miraculous is that so many people in my life cared enough about Ashley to help her find her way back. I wouldn't have even tripped over this disorder if it weren't for the nudge my mother gave me to err on the side of caution and take Ashley to the doctor—Mom, thanks for your instincts!

I am still awestruck that so many doctors, specialists, therapists and geniuses out there have researched and invented the kinds of technologies, therapies, nutritional programs, skill-building apparatus and yes, even classical compositions, that really do make a difference with this disorder—they are changing lives with their brilliance! Ashley's future, once filled with murk and uncertainty, has never been more clear and full of promise.

To all of them, I say a collective thank you, once again, for Awakening Ashley and helping us Knock Autism on its Ear!

APPENDIX A

▼

WEBSITES AND RESOURCE INFORMATION

Auditory Training (Tomatis Method)

Spectrum Center
4715 Cordell Avenue
Bethesda, Maryland 20814
301-657-0988
Valerie Dejean, O.T.R., Owner/Director

Spectrum Communication
1540 York Avenue, Suite 1A
New York, New York 10028
212-706-1930
www.spectrumcenter.com
www.tomatis.com
www.awakeningashley.com

307 E 53 St 4th Floor (212) 223-2928

The Listening Centre
599 Markham Street
Toronto, Ontario M6G 2L7
(416) 588-4136
Paul Madaule, Director
www.listeningcentre.com

When Listening Comes Alive: A Guide to Effective Learning and Communication by Paul Madaule.

Organizations

Developmental Delay Resources (DDR)
4401 East-West Highway, Suite 207
Bethesda, MD 20814
www.devdelay.org

The Interdisciplinary Council on Developmental and Learning Disabilities (ICDL)
www.floortime.org
www.ICDL.com

The Child with Special Needs: Encouraging Intellectual and Emotional Growth by Dr. Stanley Greenspan and Dr. Serena Wieder

Nutrition and Alternative Medicine Specialists

Dr. Richard Layton
Allergy and Integrated Medicine
www.allergyconnection.com

Kelly Dorfman, Nutritionist
www.KellyDorfman.com

Mozart Music and the Mozart Effect

www.MozartEffect.com

Mozart Effect: Tapping the Power of Music to Heal the Body, Strengthen the Mind and Unlock the Creative Spirit by Don Campbell.

Mozart Effect for Children: Awakening Your Child's Mind, Health and Creativity with Music by Don Campbell.

THE LISTENING
CHECKLIST

A Tool to See if You or Your Child May Have a Listening Problem

(Adapted from Appendix B, When Listening Comes Alive, Paul Madaule, Norval, Ontario, Moulin Publishing, 1993, pp 191–192.)

We cannot "see" listening. The only way to "get at it" is indirectly—through skills that are related to it in one way or another. This checklist, developed by Canadian Tomatis practitioner, Paul Madaule, offers a catalog of abilities, skills or qualities that will enable you to assess whether you or your child may have a listening problem. There is NO score. This is simply a tool for you to evaluate your own or your child's ability to listen, and thus to learn. Check as many boxes, as you feel appropriate.

Developmental History: Our early years

This knowledge about our younger years is extremely important in early identification and prevention of listening problems. It also sheds light on possible causes of listening problems.

- A stressful pregnancy

- Difficult birth
- Adoption
- Early separation from the mother
- Delay in motor development
- Delay in language development
- Recurring ear infections

Receptive Listening: Our external environment

This type of listening is directed outward to the world around us. It keeps us attuned to what's going on at home, at work, in the classroom or with friends.

- Short attention span
- Distractibility
- Over-sensitivity to sounds
- Misinterpretation of questions
- Confusion of similar-sounding words
- Frequent need for repetition
- Inability to follow sequential instructions

Expressive Listening: Our internal atmosphere

This is the kind of listening that is directed within us. We use it to listen to ourselves and to gauge and control our voice when we speak and sing.

- Flat and monotonous voice
- Hesitant speech
- Weak vocabulary
- Poor sentence structure
- Overuse of stereotyped expressions
- Inability to sing in tune
- Confusion or reversal of letters

- Poor reading comprehension
- Poor reading aloud
- Poor spelling

Motor Skills: Our physical abilities

The ear of the body (the vestibule), which controls balance, muscle and eye coordination and body image needs close scrutiny also.

- Poor posture
- Fidgety behavior
- Clumsy, uncoordinated movements
- Poor sense of rhythm
- Messy handwriting
- Hard time with organization, structure
- Confusion of left and rights
- Mixed dominance
- Poor sports skills

The Level of Energy: Our fuel system

The ear acts like a dynamo (a powerful motor), providing us with the "brain" energy we need to not only to survive but also to lead fulfilling lives.

- Difficulty getting up
- Tiredness at the end of the day
- Habit of procrastinating
- Hyperactivity
- Tendency toward depression
- Feeling overburdened with everyday tasks

Behavioral and Social Adjustment: Our relationship skills

A listening difficulty is often related to these qualities of interacting with others.

- Low tolerance for frustration
- Poor self-confidence
- Poor self-image
- Shyness
- Difficulty making friends
- Tendency to withdraw or to avoid others
- Irritability
- Immaturity
- Low motivation, no interest in school/work
- Negative attitude toward school/work

0-595-30780-9

Printed in the United States
48039LVS00003B/202-222